# INVESTING in DEVELOPMENT: NEW ROLES for PRIVATE CAPITAL?

Theodore H. Moran and contributors:

Joseph M. Grieco
Dennis J. Encarnation
Louis T. Wells, Jr.
Vincent Cable
Bishakha Mukherjee
David J. Glover
Charles P. Oman
Stephen Guisinger
David J. Goldsbrough

Series editors:
Richard E. Feinberg
Valeriana Kallab

 Transaction Books
New Brunswick (USA) and Oxford (UK)

Library of Congress Catalog Number: 86-50512
ISBN: 0-88738-044-3
ISBN: 0-88738-644-X
Printed in the United States of America

**Library of Congress Cataloging-in-Publication Data**
Main entry under title:

Investing in development;
(U.S.-Third World policy perspectives; no. 6)
1. Investments, Foreign—Developing countries.
2. International business enterprises—Developing countries.
I. Moran, Theodore H., 1943-
II. Series.
HG5993.1585   1985      332.6'73'091724      86–50512
ISBN 0-88738-074-3
ISBN: 0-88738-644-X

# Investing in Development: New Roles for Private Capital?

# Acknowledgments

*Guest Editor:*
Theodore H. Moran

*Series Editors:*
Richard E. Feinberg
Valeriana Kallab

The Overseas Development Council gratefully acknowledges the assistance of the Ford, William and Flora Hewlett, and Rockefeller Foundations, whose financial support contributes to the preparation and dissemination of the policy analysis presented in ODC's U.S.-Third World Policy Perspectives series.

On behalf of the ODC and the contributing authors, the editors wish to express special thanks to members of the ODC Program Advisory Committee and others who participated in the discussion of early versions of the papers included in this volume at the ODC's conference on "The Future of Foreign Investment in the Third World."

Special thanks for their respective roles in the editorial preparation and production of this volume are due to Patricia A. Masters, Linda Starke, Carol J. Cramer, and Lisa M. Cannon.

# Contents

Investing in Development:
New Roles for Private Capital?

# Overview and Summaries of Recommendations

# The Future of Foreign Direct Investment in the Third World

## Theodore H. Moran

The debate about the need for foreign direct investment in the Third World has changed dramatically in tone and substance—partly in response to the dire economic conditions of the debt crisis. In both North and South, there are expectations that multinational corporations can play a key role in restoring economic activity, making up for lower aid flows, and providing capital to relieve the burden on commercial bank lending—and that (together with the private sectors in the local economies) they can lead to an era of healthier and more balanced development. In the search for new sources of growth, the tone of instinctive criticism that characterized most discussions of foreign direct investment a decade ago has given way to almost unqualified support.

To what extent are these expectations about a greater and more positive role for multinational corporations justified?

This volume brings together the evidence from a new generation of research in order to reassess the impact of multinational corporate operations on Third World development and provide a basis for policy decisions about the future. It looks at how the approach of many host governments has changed over time, and at what the prospects are for new growth via foreign investment in coming years. The analyses assembled here cover not only direct equity investment in natural resources and manufacturing, but also non-equity arrangements extending to agriculture and other sectors. They assess the prospects for international corporations to "fill the gap" in the need for new commercial bank loans. They examine the possibilities for multinational firms to expand their contribution to the *least developed* countries as well as to the newly industrializing countries (NICs). they address the question of whether greater flows of outward investment are in fact in the interest of the developed countries themselves, or whether increased flows might export jobs and undermine the industrial structure of the United States and other "home countries" generating new investment. In each case, the authors draw policy conclusions for host governments, for home governments (particularly the United States), for multilateral institutions such as the World Bank and the agencies of the United Nations, and for the multinational firms themselves.

## The Impact of Multinational Corporations on Third World Development

The debate about how foreign investors affect the development process has a long and contentious history. What has been learned about how to maximize the contribution of international corporate investors to the growth of the less developed countries? Is the creation of a "good investment climate" enough, and is the maximum flow of private direct investment necessarily "good" for nations of both North and South?

As the chapter by **Joseph Grieco** shows, substantial progress has been made since the mid-1970s, when debate of investment issues was strongly affected by the Third World's call for a New International Economic Order. In that context, proponents of two opposing views—one unqualifiedly supportive of foreign direct investment, the other resolutely critical—exchanged largely unsubstantiated charges about the impact of direct foreign investment on the Third World. At the theoretical level, each side now has a more rigorous logical structure or model that can be tested against empirical data to determine its validity. The pro–foreign-investment school pictures foreign investors as adding new resources—capital, technology, management, and marketing—to the host economy in a way that improves efficiency and stimulates change. It perceives investment as creating jobs, fostering growth, and improving the distribution of income by bidding up wages while driving down the returns to capital. The opposing, *dependencia* school asserts that multinational companies soak up local capital for their projects rather than bring in many new resources; that they use inappropriate technologies developed in response to the labor/capital proportions in the home country; and that they drive domestic producers out of the market. From this perspective, the result could be outside domination of key sectors of the economy, the creation of a small labor elite and exacerbation of unemployment, and the capture of high profits for transfer to corporate headquarters far away.

A key distinction between the two schools—one that emerges repeatedly at important points throughout this volume—is the presence or absence, maintenance or disappearance, of competitive conditions in the industries in which foreign investors are involved. In the light of accumulated evidence, is it possible to conclude that one of these two schools, the pro–foreign-investment school or the *dependencia* school, is correct? On the basis of aggregate data, Joseph Grieco's answer is "no." Macro-level surveys across many countries that have sought to determine the relationship between multinational corporate investment and development show that foreign investment is, for example, associated with higher levels of income. But they do not establish whether foreign investment causes higher income levels or whether higher income levels merely attract outside investment. Attempts to generalize about the link between foreign-firm activities and income distribution, growth patterns, or other economic variables likewise have not borne fruit.[1]

Shifting from the macro to the micro level, however, there is a third school, which Grieco calls the "bargaining school," that focuses directly on the outcome of individual investment negotiations. Here the evidence is less opaque. The bargaining school has documented growing sophistication on the part of host-country negotiators; in the more successful countries, a strategy of "squeezing" foreign investors *after* their operations are in place (a process Raymond Vernon first labeled "the obsolescing bargain") has replaced an inflexible insistence on stiff entry requirements. The principal impact of such requirements was simply to keep international companies away. A large number of cases now suggest growing bargaining strength and significant gains for Third World countries: Natural resource projects show tax rates climbing by as much as 30 percentage points between the initial investment agreement and the mature production arrangement, and manufacturing projects contain the demand for "performance requirements" that increase domestic content and/or expand exports as their operations proceed.[2]

Does this settle the argument in favor of proponents of foreign direct investment? Here is where **Dennis Encarnation** and **Louis Wells** provide an important contribution. Surveying the evidence on 133 manufacturing projects in at least thirty countries over more than a decade, as well as 50 proposed projects in one country, the authors conclude that between 55 and 75 per cent of these projects would have a clear, positive effect on development. Moreover, as Grieco as well as Encarnation and Wells point out, no static analysis of the costs and benefits sufficiently captures the dynamic multiplier effect that international corporations can have on local economic growth. This is a strong endorsement of foreign direct investment's potential.

Equally significant, however, is the obverse of this finding—namely, that a large minority of the investments (between 25 and 45 per cent) have a demonstrably negative impact on the host societies. That is, the costs in terms of using scarce domestic resources inefficiently substantially outweigh the benefits to national income. What produces the detrimental impact on the host economy is not the "foreign-ness" of the investment, but the fact that it takes place in an environment shielded from competition.[3] Encarnation and Wells take a close look at the protection from import competition that many international companies insist on before establishing local production. Such protection creates distortions and a misallocation of resources. This major point of their analysis is more broadly valid as well: The benefits of a competitive environment extend beyond static ideas of allocative efficiency. For example, the presence or absence of competition also plays an important role in the foreign firm's choice of technology: The greater the pressures from competitors, the more likely the firm is to resort to labor-intensive technology.[4] Competition also speeds the gains that host authorities can appropriate by playing one corporation off against another.

These findings should inject a cautionary note into the enthusiastic tone of the bargaining school as well as provide some underpinning for what Grieco calls a new "structuralist school," which is critical of the idea that the outcome of foreign-investor–host-government negotiations will always be favorable to the latter.[5] The findings are consistent with those of members of the pro–foreign-investment school who emphasize, from a neoclassical perspective, how important it is to have markets work competitively; the findings contradict those members of the pro–foreign-investment school who focus primarily on a warm welcome for international investors.

The problem is that some form of market exclusivity is the surest means that host authorities have for stimulating foreign investment. Two decades of research have shown consistently that protection from competition has a much stronger impact than all other forms of investment incentives. For the investor, a guaranteed market share both generates profits and—unlike tax breaks, for example—reduces losses if the project is not commercially successful. For the host authorities, protection from competition is largely invisible, in that it does not generate public criticism, as generous treatment of multinational enterprises might.

Nevertheless, the conclusion from these findings is that giving up the promise of market exclusivity is in the interest of host countries of the South (and, as discussed later, in the interest of the home countries of the North as well), even though it may result in lower levels of foreign private investment. More is not *necessarily* better in the case of multinational corporate activities in the Third World.

In sum, foreign direct investment can be of great value to less developed countries. But the contemporary wisdom that friendly investment climates and greater investment flows will automatically help solve developing countries' problems has to be carefully qualified. To ensure the greatest contribution to their own development, host governments may in fact have to refuse to grant the kind of treatment that many international companies want most.[6] And in doing so, they may have to give up their strongest magnet for attracting larger investment flows.

## The Spread of Foreign Investment to the Poorer Developing Countries

Although the list of less developed countries looking to foreign investment to help stimulate domestic growth has lengthened considerably since the onset of the debt crisis, the thrust of multinational corporate activity traditionally has been concentrated in a relatively small number of newly industrializing countries. As David Goldsbrough shows, since 1973 five countries (Brazil, Indonesia, Malaysia, Mexico, and Singapore) have received 50 per cent of all direct investment flows, while forty-one low-income countries (excluding China and India) have received only 2 per cent of the total.

Does this mean that international corporate investment cannot be a vehicle for the growth of the *poorer* developing countries? How can aid flows and aid agencies be used to catalyze the spread of foreign direct investment to the least developed countries?

Three of the policy papers presented in this volume (those by Vincent Cable and Bishakha Mukherjee, by David Glover, and by Charles Oman) suggest that, while the outlook for foreign direct investment in the poorer developing countries is not bright, there may be broader possibilities for participation by international corporations in the future than past data would indicate. In poorer countries having favorable natural resource endowments, there have been successful efforts to attract foreign investors, with the terms of investment agreements in fact paralleling those reached with the NICs. The principal difference has been an enlarged role for consultants and advisers from multilateral agencies. In the resource exploration phase, the World Bank has played a crucial part in, for example, the organization of seismic data and preparation of tracts for bidding in Bolivia, Madagascar, and Tanzania. In the development phase, the United Nations helped Botswana and Papua New Guinea construct contractual arrangements that have become models for Third World use. In the negotiation process itself, advisory teams organized by the World Bank have given host-country ministries without experience in natural-resource taxation and pricing issues the needed confidence to move ahead with agreements involving politically sensitive terms. The record suggests that external assistance can function as an important catalyst for private-sector involvement.[7]

In the manufacturing sector, the prospects for foreign direct investment in the least developed countries tend to be concentrated in export-zone projects, given these countries' small domestic markets to absorb local production. As **Vincent Cable** and **Bishakha Mukherjee** point out, in only six years, Sri Lanka, for example, attracted projects accounting for 50,000 jobs and 10.5 per cent of the country's exports in its special enclave zone. Attempts to replicate this kind of success, however, have been hindered elsewhere—not by lack of welcome on the part of local governments or by the absence of cheap labor, but by inadequate infrastructure and low work-force productivity at various sites. Here again there is a potential lead part that external assistance can play—this time in the form of infrastructure loans and programs for worker training and education. The benefits from export zones remain limited, however, because of extreme competition among governments with potential sites. This suggests a need for a forum for multilateral negotiation—perhaps under U.N. or World Bank auspices—to establish a model package of investment incentives that places a limit on the special breaks that host-country bidders give away. If a coalition of host countries uniformly applied such a package, it should be able to improve bargaining terms and gain greater benefits from export platform operations without substantially retarding the investment flow. In the manufacturing sector as well as in the natural resource sector, well-constructed programs of aid and advice clearly can be a complement and a necessary ingredient for obtaining the benefits of foreign direct investment.

The study by **David Glover** suggests that for the least developed countries as well as for the newly industrializing, there may be promising opportunities for foreign involvement in commercial agriculture. In addition to advanced production techniques, international firms can offer quality control, brand-name recognition, and access to markets for processed foods with higher 'value added.' There are dangers posed for this sector, however, as international companies try to take advantage of Third World production sites while limiting their own exposure to economic nationalism. Over the past two decades, as Glover demonstrates, the companies have been progressively relinquishing direct ownership to the hands of domestic producers. While this enables local farmers to take over activities at the production level, it also has a tendency to shift the risk from market fluctuations onto the local producers themselves.

Cable and Mukherjee's analysis of international subcontracting for consumer electronics and for clothing in Haiti reinforces the point that local ownership does not necessarily mean local control in vertically integrated international industries, especially for poorer developing countries that do not have indigenous companies or state enterprises able to penetrate external markets on their own. Cable and Mukherjee, like Glover, argue that in such a situation direct equity investments might be preferable to other arrangements that seem to promise more indigenous ownership. They find that many international companies use a non-equity form of operation to lower their exposure and to reduce their commitment in a project while transferring risk to the local participants.

This point is underscored for the least developed countries and the newly industrialized alike in the study by **Charles Oman**, who finds that earlier, uncritical enthusiasm for "new forms" like management contracts, franchising, production-sharing arrangements, and licensing and subcontracting as alternatives to direct foreign investment is being replaced by the realization that "new forms" may bring new problems and new dangers by lowering the corporations' stake in the ongoing success of the projects. Oman concludes that non-equity forms nevertheless offer some new avenues to business opportunities, and that resort to them may in any case grow rather than decline—given the companies' desire to reduce their vulnerability in Third World locations.

In sum, despite the relative lack of interest that international investors have shown in the least developed countries in the past, the studies included in this volume identify some promising signs of foreign corporate interest in some sectors in some of these countries. Even this limited involvement of international companies, however, will have to be nurtured within the context of ongoing

flows of official development assistance. And there is no evidence
that direct foreign investment can simply "replace" aid or "provide
a solution" that will eliminate the need for official development
assistance.

## The Impact of Outward Investment by International Firms on the Home Country

But are efforts to encourage the flow of multinational corporate
capital to the Third World, especially in the manufacturing sector,
in the interests of the home country? What about the growing fear
on the part of organized labor in the developed nations that outward
investment leads to a loss of jobs and undermines the industrial
base of the North?[8] In the United States, union leaders have urged
that federal tax laws be changed to make foreign operations less
profitable. In Europe, one proposal would give workers and communities the right of prior approval before corporations could expand
abroad. Throughout the North, a concern about loss of jobs has led
governments to place developing-country "performance requirements" for foreign investors high on the agenda for attack during
the next round of multilateral trade negotiations under the General
Agreement on Tariffs and Trade (GATT).

What does the evidence show about outward investment and
the potential loss of jobs?

The debate has been confused to some extent by the assertion
that home countries, in particular the United States, are being led
by their own multinationals into a process of absolute "de-industrialization." This is not consistent with U.S. data. The volume of
output in manufacturing, value-added in manufacturing, investment in manufacturing, and even employment in manufacturing all
have been rising in this country. The relative share of manufacturing in the U.S. economy has declined, consistent with a long-term
expansion of the service sector. The labor-capital ratio has declined,
consistent with a long-term expansion of automation. To be sure,
some industrial sectors are hard pressed by competition from
abroad—a painful process that has been magnified by an over-
valued dollar and a lack of adequate adjustment policies at home.
Nevertheless it is premature to conclude that a process of absolute
"de-industrialization" is taking place.[9]

But this conclusion does not do justice to the fear of organized
labor that outward investment may be detrimental to the employment structure of the United States. The relevant question is: What
would the situation be like if international firms based in the
United States were kept at home? And here the test must be

indirect[10]—involving a comparison of firms that moved abroad with firms of similar characteristics in the same industry that stayed at home. The evidence suggests that the process of moving abroad may at first increase employment in the home country as the parent company exports to its own subsidiaries, but that it subsequently may reduce employment as the operations of the subsidiaries grow. The net effect is not exactly clear but appears to be negative; more important, the magnitude is relatively small and would require an exceptionally fine-tuned set of policy instruments to capture the gains and avoid the losses among a very heterogeneous range of investment projects. Moreover, the effort to maximize home-country jobs would surely provoke retaliation, depriving any one home country of many of the benefits of inward investment into its own economy. For this reason, most analysts reject the desire of American labor to impose a taxation penalty on outward investment. Instead, they conclude that the best policy is fiscal neutrality, or not trying to affect the locational decisions of international companies one way or another by means of national tax policy.

The argument of organized labor must, however, be carried one stage further. Within the neutrality framework, do not the performance requirements levied by less developed countries on international companies constitute a clear case of cheating—forcing the latter to rearrange investment patterns and distort trade flows? Here is where the study by **Stephen Guisinger** constitutes a breakthrough: In only four of the seventy-four cases would the investments have been made elsewhere in the absence of the performance requirements. Most frequently, performance requirements are used, in conjunction with other investment incentives, to galvanize international companies to push themselves in the direction comparative advantage would lead them anyway. They act as "turbochargers," mobilizing and focusing the use of the rents generated by incentive policies. Finally he notes that performance requirements and other investment incentives are largely fungible—meaning that a proscription of the former would simply prompt resort to some other form of the latter.

Still, if there is a net incentive effect that influences the location of multinational corporate operations, surely this must represent a deviation from the idea of a level playing field for investment (like the oft-discussed level playing field for trade) embodied in the concept of neutrality. But the pro-investment policies of the North as well as of the South do not constitute a unique or singularly unfair deviation. Twenty-four U.S. states and all twelve members of the European Community, for example, have investment promotion programs of a similar nature. The locational incentives of American states from South Carolina to Oregon and Michigan to Texas include investment tax write-offs, property tax breaks, industrial development bonds, publicly financed job training, and direct state loans. The European Community offers both fiscal subsidies and direct cash grants.

Consequently the idea of singling out developing-country performance requirements for attack as a central part of the next round of GATT trade negotiations is surely misdirected. Even if the attack were successful in its own terms, it would not produce the desired result. Performance requirements would simply reappear in another guise—perhaps more opaque, but with the same impact. More to the point, however, the attack is neither in the best interests of the North, nor fair to the South. Instead, the proper goal should be a common ceiling on locational incentives in the countries of the North and South alike.

## International Investors and the Debt Crisis

How much of a role can foreign direct investment play in helping to solve the debt crisis? Can multinational enterprises be counted on to lighten the burden on private commercial banks in restoring a new equilibrium to the international financial system?

The debt crisis that broke in 1982 has pushed the principal borrowing nations into a depression nearly rivaling that of the 1930s.[11] The expansion of their ability to service existing debt is now constrained by shortages of capital and foreign exchange that are unlikely to be generated simply by ever-tighter austerity programs. The shift toward the current consensus that the major debtors must "grow" out of the debt crisis presents a paradox: Commercial bankers feel that, given their current overexposure, greater lending should be made only *after* their clients demonstrate an ability to service existing debt. This leaves a large gap of $10–30 billion per year in what is considered necessary for the largest developing-country debtors to return to a steady growth path.[12] How much can be provided by multinational corporate investors?

This is where the painstaking analysis by **David Goldsbrough** fits into the broader picture. It shows that, historically, the response of the international investment community after cyclical downturns has been quite strong (an increase of 34 per cent in 1973 after a drop of 16 per cent in 1972, and an increase of more than 19 per cent in 1977–78 after a drop of 21 per cent in 1976). Goldsbrough estimates that multinational firms are similarly poised to increase their investments at the present time; from a very steep decline in foreign investment of more than 28 per cent in 1982–83, net inflows of direct investment may climb a total of nearly 40 per cent by the beginning of 1987, leveling off to an annual rate of increase of 3.25 per cent thereafter. This projection is strengthened by some support from survey data from fifty-two large international corporations conducted by the Group of Thirty (which since 1978 has explored basic problems in the functioning of the international economic system): 22 per cent of the firms expected their real investment flows to be larger in the period 1983–87 than during 1978–82, while 7 per cent expected them to be lower.[13]

What does this 'strong' recovery mean in aggregate terms? While Goldsbrough's analysis suggests a climb to $13 billion in 1987, that is a net new inflow of only $2 billion more than 1985. In short, under even a relatively optimistic scenario, the magnitude of the contribution of foreign direct investment in filling the "gap" is at best a modest fraction of what is needed.[14]

Can North and South together take additional measures to stimulate further flows? A favored initiative coming out of the 1985 World Bank-IMF meetings in Seoul is the Multilateral Investment Guarantee Agency (MIGA), which will provide political risk insurance against expropriation, breach of contract, inconvertibility, and war or civil disturbance. The hope is that the MIGA can provide security to a growing number of private investors who feel that otherwise the pressures of economic nationalism render large long-term projects too vulnerable to undertake.[15]

How much additional investment might a successful MIGA stimulate? Any estimate must be highly conjectural. Overall, it is optimistic but not implausible to conclude that MIGA will have a portfolio of projects totaling nearly $2 billion by the late 1980s, growing by approximately $500 million per year, of which roughly $200 million might be net additional flows that would not be made in the absence of MIGA.[16]

The appeal of MIGA to the international corporate community will depend, however, upon a voting structure in which investors have confidence that their potential claims will not be blocked. And the success of MIGA as a functioning institution will depend upon legal agreements through which the agency can pursue the reimbursement for claims with confidence against the member states, and upon a connection with the lending activities of the World Bank parent that gives it clout in its negotiations with Third World governments. These, however, are precisely the areas that make the MIGA proposal most controversial from the point of view of the capital-importing countries.

There may, however, be other, more promising techniques by which the World Bank can accomplish the same objectives.[17] One possibility lies in making fuller use of the way "remedies clauses" can be written into World Bank loan agreements to include a host-country commitment not to alter the fundamental laws or conditions surrounding large foreign investment projects. A second possibility lies in expanding co-financing "B" loans—arrangements in which the Bank participates in and guarantees the later maturities of loans to direct investment projects, subject to the same contractual commitments as above. A third possibility (not yet tested in actual agreements) consists of sponsor guarantees, whereby the World Bank would make parallel loans to a government and to a private investor for the same project; the loan to the private investor would include a "political force majeure" exception enabling it to trigger a default to the World Bank if the host-country government abrogates the contractual terms surrounding the project.

These techniques will not, in all likelihood, relieve foreign corporations from the multiple "squeezes" of economic nationalism, but they may help ensure that the evolution of the foreign-host relationships evolves in a non-zero sum fashion over the life of large long-term projects. And they do not run contrary to the interests of the host countries themselves. Not only do they allow projects to be launched that otherwise would remain on the drawing boards; they also reinforce the credibility of the host-country negotiators, thus strengthening their bargaining position.

By the late 1980s, World Bank project lending with remedies clauses that provide such protection for foreign direct investors could amount to $100 million per year, with co-finance "B" lending amounting to another $100 million, spreading the World Bank umbrella over $600 million in projects, of which roughly $300 million might be *additional, new* investment.[18]

In all, a well-managed and vigorous set of World Bank initiatives could generate a total of an extra half-a-billion dollars in foreign investment flows a year by the late 1980s ($200 million from MIGA and $300 million from co-financing with protective remedies clauses). This is still, however, only a small portion of what is needed to fill the "gap."

Against such an effort to stimulate greater corporate operations in the Third World must be weighed any attempt to limit the use of market protection to attract multinational corporate operations. As pointed out earlier, research on measures to promote new investment has shown consistently that the promise of shelter from competition amounts to much more leverage than other incentives in stimulating new investment. The unhappy conclusion is that concerted measures to limit protection for multinational investors will lead them to turn away from many projects—probably more than enough to offset the new flows that World Bank initiatives may stimulate.

In short, direct foreign investment flows do not offer a substitute for the additional liquidity that the South needs from the North to reinforce growth. And the responsibility of the North for managing the next phase of the debt crisis in a positive fashion does not end with the simple provision of expanded bank financing. Goldsbrough's relatively optimistic forecast of international business investment depends upon further crucial assumptions: that the countries of the North achieve an average real growth of GNP of more than 3 per cent per year, that they reduce their structural deficits by about 1 per cent of GNP, and that they not increase their protectionism against developing-country exports. As Goldsbrough himself points out, failure to achieve these goals is likely to have very adverse effects on the volume of foreign investment flows.

The importance of such measures by the North to strengthen the global macro-economic environment is reinforced in survey data from the firms themselves. In Latin America, for example, the Council of the Americas found that, whereas international firms contemplating the expansion of their operations indicated that further improvements in host-country treatment (such as the elimination of price controls, negative bureaucratic bias, and industry-specific regulations, as well as the alleviation of political instability) were desirable, their investment plans were far more affected by obstacles arising from unfavorable macro-economic conditions. The Council's report concluded that "economic stagnation is a higher business concern currently than government rules or policies."[19]

It is clear, therefore, that public policy decisions undertaken by the developed countries themselves will strongly influence the ability of foreign direct investment to play a role in helping the Third World work its way through the next phase of the debt crisis.

## Policy Implications

The analysis presented in this volume does not offer a single, simple vision of multinational corporate investment in the developing countries. Instead, the picture is complex, with both sharp contrasts and subtle nuances. Foreign direct investment can make a valuable contribution to Third World development, but not all foreign direct investment does so. Greater flows of direct foreign investment are needed, but more is not always better. A good investment climate in less developed countries is important, but a good investment climate is not synonymous with what corporations prize the most. The benefits from multinational corporate investment may extend beyond the newly industrializing countries to some of the less developed countries, but the possibility of such investment does not offer a solution that can take the place of aid. International firms can help the Third World countries "grow" their way out of the debt crisis, but they will not replace the need for ongoing and expanding commercial-bank loans backed by larger infusions of multilateral public finance. The South has a responsibility to provide an environment in which the private sector can function effectively, but the North has the equally large responsibility to create global macro-economic conditions that make possible the expansion of private sector investment.

What policy lessons and recommendations emerge from our analyses for each of the major actors on the foreign investment scene?

*For host-country governments in the Third World:*

- Most foreign investment projects *do* generate substantial positive economic benefits for the Third World. An investment climate that rewards the investors sufficiently to compensate them for their risk is necessary to attract foreign corporations.

- The vulnerability of some of the largest potential investment projects to major contractual changes is sufficiently great that special guarantees (perhaps via the World Bank) may be needed to enable the projects to be launched in the first place.

- Not all conditions that are appealing to multinational corporations should be acceptable to host authorities attempting to create a good investment climate. Especially if such conditions involve sheltering the investors from competition, they are likely to be detrimental to the host economy.

*For multilateral institutions:*

- The World Bank and the United Nations can play an important catalytic role in helping the Third World to design policies to attract and manage foreign direct investment. This role can be strengthened and expanded with low cost and high effect.

- The World Bank, in particular, can play an important part in helping to enhance the credibility of host-government commitments to foreign investors.

- Among the techniques for stimulating private investment flows open to the World Bank, the Multilateral Investment Guarantee Agency (MIGA) is only one option—and perhaps not even the one with the largest potential impact.

*For multinational investors:*

- International corporate strategy should be based on genuine comparative advantage rather than on special local advantages, especially those associated with protection.
- Within the context of international comparative advantage it should be possible to defend investment decisions on a global basis—before diverse constituencies worldwide—in terms of their contribution to growth, exports, and jobs.
- For large-scale projects that are especially vulnerable to economic nationalism, new initiatives by the World Bank may offer an unprecedented vehicle for narrowing the margins within which the swings of renegotiation take place.

*For home-country governments (especially the United States):*

- Outward investment to the Third World does not represent a loss in exports and employment to the home countries that requires countermeasures such as tax constraints to keep it at home. Instead, home-country tax policy should be neutral as between domestic and outward investment.
- While it is in the home-country interest to press for greater trade liberalization via the GATT, the single-minded focus on developing-country performance requirements should be replaced by an effort to establish a common ceiling on locational incentives in both North and South.
- If multinational corporate investment is to contribute to Third World development, the North has at least as great a responsibility as the South for creating a good global investment climate via responsible macro-economic policies at home, a rollback of protectionism, and the provision of more liquidity to the newly industrializing countries and more concessional assistance to the poorest developing countries.

With alternative sources of capital in scant supply, there will be a continuing temptation to look to the international corporate community as the most promising source, if not the main source, for bringing new prosperity to the less developed world—if only developing-country governments will provide a warm and enthusiastic welcome. Surely there is an irony in the fact that the greatest danger lies not in the prospect that multinational corporations will be *under*appreciated, but that they will be *over*appreciated as a panacea for solving Third World problems at least over the medium term. Foreign direct investment can indeed play a dynamic role in contributing to the growth and development of Third World nations. But that role is smaller, takes longer to build up, and carries more dangers than conventional wisdom currently suggests. Moreover, the extent to which foreign direct investment can play a dynamic role at all is highly dependent upon a larger macro-economic framework that will require, as outlined above, sensible and disciplined decisions to be taken as much in the public policy arenas of the North as in those of the South.

## Notes

[1] For a critical analysis of such aggregate studies, reaching the same conclusion as Grieco, see Richard E. Caves, *Multinational Enterprise and Economic Analysis* (New York: Cambridge University Press, 1983), Chapter 9.

[2] For an assessment of the problems as well as of the successes of foreign-investor–host-country bargaining in natural resource and manufacturing industries, see Theodore H. Moran, *Multinational Corporations: The Political Economy of Foreign Direct Investment* (Lexington, Mass.: D.C. Heath, 1985). On high-technology industries, Joseph Grieco's own study of the computer industry in India provides an instructive case study of the pitfalls and ultimate accomplishments of alternative policy approaches in one host country. Joseph Grieco, *Between Dependency and Autonomy: India's Experience with the International Computer Industry* (Berkeley: University of California Press, 1984).

[3] Encarnation and Wells do not deal with issues of social structure, culture and tastes, and political influence raised by the presence of foreign corporations. For comment on these issues, see the chapter by Grieco. The analysis by Encarnation and Wells concentrates on the cost-benefit ratio; the "bargaining school" focuses on the evolution of the negotiating relationship between foreign investor and host government over time. It should be noted that the assessment of costs and benefits for development, the generous or stringent treatment of foreign corporations, and the stability or renegotiation of investment agreements are all logically independent. That is, an investment agreement that treats the foreign investor generously can be good or bad for the host country's development; an investment agreement that imposes stringent requirements on the foreign investor can similarly have a beneficial or detrimental impact on development; and an investment agreement that begins generously and is renegotiated stringently over the life of the project can also have a beneficial or detrimental impact on development. A key distinction in determining what the impact is in all of these situations is the presence or absence of a competitive environment surrounding the foreign corporate operations at any given point in time.

[4] Wayne Yeoman has found, for example, that the weaker the price competition faced by the local subsidiary, the greater the propensity of the multinational to utilize the production techniques used in the home country without adapting them to the Third World setting. Competition, in contrast, pushes the foreign company to modify its operations so as to employ more labor. Wayne A. Yeoman, *Selection of Production Processes for the Manufacturing Subsidiaries of U.S.-Based Multinational Corporations* (New York: Arno Press, 1976). Louis Wells has argued that a lack of competition allows "engineering man," who admires technological sophistication for its own sake, to take precedence over "economic man," who wants to minimize production costs by using greater labor inputs. Louis T. Wells, "Economic Man and Engineering Man: Choice in a Low-Wage Country," *Public Policy*, 21 (Summer 1973), pp. 319–42.

[5] As Grieco points out, the "structuralist school" also asserts that, due to domestic political alliances, the balance of host-country bargaining power vis-à-vis multinationals may decline rather than rise over time. In addition, Grieco reviews the question of leakage of revenues via transfer pricing.

[6] The chapter by Encarnation and Wells suggests how screening mechanisms can help Third World countries sort out beneficial from detrimental foreign investment projects.

[7] In addition to the papers in this volume, see Theodore H. Moran, "Does the World Bank Belong in the Oil and Gas Business?," *The Columbia Journal of World Business*, Vol. XVII, No. 1 (Spring 1982), pp. 47–52.

[8] Cf. Sol C. Chaikin, "Trade, Investment and Deindustrialization: Myth and Reality," *Foreign Affairs*, Vol. 60, No. 4 (Spring 1982), pp. 836–51; and *Resolution on International Trade and Investment*, adopted by the 16th Constitutional Convention of the AFL-CIO, October 1985.

[9] Robert Z. Lawrence, *Can America Compete?* (Washington, D.C.: The Brookings Institution, 1984).

[10] For the analysis of this issue, see Theodore H. Moran, *Multinational Corporations: The Political Economy of Foreign Direct Investment*, op. cit.; C. Fred Bergsten, Thomas Horst, and Theodore H. Moran, *American Multinationals and American Interests* (Washington, D.C.: The Brookings Institution, 1978); Richard T. Frank and Richard T. Freeman, *Distributional Consequences of Direct Foreign Investment* (New York: Academic Press, 1978); Robert E. Lipsey and Merle Yahr Weiss, "Foreign Production and Export of Individual Firms," *Review of Economics and Statistics*, May 1984.

[11] See Richard E. Feinberg and Valeriana Kallab, eds., *Adjustment Crisis in the Third World*, and *Uncertain Future: Commercial Banks and the Third World* (New Brunswick, N.J.: Transaction Books, for the Overseas Development Council, 1984).

[12] At the low end of the estimates of the "gap" is the Baker Plan, which envisages $9 billion per year for three years of net new lending (plus an unspecified amount of new foreign direct investment). Other estimates put the "gap" at $15–30 billion per year. See Donald R. Lessard and John Williamson, *Financial Intermediation Beyond the Debt Crisis* (Washington, D.C.: Institute for International Economics, September 1985); Albert Fishlow, "Capital Requirements for the Developing Countries in the Next Decade," Paper prepared for the U.N. Committee for Development Planning, November 1985 (draft).

[13] Group of Thirty, *Foreign Direct Investment, 1973–87* (New York: Group of Thirty, 1984). As Goldsbrough points out, his analysis is actually more cautious than the Group of Thirty survey. His baseline scenario suggests a slightly lower real value of foreign direct investment flows 1983–87 in comparison to 1978–82; theirs suggests a slightly higher real value of foreign direct investment flows.

[14] In addition, Helleiner points out that approximately half of the foreign direct investment in one survey led to new debt obligations. G. K. Helleiner, *Direct Foreign Investment and Manufacturing for Export in Developing Countries: A Review of the Issues* (London: Commonwealth Secretariat, 1984), cited by Cable and Mukherjee.

[15] See Srilal Perrera, "Techniques in Protecting Foreign Investment Against Political Risk," Georgetown University Department of Government, November 1985 (unpublished Ph.D. thesis).

[16] The MIGA initiative envisions an initial capital base of SDR 1 billion, with guarantees for 70–95 per cent coverage of projects, starting at 1.5 times the capital and growing to 5 times the capital. A study of the need for political risk insurance by Arthur Young & Co. in 1982 suggested that between 25 per cent and 82 per cent of the investments covered by such insurance (in their study, by the Overseas Private Investment Corporation) would not go forward without the coverage. If one chooses the higher figure (82 per cent) for MIGA projects and assumes arbitrarily that 50 per cent of the MIGA coverage is not a direct substitute for private or bilateral political risk insurance, a growth rate of $500 million in new coverage per year would yield an "additionality" figure of approximately $200 million per year ($500 million $\times$ 50 per cent $\times$ 82 per cent = $205 million). Arthur Young & Co., *A Study of "Additionality" of OPIC Assistance to U.S. Private Direct Investment in Developing Countries* (Washington, D.C.: May 1982).

[17] See Theodore H. Moran, Stephen Kobrin, and Fariborz Ghadar, *Managing International Political Risk: Strategies and Techniques* (Washington, D.C.: Ghadar Associates, 1983); Perrera, op. cit.; John Purcell and Michelle Miller, "The World Bank and Private International Capital," in Richard E. Feinberg and Valeriana Kallab, eds., *Between Two Worlds: The World Bank's Next Decade* (New Brunswick, N.J.: Transaction Books, for the Overseas Development Council, forthcoming 1986).

[18] This estimate assumes a 4 to 1 ratio of foreign investment to World Bank loan, with half of the co-financing "B" loans not also having remedies clauses. Using an arbitrary 50 per cent additionality hypothesis (and no overlap with MIGA), by 1987, a flow of $300 million per year could be stimulated by this protection of the World Bank.

[19] Council of the Americas, *Debt, Economic Crisis and United States Companies in Latin America* (New York: Council of the Americas, September 1984).

# Summaries of Recommendations

## 1. Foreign Investment and Development: Theories and Evidence (Joseph M. Grieco)

An enormous amount of research is available on the questions of whether and how multinational enterprises help or hurt the prospects for growth in the Third World. These studies address three central questions: What is the distribution of gains between foreign firms and developing host countries? What shapes the distribution of gains between these two sets of actors? And what policies should developing countries pursue toward foreign enterprises?

At least four quite different schools of thought—the pro–foreign-direct-investment, *dependencia,* bargaining, and structuralist approaches—seek to respond to these questions. In addition, a large number of empirical studies have focused on: the impact of foreign capital on developing-country aggregate growth and distribution of national income; the introduction of new technology and its implications for the generation of employment and exports; the transmission of cultural norms and consumer tastes from advanced to developing countries; and the effects of foreign firms on political structures within developing countries. But neither the theoretical analyses nor the empirical studies have reached a firm consensus on whether and how multinationals nurture or constrain development in host countries in the Third World.

21

Keeping in mind the great differences across the four schools of thought and the absence of empirical consensus concerning MNCs and developing countries, the author derives from the literature the following lessons and policy recommendations:

- Developing-country governments should both encourage the inflow of foreign direct investment *and* construct policy institutions that can ensure the transparency of the operations of foreign firms within their respective economies.

- Developing countries can greatly enhance their prospects for receiving substantial gains from foreign capital if they undertake policies consciously aimed at fostering competition among foreign firms, between foreign firms and national enterprises, and between imports and goods locally produced by foreign enterprises.

- Host developing countries should consider acceptance of internationally defined limitations, which could be negotiated at the regional level, on the use of foreign investment incentives and performance requirements. In general, developing countries have an interest in phasing out artificial inducements or restrictions on the local operations of foreign firms, for the very success of these policies increasingly contributes to protectionism in the advanced countries.

- International organizations such as the World Bank's International Centre for the Settlement of Investment Disputes and its proposed Multilateral Investment Guarantee Agency (MIGA) can play a very helpful role in promoting foreign direct investment in developing countries and in facilitating conflict resolution between multinationals and host governments.

- The World Bank or the International Monetary Fund could serve as a convenient forum for the negotiation of model regional agreements on performance requirements and investment incentives. Moreover, the Bank or the Fund, or more specialized affiliated organizations such as the Bank's International Finance Corporation or its Centre for the Settlement of Disputes, could assist in implementing and monitoring such regional accords.

- The debate on multinationals in the Third World may provide U.S. policy makers with important insights into why developing-country officials feel the need to screen, harness, and ensure some formal measure of control over multinational activities. In the absence of some form of host-country regulation, developing countries feel they will be unlikely to achieve what in their view is a fair share of the gains from the local operations of multinational corporations.

## 2. Evaluating Foreign Investment (Dennis J. Encarnation and Louis T. Wells, Jr.)

Foreign investment can aid economic development if it contributes more to national income than it extracts. The majority of foreign projects do indeed make such a positive contribution, but those that do not are a very significant minority. The principal finding of new research conducted by the authors—corroborating earlier, more tentative studies—is that more than 30 per cent are actually an economic drain on host economies. The most important explanation of these negative effects is the high rate of trade protection enjoyed by investors in import-substituting industries, although government subsidies and overvalued exchange rates are, to a lesser extent, also responsible.

As a result of these government policies, foreign investors continue to find projects financially attractive even if these are economically costly to developing countries. To rectify this disjuncture, most developed-country economists recommend that developing countries lower import protection and diminish subsidies. But such structural adjustment is difficult to achieve. In its absence, a second-best solution is the screening of foreign investment.

Host-country screening of investment of course is not a new practice. Irrespective of their contribution to national income, foreign investors have long faced tedious negotiations with host-country government agencies and state enterprises before being allowed to enter most developing countries. Such screening mechanisms were typically organized in four ways—depending upon their degree of fragmentation—with wide variation across countries, among different industries in the same country, and over time in the same country. Each mechanism has its advantages and impediments, which shape the country's subsequent choice. That organizational choice is also related to a country's attitude toward foreign investment, the political importance of the proposed project, and the level of competition among governments seeking to attract foreign investment.

Even though all screening mechanisms, when implemented, have serious faults, the screening process can be simplified and improved. For example, export projects that consistently generate positive contributions to national income can be screened separately and swiftly, while projects in import-competing industries—especially those with high rates of effective protection—merit much closer scrutiny. Assistance from the World Bank and the OECD developed countries in devising workable screening mechanisms is preferable to exhortations for their removal prior to structural adjustment. Indeed, in the absence of such reform, developing countries have good reason to ignore the exhortations from Washington that they remove barriers to foreign investment—especially when such advice for liberalization is inconsistent with other advice and with policies in the OECD countries themselves.

## 3. Foreign Investment in Low-Income Developing Countries
## (Vincent Cable and Bishakha Mukherjee)

There is a growing interest in the role that foreign investment can play in the development process not only for the more advanced developing economies, but also for the low-income countries, which, with a few exceptions, have so far attracted little investor interest.

However, on the basis of evidence from Commonwealth countries, the authors conclude that, although there are some promising possibilities, it would be unrealistic to expect low-income countries to derive benefits from an improved climate for foreign investment. Even if these countries take the steps necessary to improve the investment climate and offer inducements, most of them will continue to find it difficult to stimulate investor interest because of their lack of a substantial home market, their poor infrastructure, or their paucity of resources. Moreover, many of these countries, especially those of Sub-Saharan Africa, are currently experiencing extreme external financing and debt problems that have led them to take actions, such as controls over remittances, that are inimical to new inflows.

## 4. Multinational Corporations and Third World Agriculture
## (David J. Glover)

In agriculture, as in other sectors, the involvement of foreign investors in developing countries has taken a variety of forms in recent years. Foreign direct investment through plantation ownership has been supplemented and to some extent replaced by systems that involve local farmers in crop production. Production contracting, often including host-country governments as intermediaries or sources of finance, appears to satisfy the nationalist sentiments of the host while lowering the financial and political exposure of the investor. Farmers can benefit from access to export markets, technology, and credit. These new forms of involvement in agriculture may thus contain potential for mutual benefits.

The author surveys the variety of forms—ranging from plantations to contract farming to arm's-length sales—through which foreign firms interact with developing-country agriculture. He argues that new forms of involvement must be carefully considered and selectively applied if the potential benefits are to be realized. In some cases, the replacement of plantations with new forms of involvement has shifted risk and financial burdens from foreign firms to host-country governments and producers. In cases where local producers are themselves employers, wages and working conditions have frequently deteriorated with the transfer of production from foreign firms to local ones.

Negative effects have been most common in situations where production contracting has been imposed on unwilling firms, and where decentralized smallholder production is more costly than centralized production. Small farmers have most often benefited when producing high-value, labor-intensive crops, such as fruits and vegetables, and, to some extent, when producers' associations are involved.

The author recommends that new forms such as contract farming not be considered as panaceas and that production systems be matched to the economic and technological imperatives of particular crops and markets. In some cases, plantation production with an effective taxation system may be more beneficial to labor and to the economy as a whole than inefficient production contracting.

Host-country governments can enhance the viability of production-contracting schemes by adopting realistic pricing policies, by permitting or promoting farmers' associations, by exploring the greater incorporation of food crops in predominantly cash-cropping schemes, and by developing local markets for surplus and rejected produce intended for export markets.

Since the U.S. Agency for International Development actively promotes the new forms of involvement in agriculture, the United States can exert some leverage in choosing forms that will benefit small farmers. It might, for example, insist on the inclusion of growers' organizations in agricultural projects, or it could request greater financial participation from the private sector. Reducing tariff and non-tariff barriers to agricultural imports would provide major benefits to developing countries. The relocation of some production from the United States to developing countries would also reduce the demand for unskilled agricultural labor in the United States, much of which is satisfied by illegal immigration.

## 5. New Forms of Investment in Developing Countries
### (Charles P. Oman)

New forms of investment—such as joint ventures, licensing, franchising, and turnkey and management contracts—are business operations that lie in a gray area between the traditional international activities of firms, namely arm's-length exports and wholly or majority-owned foreign direct investment. The importance of these new forms has grown significantly in the North-South context since the early 1970s. This growth reflects, and may reinforce, a changing division of risks and responsibilities among the three principal participants in international investment in developing countries: multinational firms, international lenders, and host countries.

Many developing countries are today reassessing their policies on traditional foreign direct investment, often with a view to attracting more of it. At the same time, multinational firms—including both "majors" and "newcomers" or market-share "followers"—are finding that new forms of investment can hold important advantages, especially in reducing exposure and shifting risks onto lenders or host countries.

It has to be recognized that in this context foreign investment cannot to any significant extent reduce the need for long-term concessional finance. This is especially true in relation to funding public-sector projects for physical infrastructure and social development, which foreign investment may help to stimulate, but which it cannot finance.

Against the background of this analysis, the authors offer the following conclusions and recommendations:

- Higher levels of concessional aid flows to low-income developing countries are required to help create both the improved infrastructure and the general economic conditions that are necessary to induce foreign investment flows.

- In view of the small domestic markets of many low-income developing countries, export-oriented investment needs particular encouragement. A key factor influencing such investment is access to major markets. The removal of protectionist barriers in the industrial countries is therefore important to investment flows as well as to trade. Where major barriers present serious problems—notably the Multi-Fibre Arrangement in the case of textiles—liberal provision should be made for low-income and small exporters.

- Agencies such as the International Finance Corporation (IFC) and the Commonwealth Development Corporation (CDC) have a particularly important role in low-income developing countries in providing catalytic financing for foreign direct investment where investors are reluctant to take financial risks. The IFC currently has only a modest proportion of its financial commitments in these countries, but the recent capital increase and reorientation of its lending program should enable it to play a much bigger role.

- For host countries seeking to maintain an inflow of foreign investment over a long period, there is little alternative to redefining domestic economic policy to be more sympathetic to private-sector activity as a whole and to providing a growth environment. In the short run, some interesting possibilities for investment do exist in, for example, mining, tourism, and some variants of export-oriented manufacturing. Moreover, a variety of techniques can be used more widely to introduce a greater equity element into foreign collaborations and to attract both new overseas investment and profit reinvestment in existing foreign enterprises.

For the host countries, the most important advantage of new forms of investment is the potential for both increased domestic control over investment and a larger local share of returns. A country's ability to benefit from that potential appears to depend less on its regulation of foreign investment per se than on the coherence and effectiveness of its industrial and macro-economic policies, and on its ability to take advantage of rivalry among foreign firms. The latter of course also depends on the size and perceived dynamism of the local market, and on the levels of local technological, managerial, and entrepreneurial skills.

One potential risk of new forms of investment for host countries is continued dependence on foreign firms—for example, for access to new technology or to world export markets—under conditions where those firms are less committed to the long-run success of the investment than under traditional foreign direct investment. There is a danger that any gains that host countries derive from new forms of investment will not be commensurate with the increased risks and costs that they assume.

Another danger is that decisions on whether to invest and how much capacity to install may be de-linked from world market conditions and technology supply. In new forms of investment, these decisions are often taken by host-country participants instead of multinational corporations, which usually have greater mastery of world-market conditions and of technology supply. Such de-linking may exacerbate tendencies in some industries toward over-production or excess capacity—imbalances that can imply major costs and risks for firms in those industries in developed as well as developing countries. The result may be—and already has been in some cases—aggravated international trade and investment relations, notably in the North-South context, but also among the industrial countries. Such imbalances can lead to increased pressures for state intervention in trade (including anti-dumping measures and other forms of protectionism), in financial markets, and even in investment activities.

On the policy front, two further points deserve emphasis. First, most international investment by firms takes place, and increasingly so, within the major industrial countries. Thus any negative impact of certain new forms of North-South investment on the global economy could at most be one of exacerbating in some industries difficulties that originate in industrial countries and must be resolved in these countries (by industrial restructuring and resisting protectionism).

Second, government policies most likely to enhance the potential advantages of new forms of investment—for both host countries and the global economy—are policies that encourage firms to make long-term commitments to investing in production in developing countries. Such commitments—as opposed to a sometimes myopic emphasis on risk avoidance and on short-term cash flows—can be encouraged in the leading industrial countries by policies that promote stability and predictability of interest and exchange rates, that resist protectionism, and that enhance the transparency and international coordination of industrial policies.

## 6. Host-Country Policies to Attract and Control Foreign Investment (Stephen Guisinger)

National policies designed to attract and control direct foreign investment have come under intense scrutiny in both developed and developing countries in recent years. Debt-burdened developing countries are seeking the most efficient means of attracting new inflows of foreign equity in order to achieve investment growth targets. Developed countries, particularly the United States, have become concerned that the web of non-trade incentives and controls now in place in many countries may soon rival tariffs as distorters of world-wide patterns of trade and investment—especially now that many countries make incentive awards contingent on a firm's willingness to expand exports or reduce imports.

Three important questions about investment incentives and controls are the following: Do countries use incentives to compete for foreign investment? Are incentives effective in increasing foreign investment levels? And have performance requirements influenced international patterns of trade and capital flows? The author finds that little useful empirical research has been conducted on any of these issues. One reason for this is the absence of any clear consensus on the definition of "incentives."

Guisinger finds that if "incentives" are broadly defined to include tariffs and trade controls along with tax holidays, subsidized loans, cash grants, and other fiscal measures, they comprise more than forty separate kinds of measures. Moreover, the author emphasizes, the value of an incentive package is just one of several means that governments use to lure foreign investors. Other methods—for example, promotional activities (advertising, representative offices) and subsidized government services—also influence investors' location decisions. The author points out that empirical research so far has been unable to distinguish the relative importance of fundamental economic factors and of government policies in decisions concerning the location of foreign investment—let alone to determine the effectiveness of individual government instruments.

The author reports the results of a survey of multinational enterprises in four industries—automobiles, chemicals, computers, and food products—as evidence that government policies do make a difference. The survey (conducted as part of a research project on investment incentives and performance requirements and sponsored by the World Bank) indicated that, in almost two-thirds of the cases studied, the hypothetical absence of incentives would have altered the firm's location decision if competitor countries had simultaneously maintained their own incentive packages at traditional levels.

The same survey found that more than half of the seventy-four cases studied were subject to some form of performance requirement. These performance requirements acted as turbochargers, accelerating and redirecting the rents generated by incentives toward national objectives such as export promotion and import substitution. However, it was impossible to tell exactly what impact these performance requirements had on the investment projects surveyed because many were redundant, unenforced, or altered during the lifetime of the investment.

Several policy conclusions emerge from this study:

- Incentives and performance requirements probably do affect worldwide patterns of investment and trade, but much more research is needed to document the extent and significance of these measures.

- Where governments use incentive measures to compete for foreign investment, the trap of competitive bidding for investments can be obviated by agreements to limit the value of incentives granted. Because of the number and complexity of incentive measures, however, establishing limits will not be easy, and enforcing the limits will be even more difficult.

- Finally, because performance requirements are not independent of investment incentives, international negotiations on performance requirements cannot avoid drawing all national investment promotion measures into the discussions. If the elimination of trade-related performance requirements is the goal of these negotiations, then all parties should be prepared to accept major compensating changes in national investment incentive systems as an inevitable product of these negotiations.

## 7. Investment Trends and Prospects: The Link with Bank Lending (David Goldsbrough)

Although they declined significantly during the recent recession and debt crisis, flows of foreign direct investment into capital-importing developing countries have grown at a trend rate of around 4.5 per cent in real terms since the late 1960s. During the 1970s, however, foreign direct investment flows were overshadowed by the large increase in bank lending to developing countries.

The prospects for greater inflows of foreign direct investment substituting for the now sharply reduced level of bank lending depend in part on the policies adopted in the industrial countries. The shift in the source of net international savings from oil-exporting countries back toward industrial nations should encourage foreign direct investment because of the greater preference for equity investments in portfolio choices in the latter. However, total private capital flows, including foreign direct investment, will remain constrained as long as a large share of private savings is channeled into the financing of fiscal deficits in many industrial countries.

The policies in developing countries that will most encourage increased foreign direct investment are those that promote internal and external macro-economic balance, including exchange-rate and interest-rate policies which ensure that capital inflows are used to finance increased investment rather than consumption or capital flight.

On the assumptions of moderately favorable macro-economic policies but no major changes in specific policies concerning foreign direct investment, a partial recovery in the level of foreign direct investment flows—broadly similar to the recoveries that occurred after earlier recessions—can be expected through 1986, followed by sustained real growth of a little over 3 per cent. The adoption of less favorable policies, particularly with respect to exchange rates, monetary growth, and fiscal deficits in developing countries, could create a poorer investment climate that would cause foreign direct investment to decline in real terms.

# Investing in Development: New Roles for Private Capital?

# Chapter 1

# Foreign Investment and Development: Theories and Evidence

Joseph M. Grieco

During the past two decades, scholars have devoted enormous attention to the question of the effects of multinational corporations (MNCs) on developing countries.[1] This chapter reviews the major schools of thought and the leading empirical studies of foreign direct investment (FDI) and Third World development. In addition, it suggests how the scholarly debate on multinationals can help guide policy choices on these issues by all of the decision makers involved: developing host-country governments, multinational enterprises, international organizations, and home-country governments—with particular focus here on the United States.

## Four Major Theoretical Approaches

The literature on multinationals in the Third World is concerned with three central questions: Do developing countries *benefit* from foreign direct investment? What forces shape the *distribution of gains* between foreign firms and developing host countries? And what *policies* should developing countries follow toward multinationals?

### Proponents of Foreign Direct Investment

One set of responses to these questions is based on the general belief that national and foreign private-sector enterprises, if permitted to operate in competitive market conditions, offer developing countries the best prospects for speedy national economic growth.[2] Analysts who favor this pro-foreign direct investment perspective, described in detail in this section, do not, however, view multinational capital as a panacea for the Third World. For example, P. T. Bauer offered only a few (albeit highly favorable) references to foreign capital in his most recent discussion of the problem of development.[3] And Peter Drucker has emphasized that MNCs can "energize domestic potential," but that "by themselves, multinationals cannot produce development; they can turn the crank but not push the car."[4]

Although the pro-FDI approach does not find foreign capital to be a miracle cure-all for developing countries, its proponents do strongly believe that foreign direct investment helps Third World countries. Harry Johnson, for example, has argued that foreign investment brings to the host country "a 'package' of cheap capital, advanced technology, superior management ability, and superior knowledge of foreign markets for both final products, and capital goods, intermediate inputs, and raw materials."[5] Johnson has suggested that, because of continuing barriers to trade, migration, and capital flows, the diffusion of technology and the transfer of management expertise from industrial to developing countries are the most important external means by which the latter can improve their standard of living. Thus MNCs are useful to developing countries, according to Johnson, for "the activities of the multinational enterprise are now the major way in which the transmission and diffusion of advanced technology occur."[6]

In addition to transmitting technology, multinationals, according to the pro-FDI approach, serve as a major avenue for developing-country exports. Drucker, for example, has argued that developing countries need to employ export-oriented development strategies in order to meet their foreign-exchange and employment-creation requirements, and that such an orientation is much more likely to succeed if these countries can acquire "captive" export markets. Such markets, he maintained, are precisely what MNCs, with their worldwide sourcing and marketing, can offer.[7] In a similar vein, John Diebold has indicated that the generation of exports may be the single most important benefit that multinationals can provide Latin American countries.[8] More generally, Drucker has argued that the solution of many developing countries' unemployment problems "will to a very large extent require the presence of the multinationals—their investment, their technology, their managerial competence, and above all their marketing and export capabilities."[9]

Moreover, according to the pro-FDI approach, a number of the benefits that multinationals offer developing countries are the result of their normal business operations. Thus Johnson has suggested that "the international corporation has a hard-headed commercial interest, and not merely an ineffectual humanitarian interest, in promoting economic development in this way, the motivation being to tap new and profitable markets and to take advantage of relatively cheap labour."[10] Similarly, Drucker has argued that "for the multinational in manufacturing, distribution, or finance locating in a developing country, rapid economic development of the host country offers the best chance for growth and profitability. The multinational thus has a clear self-interest in the multiplier impact of its investment, product, and technology."[11]

Finally, Third World countries can enjoy these external benefits, according to the pro-FDI approach, while they augment their indigenous economic capabilities. For example, managers and workers trained by MNCs can be available for local enterprises, and the very competition presented by multinationals induces local firms to aspire to greater efficiency.[12]

On the grounds of the arguments sketched above, the pro-FDI approach strongly recommends that host countries avoid restrictive policies that might impede or deter foreign investors. Johnson, for example, has found that restrictions on foreign investment are almost never a "first-best" solution to national economic problems.[13] Other pro-FDI authors have favored the use of policy instruments on a highly constrained basis. Diebold, for example, agreed that developing countries ought to band together to counter efforts by multinationals to engage in tax evasion through transfer-pricing.[14] In addition, Drucker indicated that developing countries should "encourage" MNCs to commit themselves to make local facilities a part of their worldwide sourcing systems as soon as possible.[15] But these policy prescriptions are meant to underline the overall pro-FDI view that, in general, the key policy goal for developing countries is not to prevent being harmed by multinationals, but to accelerate the pace at which they receive a multitude of benefits from foreign enterprises.

### The Dependencia School

In contrast to the pro-FDI perspective, the *dependencia* school has emphasized the risks that multinationals pose for the Third World.[16] Theotonio Dos Santos argued that developing countries' economic difficulties do not originate in their isolation from the advanced countries but that "the most powerful obstacles to their full development come from the way in which they are joined to this international system."[17] Ronald Muller concluded that MNCs transfer technologies to developing countries that result in mass unemployment; that they monopolize rather than inject new capital resources; that they displace rather than generate or reinforce local businesses; and that they worsen rather than ameliorate these countries' balance-of-payments problems. Overall, there is "little doubt," Muller maintained, that multinationals "can only contribute to the further impoverishment of the poorest 60 to 80 per cent of Third World populations."[18]

While Muller found very little shared interest between multinationals and developing countries, Fernando Henrique Cardoso argued that MNCs "put a dynamic element into operation in the internal market" of many Latin American countries, and therefore "*to some extent*, the interests of the foreign corporations become compatible with the internal prosperity of the dependent economies. In this sense, they promote growth." Cardoso suggested, however, that the costs of this pattern of development include income concentration, too great an emphasis on luxury consumer durables, foreign indebtedness, and unemployment.[19] Dependent development may promote growth for an "urban-industrial sector," but, according to Cardoso, the net result might be "increasing relative misery."[20] Finally, Cardoso and Enzo Faletto found that many Latin American countries did achieve partial industrialization through acceptance of foreign capital, but that they did so "at the expense of the autonomy of the national economic system and of policy decisions for development."[21]

*Dependencia* writers have emphasized at least three factors in explaining how developing countries find themselves in highly undesirable relations with multinational corporations. First, currently unequal relations are deeply rooted in history. While serving as raw-material or natural-resource exporters (usually under the tutelage of foreign enterprises), many Third World countries—according to Furtado and to Charles Wilber and James Weaver—experienced extreme concentrations of income in elites that aspired to the consumption standards of the "metropolitan" economies.[22] Later these elites would permit entry of foreign firms in order to gain access to advanced-country consumer goods, thus opening the doors to new dependency. Second, MNC control of technology and of consumer preferences has reinforced their influence in the less developed countries; Furtado, for example, argued that these two forms of control have been "a decisive factor" in the domination of developing countries by multinational enterprises.[23] Third, dependency relations have been solidified in recent years by the operation of an "alliance" between foreign capital, host-country governments, and externally oriented segments of the local business community. Adjustments in the distribution of gains among alliance members that might emerge from more aggressive host-country policies have not helped the majority within the developing country, for, as Cardoso and Faletto maintained, "the entrepreneurial-repressive state *dissociates* itself from the nation."[24]

Overall, the *dependencia* school rejects the pro-FDI analysts' depiction of the benefits derived from participation in the international economy; indeed, Dos Santos has argued that neo-classical trade theory, from which the pro-FDI perspective is derived, "seeks to justify the inequalities of the world economic system and to conceal the relations of exploitation on which it is based."[25] Thus some *dependencia* writers have urged developing countries to "delink" at least temporarily from the international economy. Dieter Senghaas, for example, suggested that "in the long run, the Third World has a chance of building up self-reliant and viable economies and societies only if it dissociates itself temporarily from the prevailing international economy, i.e., the metropolitan economies."[26] Cardoso and Faletto indicated that, in the Third World, "it is not realistic to imagine that capitalist development will solve basic problems for the majority of the population." For them, the issue was not simply national growth and autonomy: "In the end what has to be discussed as an alternative is not the consolidation of the state and the fulfillment of 'autonomous capitalism,' but how to supersede them." They concluded that "the important question, then, is how to construct paths to socialism."[27]

## The Bargaining Approach

The pro-FDI and *dependencia* approaches each predict a specific, although very different, distribution of benefits between multinationals and developing countries. A third approach, that of the bargaining school, has suggested that distributions of gains emerge from negotiations between foreign firms and host-country governments. The bargaining school has found that foreign direct investments often occur in industries in which market imperfections create opportunities for firms to enjoy relatively high profits through foreign operations.[28] At the same time, the bargaining school has assumed that a host government can veto a firm's entry if it finds the latter's proposed terms to be wholly unacceptable. In these circumstances, the enterprise's terms of entry (which determine the distribution of gains between the host country and the enterprise) result from negotiations between the government and the foreign firm.[29]

The indeterminacy of gains and the necessity of bargaining are two core insights of the proponents of the bargaining approach. In addition, this approach has suggested that bargains struck between multinationals and host countries often initially favor the former but that, as a result of renegotiations of the terms of the relationship between the two over time, the balance of benefits tilts increasingly in favor of the latter. One key cause for this "obsolescing bargain" is that failed—and therefore costly—investments (in a natural resource industry, for example) are not taken into account by a host government as it assesses the return to a foreign firm on what develops into a successful investment. As Raymond Vernon noted, "The projects that succeed take the limelight; what was once a wistful hope becomes a tangible bonanza."[30] Once a foreign natural-resource subsidiary is successful, Theodore Moran has observed, "the whole atmosphere that surrounds the foreign-host relationship changes and old doubts are forgotten, and the terms of the relationship no longer correspond to the 'realities of the situation'."[31] Thus the initially high level of risk associated with the investment declines, and the host government no longer believes that the high returns to the firm are justified. In addition, once a raw material has been located or a developing-country market has proved to be profitable, other foreign investors, engaging in what Frederick Knickerbocker has termed "oligopolistic reaction," seek entry into the country, thus enhancing the latter's bargaining power with each investor.[32]

Reductions in risk and international oligopolistic rivalry are two of the factors that operate to the long-term advantage of the developing country. A third factor is the establishment of host-country institutions and processes capable of exploiting these favorable conditions. (A useful overview of the range and characteristics of these institutions and processes is provided in Chapter 2 of this volume.) At first, host-country governments may not have the technical skills needed to assess the real risk associated with an investment and thus may agree to terms that in retrospect seem excessively favorable to the foreign firm. But this problem may be self-correcting; as Moran has noted: "Successful ventures . . . provide an incentive for the host country to develop skills and expertise appropriate to the industry. Beginning with elementary attempts to tighten the bargaining process, the country starts to move up a learning curve that leads from monitoring industry behavior to replicating complicated corporate functions."[33]

Overall, the initial success of foreign firms triggers national institution-building needed for more effective bargaining; as Alfred Stepan has suggested, "there is thus reason to think that the multinational corporations may well encourage the rise of countervailing bureaucracies in which the state will play a major role."[34]

According to the bargaining perspective, developing countries can learn how to extract greater benefits from multinationals. The key policy prescription that has emerged from the bargaining school's analysis is that foreign direct investments ought to be permitted, even encouraged, by host governments *and* that these governments ought to build the national institutions needed to enhance the country's share of the resulting benefits. The bargaining school has been less sanguine than the pro-FDI approach that the host developing countries will automatically enjoy gains as a result of their acceptance of foreign direct investments. On the other hand, in contrast to the *dependencia* school's view that multinationals increase their power over host countries or co-opt their national elites, the bargaining school has found that the cleavage between host governments and foreign firms remains very deep and that the former do seek, with ever-greater levels of success over time, to extract increasingly significant gains from multinationals.

### The Structuralist Approach

More recently, a new body of literature has emerged, however, that challenges the bargaining school's optimism about the long-term negotiating prospects of the Third World. What might be labeled the structuralist school has argued that developing countries may in fact experience a long-term *decrease* in their power over high-technology manufacturing MNCs. The bargaining school itself had been hesitant to extend its understanding of the "obsolescing bargain" in natural-resource industries to cases involving manufacturing. By the late 1970s, however, Vernon, Bergsten, Moran, and Horst were suggesting that, except for MNCs in extremely advanced technology industries, multinational manufacturers would increasingly succumb to host developing-country pressures. My own observations on this issue suggested that developing countries such as India and Brazil might be successful even with respect to seemingly invulnerable high-technology multinationals, such as those in the data-processing industry.[35] The newest body of literature, in contrast, argues that the structural characteristics of international oligopolies and developing-country elites may interact in a way that reduces the power of host governments as foreign firms become entrenched in the local economy. As Douglas Bennett and Kenneth Sharpe have suggested of high-technology, consumer-goods industries such as automobiles, "other things being equal, the balance of bargaining power in such a manufacturing industry may with time shift toward the transnational firms rather than toward the LDC."[36] Gary Gereffi also found that manufacturing multinationals may be at their weakest prior to entry into a host economy, for, "once established, manufacturing TNCs begin to acquire domestic allies and their bargaining position vis-à-vis the government improves."[37]

Gereffi and Richard Newfarmer have offered three explanations of why the bargaining power of host countries vis-à-vis manufacturing multinationals can be very limited. First, there has continued to be the problem of technology: "In industries with technological barriers . . . the control of R&D by the home office has meant that any attempt to increase national control over the industry will run the risk of severing the lifeline of new innovations so crucial to the industry's progressive development."[38] A second limitation is the issue first noted by Cardoso and Faletto and by Peter Evans—that is, the operation of an alliance involving foreign firms, the government, and segments of local business, including the advanced labor and middle classes: "The shifting alliances upon which government support rests require an articulation and mediation of these private interest groups, and this has circumscribed the 'political will' of the state in its bargaining with TNCs over the structural dimensions of their participation in the market."[39] Third, bargains once struck between host governments and foreign firms in manufacturing—in contrast with those in natural resource industries—may be less susceptible to obsolescence. This is because of the integration of the country's productive resources into the worldwide system of the foreign corporation, the lower salience of a host-country learning curve, and the domestic political linkages to the multinationals.[40]

The structuralists' analysis of MNC effects on Third World economies has been in basic agreement with that of the *dependencia* approach as articulated by Cardoso and Faletto. However, the structuralists have not found that either de-linkage or socialism are valid options for the developing world. Taking a position much closer to the bargaining school, Evans found in Brazil that "the global rationality of the multinationals seriously detracted from their national contribution to local accumulation, but that the contradictions between their global strategies and local priorities were resolvable by bargaining."[41] Similarly, Gereffi and Newfarmer have suggested that "assertive public policy can substantially increase the benefits of transnational trade and investment accruing to developing countries." They indicate, however, that bargaining alone will not reduce the extreme inequalities in income that characterize many developing economies, and they suggest that "ultimately, the development task of the future is to build domestic political coalitions favoring the emergence of appropriate policies that do redress the worsening inequalities in many Latin American countries."[42]

These, then, are the four main contending schools of thought on the question of multinational enterprises in the Third World.

The pro-FDI approach is useful in that it outlines the range of benefits that, at least in principle, MNCs can offer developing countries. However, if this approach's high-competition assumption does *not* characterize the industry in which foreign investments are being made, then potentially severe problems may arise concerning the distribution of gains between foreign firms and host countries. In addition, the pro-FDI approach often does not offer a very complete accounting of the political problems associated with foreign capital. Johnson, for example, suggested that, if multinationals produce inappropriate luxury consumer durables in developing countries because these countries have highly unequal distributions of income, then the problem of inappropriate production by MNCs ought to be mitigated by national income-redistribution policies; yet this begs the question of whether the national governing coalition would be willing to implement such policies.[43]

The *dependencia* school has recognized the ways in which multinational corporations can contribute to, if not exacerbate, social inequality within developing countries. However, even the analysis presented by Cardoso and Faletto suffers from assigning too great a degree of significance to MNCs as a force in the Third World; moreover, while these authors suggested that socialism may enhance the prospects for advancement of the majority of the population in many developing countries, they did not explain how socialist Third World states, which would still be characterized by relatively small economies and underdeveloped technological capabilities, would be materially *less* dependent on the more developed capitalist and socialist countries.

The bargaining school has a better understanding than the pro-FDI approach of the structural weaknesses of developing countries in the international economy and thus of the difficulty of assuring the transfer of gains to them. In addition, the bargaining school has a better sense than the *dependencia* school of the realistic possibilities for developing states at least to learn to manage their circumstances of dependency in ways that yield a progressively larger share of the gains. The bargaining school has difficulties, however, on the internal distribution issue. It has tended to focus on increases in the extraction of greater overall, national gains from multinationals by developing-country governments; what it has not yet addressed sufficiently is the question of which societal groups within developing countries actually are able to enjoy these gains.

The structuralist approach, which combines elements of the *dependencia* and bargaining schools, understands that there may be both substantial opportunities for enhanced host-country gains from multinationals and tight limits on the degree to which host countries can reduce their dependency and increase their shares of the gains. The structuralist approach also provides a potentially better understanding than the bargaining school of the problem that enhanced national gains may not be widely distributed within the host developing societies. A drawback of the structuralist perspective (shared by the bargaining school to some degree) is that it has not yet established valid benchmarks for a realistic assessment of "true" improvement in a developing country's position vis-à-vis multinationals. In addition, the structuralist school has suggested that it is the international oligopolistic character of MNCs that causes them to have interests at odds with those of developing countries. But it is not clear that national private enterprises, if they could take the place of the foreign firms, would act in ways more favorable to the developing country. This last point raises the question of what scholars have learned empirically about the behavior and effects of multinationals in the Third World.

## Empirical Issues, Studies, and Findings

One very basic issue addressed by a number of empirical studies is the effect of foreign direct investment on the aggregate growth of developing countries. Volker Bornschier and his associates, for example, have argued that FDI inhibits developing-country growth.[44] In a multiple-regression analysis of variance in the rates of growth of gross national product (GNP) per capita in seventy-six developing countries between 1960 and 1975, Bornschier and Jean-Pierre Hoby have argued that flows of foreign direct investment were associated *positively* but stocks were associated *negatively* with growth in income per capita. They have suggested that flows of foreign direct investment inject new capital into a country and thus initially spur growth; over time, however, the more powerful negative effects of multinationals begin to work their way through the economy and constrict further growth. They have argued that this negative relationship holds across mining, agriculture, and manufacturing.[45] Bornschier, Christopher Chase-Dunn, and R. Rubinson found that relatively richer Third World countries experience a greater constriction of long-term growth because of foreign investment stocks than do poorer countries. Finally, the differences between the effects of flows and stocks of foreign investments was held to obtain across Latin America, Asia, and Africa.[46] Significantly, a multiple regression analysis conducted by Michael Dolan and Brian Tomlin of per capita GNP growth in sixty-six developing countries between 1970 and 1973 appeared basically to confirm

Bornschier's observations of the differential impact of flows and stocks of foreign direct investment.[47]

However, these studies by Bornschier and his associates have been challenged on both methodological and empirical grounds. On methodology, Richard Caves has demonstrated that because two of Bornschier's independent variables—stocks of foreign direct investment and income per capita in 1950—are positively related to one another, then a negative statistical relationship must result between stocks of foreign investment and growth in per capita income; this negative relationship, in other words, might have been a statistical artifact of Bornschier's specification of independent variables.[48] On the empirical side, Robert Jackman, in a regression analysis of growth of per capita GNP in seventy-two developing countries between 1960 and 1978, employed as independent variables not only the indicators of foreign direct investment flows and stocks, domestic capital formation, and initial national wealth that were used in the studies cited above, but also initial population size and growth in population. Jackman found stocks of foreign direct investment to be positively associated—at a statistically significant level—for relatively *poorer* developing countries, and negatively associated—but not at a statistically significant level—for relatively *more advanced* economies. He also found that the growth of foreign direct investments was not statistically related to growth in lower-income developing countries but was positively related at a statistically significant level for relatively richer developing countries. Jackman concluded that, once the size of developing countries is taken into account, the level of foreign direct investment "has no consistent effect on growth, one way or another."[49]

Moreover, John Rothgeb, in his analysis of growth of per capita income in eighteen developing countries between 1950 and 1976, found stocks of U.S. foreign direct investment to be negatively related to growth at a statistically significant level for the sample as a whole but not for a sub-sample composed of Jamaica and seven Latin American countries. His sectoral findings were even more curious: Stocks of U.S. investments in agriculture, manufacturing, transportation and communications, and domestic trade were often positively related to growth of sectoral income (although rarely at statistically significant levels) in the full sample and especially in the Latin American (and Caribbean) subgroup.[50]

In addition to the question of changes in aggregate national growth, empirical studies have examined the *dependencia* proponents' argument that multinationals induce a more concentrated distribution of income in developing countries. Bornschier and his associates, for example, have reviewed a number of quantitative studies and concluded that foreign direct investment is associated with a worsening in the income distribution of developing countries.[51] Vincent Mahler's analysis, relating sector-specific foreign direct investment in 1967 to income inequality in 1970 in sixty-eight developing countries, found a statistically significant association between income concentration in the top 20 per cent of the population and foreign investment in manufacturing, but not in mining or agriculture. Mahler reported statistically significant associations between foreign investment in all three sectors and the income concentration of the top 5 per cent of the population.[52] However, Dolan's and Tomlin's analysis of the effects not just of foreign direct investment, but also of exports and foreign aid, found that none of these external linkages were associated with income inequality at statistically significant levels—although the authors did find a "weak" positive impact of foreign investment. They concluded that external linkages are "generally unrelated to a developing country's income inequality," indicating the relatively greater significance of internal economic and political forces.[53]

Beyond these studies of the *overall* impact of multinational corporations on the growth and distribution of national income in developing countries, a number of analyses have focused on more *specific* aspects of multinational corporate operations in the Third World. Several studies have sought to estimate the economic desirability of the technology brought to developing countries by multinational enterprises. One key question concerns the effective price that multinationals have charged for technology. Constantine Vaitsos's early and highly influential study found that royalty payments, technical fees, tie-in clauses leading to the purchase of overpriced intermediate goods, export restrictions, and other limitations had led technology acquisition during most of the 1960s to become a major burden on the balances of payments of the countries of the Andean region.[54] More recently, Richard Newfarmer found that, during the mid-1960s, less developed countries paid approximately one-third more than developed countries for imported heavy electrical equipment such as turbines, generators, transformers, and electrical switching-gear.[55]

However, many developing countries appear to possess the capacity to manage—at least to some degree—the problem of high-priced foreign technology. Vaitsos found that Colombia in the late 1960s was able to mitigate balance-of-payments problems associated with technology payments through an investment-screening process managed by a new institution, the Comité de Reglias. This new state institution restructured royalty agreements so that payments in 1970 were 40 per cent lower than in 1967, a savings of $8 million; in addition, the Comité sharply curtailed the use of other costly practices associated with earlier technology transfers.[56] More generally, Daniel Chudnovsky found that governments in a number of Latin American countries, acting individually or (if members) through the Andean Pact, were able to reverse during the mid-1970s what up to that point had been a decade-long upward trend in royalties and technical fees to U.S. enterprises. Most interestingly, Chudnovsky concluded that the subsequent increase in dividends and interest payments did not make up for the reduction in technology payments, and total remittances by U.S. firms declined during the 1970s relative to overall U.S. investment in the region. This suggests that U.S. firms, unable to repatriate profits through high prices for technology transfers, apparently chose to reinvest earnings rather than to seek repatriation through dividends and interest payments to corporate headquarters.[57]

Another key issue relating to technology is whether multinational enterprises have chosen to use equipment appropriate to the relative abundance of labor in most developing countries. Gerald Helleiner, and Sanjaya Lall and Paul Streeten, for example, have explained how MNCs can exacerbate developing countries' already severe employment and income-distribution problems if they employ capital-intensive, labor-saving technologies in economies characterized by high rates of unemployment.[58] Richard Newfarmer has demonstrated that the bulk of the scholarly literature suggests that multinationals are not highly adaptable to local factor endowments in terms of changing production methods originally used in the industrial countries; he also has observed, however, that the literature does not find that local firms perform demonstrably better in this regard.[59] Indeed, Louis Wells, on the basis of his analysis of foreign and local manufacturers in Indonesia, has suggested that "foreign-ness" may be less useful as an explanation of non-adaptability of techniques than the level of price competition within a particular industry: Those industries with very high levels of protection—i.e., an absence of competition—also tended to be the least adaptable to local abundancies of labor.[60] From their review of a number of empirical studies, Bergsten, Horst, and Moran have concluded that, "to the extent host-country authorities encourage competition among foreign investors or between foreign investors and local firms, they encourage multinationals to use labor-intensive technologies."[61]

This thesis, linking competitive market structures and labor-intensive processes, was dramatically demonstrated by Gustav Ranis and Chi Schive in their study of foreign direct investment in Taiwan. They found that within a given industry, foreign firms that were oriented to the Taiwanese domestic market employed twice the amount of fixed assets per worker as foreign firms in the same industry that were oriented to the relatively more competitive international market. They also found that, controlling for industry, exports generated almost twice as much employment as did domestic sales.[62] Finally, very dramatic illustrations are available of multinationals adapting both their products and their manufacturing processes: Susumu Watanabe, for example, described the emergence of "Asian utility vehicles" in the ASEAN region during the 1970s, a process undertaken by major international automobile enterprises to produce passenger cars based on simplified designs, more local content, and relatively more labor per unit than in the industrial countries.[63]

Concerning the overall impact of multinationals on Third World employment, Muller has argued that "MNCs are eliminating many more jobs than they are creating."[64] This argument assumes that a given investment undertaken by a national as opposed to a foreign firm would yield greater host-country employment; yet a report by the International Labour Office (ILO) indicates that the question of the hypothetical employment effects of national investments "cannot be answered in any satisfactory way."[65] However, in their recent study comparing the actual employment effects of U.S. and local investments in the same set of manufacturing industries in seven Latin American countries during 1966–1970, Patricio Meller and Alejandra Mizala found that U.S. affiliates do use labor-saving processes to a greater degree than local firms in the same manufacturing branch. In manufacturing generally, however, the rate of growth in employment of U.S. affiliates during 1966–1970 (3.1 per cent annually) was found to be similar to that of Latin American manufacturing as a whole. And although U.S. affiliates created less employment per unit of value added than the manufacturing branch as a whole in Argentina, Chile, Mexico, and Venezuela, the opposite was true in Brazil, Colombia, and Peru. On average, American firms produced only some 5 per cent fewer jobs than the manufacturing branch as a whole in the seven countries.[66]

Finally, studies have not yet determined how to assess the magnitude of a foreign investment's *indirect* employment-creation effects in spurring the emergence of subcontractors or suppliers—that is, backward-linkage effects of foreign direct investment. However, a report prepared for the ILO on foreign electronics firms in Singapore and a study by the United Nations Centre on Transnational Corporations (UNCTC) on international automobile firms in India, Morocco, and Peru have both suggested that such indirect effects can be substantial and positive. (The UNCTC report emphasized that national governments need to pressure foreign firms in order to bring about these positive second-order effects in the host economy.[67])

In addition to technology payments, another potentially important foreign-exchange problem that multinationals create for developing countries is transfer-pricing. Sanjaya Lall found that transfer-pricing is difficult to document and control, and that different
industries may have differing propensities regarding transfer-pricing as a method of earnings repatriation.[68] However, even if developing countries learn how to control excessive earnings repatriations,
there still remains the question of whether or not MNCs contribute
to the solution of developing-country balance-of-payments problems
by generating exports. Rhys Jenkins, for example, found that locally owned firms in Mexico exported 19.5 per cent of turnover
while foreign affiliates exported 12.6 per cent of sales in 1974.[69] On
the other hand, Sanjaya Lall and Sharif Mohammed found that
industries in India characterized by a relatively high presence of
foreign firms were more export-oriented than industries in which
the foreign presence was low—although the relationship was not
statistically significant.[70] Newfarmer has concluded that multinationals do not materially contribute to developing-country exports,
although he noted that these countries can use bargaining strategies to induce foreign firms to improve their export performance.[71]

In addition to these economic investigations, a number of studies have sought to estimate the non-economic effects of multinational corporations in developing countries. For example, Armand
Mattelart has suggested that multinationals are an important
mechanism by which the advanced countries dominate the cultures
of the Third World. MNCs create bonds of cultural dependency,
according to Mattelart, through their control of cross-border data
flows, international advertising, the diffusion of news, and the
production of books, magazines, television programs, and motion
pictures.[72] In a study for UNESCO, Jean-Louis Reiffers and associates have suggested that multinational corporate control over the
perceptions, values, and tastes of host countries is so great that "it
is perhaps appropriate then to speak of a risk of 'ethnocide,' i.e., a
destruction of cultures."[73]

Numerous analysts have offered concrete examples of such a
transmission of tastes and perceptions. Michael Bader has argued
that multinational food and pharmaceutical enterprises resorted to
a wide range of marketing techniques to substantially increase the
consumption of infant formula in Latin America. Mattelart has
suggested that similar techniques were employed to induce consumers in the Ivory Coast to begin using a protein supplement
produced by Nestlé.[74] Fernando Reyes Matta studied newspaper
reportage by the major international news services (Associated
Press, United Press International, and Reuters) in Latin America
and found that regional news was consistently under-reported com-

pared with events in the industrial countries such as the United States.[75] And Colin Leys has suggested that resident multinational corporate executives in Kenya have set the standards for housing and personal consumption among the local elite.[76]

On the other hand, Stephen Kobrin has hypothesized that middle- and upper-income groups tend to be oriented to the acquisition of consumer goods regardless of whether they find themselves in industrial or developing countries; hence, purchasing patterns in developing countries may be due less to the marketing efforts of multinationals or the presence of MNC executives than to the emergence of a materialistic middle class in these nations.[77] Critics of multinational enterprises may argue that foreign firms are responsible for the emergence of this middle class, but this assumes that national corporations would not produce virtually the same group of consumption-oriented individuals.

Several studies have sought to assess the effects of multinational enterprises on the political structures of developing countries.[78] Thomas Biersteker, for example, has suggested that MNCs were partly responsible for the emergence of a *comprador* group that has squandered national resources in Nigeria.[79] Colin Leys has found that, in Kenya, foreign enterprises had direct access to central government ministries and used these contacts to prevent the emergence of a strong, independent labor movement in that country.[80] Gary Gereffi has reported that in Mexico, multinational drug firms have used their networks of local suppliers as well as national business organizations against a state enterprise, Proquivemex, which had tried to raise the price of *barbasco*, a raw material used in the production of steroid hormones.[81] Studies by Franklin Weinstein and by Thomas Biersteker suggest that foreign firms have exploited weaknesses in the enforcement structures of developing countries to evade compliance with the letter or the spirit of assertive national policies, while Lynn Krieger Mytelka has found that international agreements such as the Andean Pact's Decision 24 are extremely difficult to implement.[82] In addition, Bennett and Sharpe reported that the U.S., West German, and Japanese governments pressured the Mexican government on behalf of "their" respective international automobile firms during negotiations over the entry and expansion of the latter in the early 1960s; and Gereffi found that the U.S. government acted in a similar manner on behalf of American pharmaceutical enterprises in Mexico during the mid-1950s.[83]

While these studies have emphasized the power of multinationals in developing countries, other investigations have pointed to the limitations that may affect them. For example, Adalberto Pinelo reported that, during the 1960s, the previously powerful International Petroleum Company (IPC) increasingly became a pawn in Peruvian politics (tarring an opponent with association with the company had become very effective politics) and was eventually nationalized.[84] Charles Goodsell found that the U.S. government was often "out of step" with IPC as the latter negotiated with the Peruvian government over taxes and later over the disposition of its assets: In 1964 the U.S. government, contrary to company wishes, imposed sanctions on Peru, and in 1969 it declined to apply the Hickenlooper amendment.[85] Theodore Moran found that in the case of Chile, alliances between conservative national business groups and foreign copper companies were very fragile; and that during the course of twenty-five years, an extraordinary range of highly divergent national groups came to define their interests in terms of joining or supporting an attack on the Anaconda and Kennecott companies.[86] Finally, my own work indicates that local groups seeking to influence Indian computer policy found that accusations of collaboration with "foreign elements"—i.e., foreign computer firms—were a most effective tactic against their opponents.[87]

These studies have highlighted the point that multinational enterprises, as they enter and operate in developing countries, encounter and must adapt to highly complex societies with important political, economic, and cultural dynamics already at work. Indeed, Albert Hirschman has suggested that a key problem concerning MNCs is that they may accept too easily the social and political order within many Third World countries even if, for the purpose of real development, the institutions of these countries require drastic reform. He concluded that "the trouble with the foreign investor may well be not that he is too meddlesome, but that he is too mousy!"[88]

In sum, a wide range of often conflicting empirical studies have considered how multinational corporations in developing countries affect the rate of aggregate growth of these countries and the distribution of income within them; to estimate the cost and appropriateness of the technology transferred by MNCs; to gauge the overall export and employment-creation performance of foreign firms; and to determine how multinationals affect cultures and domestic political structures. At least two overall comments can be made about the empirical literature. First, many of the quantitative studies on the effects of multinationals on aggregate growth and income distribution are so overburdened with methodological uncertainties, and so many of their conclusions are based on technically non-significant factors, that one cannot at this time draw conclusions from them with any minimally acceptable level of confidence. Second, many studies indicate that multinationals are highly adaptive social agents, and therefore the degree to which these foreign enterprises help or hurt developing countries will be heavily influenced by the policy choices of the host countries themselves.

Each developing country will need to devise its own preferred mixture of assertive and accommodating policies toward multinational enterprises. It should be noted, however, that many of the studies point to the benefits of making the MNC operations more transparent to the host country and, perhaps even more significant, of exposing foreign firms to the competitive pressures of national firms and, especially, to those of other foreign firms. *Transparency* and *competition* appear to be the essential ingredients of bringing about a division of gains between the foreign enterprises and the host country that is progressively more favorable to the latter.

## Conclusion

This chapter has reviewed the major schools of thought on the relationship of multinational corporations and developing countries and considered some of the main empirical efforts to understand the implications of foreign capital for the Third World. How can these debates within the scholarly community help guide the policy choices of various actors interested in the impact of multinationals on Third World development?

First, developing countries are probably correct in estimating that some form of policy structure and some degree of regulation are needed to ensure the receipt of an equitable share of the gains from the operations of foreign firms within their nations. Yet policy should seek less to direct MNC operations than to ensure that foreign firms recognize that they must perform well or be displaced by national or other foreign firms.

In addition, a wide range of developing countries—including Brazil, Colombia, India, Indonesia, Mexico, Nigeria, and Venezuela—should carefully consider the thesis that they have in large measure already demonstrated their power vis-à-vis multinational enterprises. Indeed, their problem increasingly may stem not from too few but rather from too many successful efforts to shape and control local MNC operations—for the unintended negative consequences of host-country influence may soon outweigh the gains achieved by the application of such power. For example, protectionist pressures in the industrial countries may in some measure be traced to the greater success of countries such as Brazil, Mexico, and (using different policy instruments) the Republic of Korea to press multinational firms to bring about greater exports from their countries.

The United States has already raised the question of international constraints on host-country performance requirements and investment incentives within the General Agreement on Tariffs and Trade (GATT); these policy instruments, as they are employed both by developing *and* developed countries, are identified and analyzed in depth in this volume by Stephen Guisinger. If the developing countries wish to avoid pressures on this issue from the United States and other industrial countries within the GATT and elsewhere, they must consider accepting some form of limitation on the use of their power to attract and control multinational enterprises. If they are reluctant to work on this issue with the advanced countries within the GATT, one possibility is for them to agree at a regional level on mutual restraints on performance requirements and investment incentives. The key point is that developing countries may soon, or indeed may already, face a new challenge: Policy effectiveness vis-à-vis multinationals may be defined not just in terms of acquiring and then using power, but also in terms of learning how to construct limitations on the use of that power.

International organizations might be able to play a positive role in the construction of such regional pacts on performance requirements and investment incentives. Broader negotiations under the auspices of the World Bank (and especially the Bank's International Center for the Settlement of Investment Disputes) or the International Monetary Fund could produce a model agreement that could be adapted to the special conditions and concerns of states within particular regions, such as the Andean region or perhaps all of Latin America, South Asia, China and Southeast Asia, and Africa. Such broader guidepost negotiations for regional pacts could be related to renewed efforts to conclude a Code of Conduct on Transnational Corporations, currently deadlocked in the United Nations.

In addition, the World Bank's new Multilateral Investment Guarantee Agency (MIGA), whose main proposed features are outlined in this volume by Theodore Moran, may promote foreign direct investments in the developing countries in a way that does not distort trade to the detriment of the United States and other industrial countries. One possible problem is that, in the course of defining itself as an 'insurer,' MIGA might choose to charge higher insurance premiums to corporations that 'give in' too easily in contract disputes. Such a policy would have the effect of rewarding intransigence rather than flexibility on the part of corporations as they bargain with their host governments. MIGA's standards for premiums must take into account the problem of moral hazard; but care must be taken to assure that a perfectly good method to reach the goal of managing the problem of moral hazard will not have the unintended consequence of impeding progress toward the equally valued goal of conflict resolution between MNCs and developing countries. One way to calibrate premiums to promote conflict resolution is to charge lower rates to companies that agree in advance to some form of third-party arbitration in the event of a contract dispute.

Many of the multinationals themselves have had sufficient experience in developing countries to recognize that, over time, host governments are likely to impose ever greater demands upon them. Yet MNC managers still may not be fully aware of the deeply ingrained concerns of many host-country policy officials that serve as the backdrop to national assertiveness on equity-sharing, profit repatriation, and technology transfer. Instead, corporate decision makers may consider a host country's increasingly harsh demands to be arbitrary, or not economically rational. Such corporate misestimation of host-country fears of multinationals is especially likely in the case of companies in technology-oriented manufacturing industries. These firms have the least experience in the Third World, and their managers may be substantially unaware of the often-difficult historical relationships between many host countries and MNCs in natural-resource industries.

This suggests that multinationals should take special care to ensure that their staff members who interact with host-country officials are aware not only of the particular contributions made by the company to the country—although major efforts should be made to estimate such benefits and to emphasize them—but also, more generally, of the country's history of experience with multinational enterprises. Moreover, MNC managers should have some familiarity with the critical literature on multinationals, for in many developing countries (especially in Latin America) these analyses have had a substantial impact on the universities and the national media, and therefore at least indirectly on the policy elites. Greater awareness of a country's historical experience and intellectual debate concerning MNCs may not be the foremost influence on the position of a multinational in a particular bargaining situation; however, such knowledge might help the corporation to craft proposals that address in a more constructive fashion relevant concerns that may not always be fully articulated by host-country negotiators.

Finally, this review of scholarly research yields a number of suggestions relevant for U.S. policy concerning foreign investments in developing countries. At first glance, the academic debate on these questions does not seem to lend itself readily to guidelines for U.S. policy. The U.S. government's traditional belief in the overall efficacy of foreign capital in the development process is indeed deeply ingrained. Moreover, even if decision makers were open to new perspectives on multinationals, the extreme diversity of views—both in terms of overall theories of foreign investments and development and of more narrowly defined empirical studies— might lead them to conclude that there is insufficient consensus within the scholarly community for the latter to serve as a source of guidance for concrete policies.

Yet the scholarly debate provides one key insight of great relevance: U.S. policy officials may wish to consider the proposition that while many Third World leaders' views on multinationals reflect the analyses presented by the structuralists and even the *dependencia* approach, their actions reflect the bargaining approach. Foreign direct investments may be viewed as potential sources of benefits as well as potential sources of problems for the host country, and many Third World policy makers may believe that only specific government actions will maximize the benefits and minimize the costs of accepting multinational enterprises. Hence, the bargaining, structuralist, and *dependencia* schools offer useful insights into the frame of reference within which many Third World policy statements and concrete measures on foreign direct investment are formulated.

If this analysis is correct, then most developing-country governments are unlikely to accept at face value the recent arguments presented by the Reagan administration that international rules should be formulated to constrain and eventually to dismantle the performance requirements and investment incentives that both industrial and developing countries have formulated with respect to foreign direct investment.[89] From the viewpoint of many developing countries, performance requirements may be especially important in their efforts to control multinationals and to ensure receipt of a "fair share" of the benefits arising from foreign corporate operations. And U.S. attempts to bring about international constraints on such requirements may be viewed by developing countries as an effort—whether intentional or not—to reverse developing-country advances in constructing more equitable balances of benefits between themselves and the industrial world. Indeed, the fact that the key home country is seeking to constrain the use of performance requirements may lead many developing-country governments to conclude that such requirements are in fact inducing a shift in benefits in their favor.

Finally, even if U.S. policy officials prefer the pro-FDI approach's general skepticism concerning the usefulness of performance requirements and other assertive developing-country policies toward multinationals, they may wish to note that the United States itself, both in its domestic economy and in its treatment of foreign enterprises, has instituted a number of policies reflecting the general analytical orientation of the bargaining and structuralist schools. The wide range of American anti-trust, food and drug, occupational health and safety, and consumer safety policies reflects a basic recognition that, in the absence of selective government intervention, market imperfections and other factors often can lead the private sector to generate highly unfavorable economic and social outcomes. This is not to say that the U.S. government should accept all host-country performance requirements, but rather, that it should acknowledge that market forces alone may not always lead to an acceptable generation and distribution of benefits between foreign enterprises, home-country economies, and host countries. Hard-nosed bargaining between MNCs and developing countries is likely to be an enduring feature of the international political economy. But better understanding of the concerns and objectives of host countries can enhance the prospects for successful resolution of future conflicts between these countries and multinational enterprises.

## Notes

Note: The author wishes to thank Richard E. Feinberg, Theodore H. Moran, and Daniel A. Sharp for their comments on earlier drafts, and to express his gratitude to the German Marshall Fund of the United States and to the Center for International Affairs at Harvard University for their support during the preparation of this essay.

[1]Helpful bibliographies in this field include United Nations, Centre on Transnational Corporations, *Bibliography on Transnational Corporations* (New York: United Nations, 1979); and Tagi Sagafi-nejad, *Transnational Corporations, Technology Transfer, and Development: A Bibliographic Sourcebook* (New York: Pergamon Press, 1980).

[2]American business-oriented statements on the question of multinationals in the Third World often frame their arguments in this manner; see, for example, Orville L. Freeman, *The Multinational Company: Instrument for World Growth* (New York: Praeger, 1981).

[3]P. T. Bauer, *Reality and Rhetoric: Studies in the Economics of Development* (Cambridge, Mass.: Harvard University Press, 1984), pp. 32–33.

[4]Peter F. Drucker, "Multinationals and Developing Countries: Myths and Realities," *Foreign Affairs*, No. 53 (October 1974), pp. 126–27.

[5]Harry Johnson, "Economic Benefits," in H. R. Hahlo, J. Graham Smith, and Richard W. Wright, eds., *Nationalism and the Multinational Enterprise: Legal, Economic, and Managerial Aspects* (Leiden, The Netherlands: A.W. Sijhoff, 1977), p. 168.

[6]Ibid., p. 169.

[7]Drucker, "Multinationals and Developing Countries," op. cit., p. 128.

[8]John Diebold, "Multinational Corporations . . . Why Be Scared Of Them," *Foreign Policy*, No. 12 (Fall 1973), p. 83.

[9]Drucker, "Multinationals and Developing Countries," op. cit., p. 134.

[10]Johnson, "Economic Benefits," op. cit., p. 169.

[11]Drucker, "Multinationals and Developing Countries," op. cit., p. 126.

[12]Johnson, "Economic Benefits," op. cit., p. 169.

[13]Harry Johnson, "The Efficiency and Welfare Implications of the International Corporation," in Charles P. Kindleberger, ed., *The International Corporation* (Cambridge, Mass.: MIT Press, 1970), pp. 56–57.

[14]Diebold, "Multinational Corporations," op. cit., p. 89.

[15]Drucker, "Multinationals and Developing Countries," op. cit., p. 129.

[16]For overviews of this literature, see Thomas J. Biersteker, *Distortion or Development: Contending Perspectives on the Multinational Corporation* (Cambridge, Mass.: MIT

Press, 1978), pp. 1–27; J. Samuel Valenzuela and Arturo Valenzuela, "Modernization and Dependency: Alternative Perspectives in the Study of Latin American Development," *Comparative Politics*, Vol. 10 (July 1978), pp. 535–57; and Tony Smith, "The Underdevelopment of Development Literature: The Case of Dependency Theory," *World Politics*, Vol. 31 (January 1979), pp. 247–88.

[17]Theotonio Dos Santos, "The Structure of Dependence," in Charles K. Wilber, ed., *The Political Economy of Development and Underdevelopment* (New York: Random House: 1973), p. 116. For similar assessments, see Osvaldo Sunkel, "Transnational Capitalism and National Disintegration in Latin America," *Social and Economic Studies*, Vol. 22 (March 1973), p. 136; and Celso Furtado, "The Brazilian 'Model'," *Social and Economic Studies*, Vol. 22 (March 1973), p. 122.

[18]Ronald Muller, "The Multinational Corporation and the Underdevelopment of the Third World," in Wilber, *Political Economy*, op. cit., p. 173.

[19]Fernando Henrique Cardoso, "Associated Dependent Development: Theoretical and Practical Considerations," in Alfred Stepan, ed., *Authoritarian Brazil: Origins, Policies, and Future* (New Haven, Conn.: Yale University Press, 1973), p. 149 (emphasis in original). Cardoso stressed the difference between himself and *dependencia* writers who perceived only underdevelopment of the Third World in "The Consumption of Dependency Theory in the United States," *Latin American Research Review*, Vol. 12, No. 3 (1977), p. 125.

[20]Ibid., p. 157.

[21]Fernando Henrique Cardoso and Enzo Faletto, *Dependency and Development in Latin America* (Berkeley: University of California Press, 1979), p. 162.

[22]Celso Furtado, "The Concept of External Dependence in the Study of Underdevelopment," in Wilber, *Political Economy*, op. cit., pp. 119–20; see also James H. Weaver and Charles K. Wilber, "Patterns of Dependency: Income Distribution and the History of Underdevelopment," in Charles K. Wilber, ed., *The Political Economy of Development and Underdevelopment*, 2nd ed. (New York: Random House, 1979), pp. 120–25.

[23]Furtado, "External Dependence," op. cit., p. 120.

[24]Cardoso and Faletto, *Dependency and Development*, op. cit., p. 212 (emphasis in original).

[25]Dos Santos, "Structure of Dependence," op. cit., p. 116.

[26]Dieter Senghaas, "The Case for Autarchy," in Charles K. Wilber, ed., *The Political Economy of Development and Underdevelopment*, 3rd Ed. (New York: Random House, 1984), p. 212.

[27]Cardoso and Faletto, *Dependency and Development*, op. cit., p. xxiv.

[28]Stephen Hymer developed this linkage between market imperfections and overseas direct investment; see Stephen H. Hymer, *The International Operations of National Firms: A Study of Foreign Direct Investment* (Cambridge, Mass.: MIT Press, 1976). Later he articulated a much more critical view of multinationals; see his collected essays in *The Multinational Corporation: A Radical Approach* (Cambridge: Cambridge University Press, 1979). Raymond Vernon's product-cycle model also attributed foreign investments to oligopolistic market imperfections; see Raymond Vernon, "International Investment and International Trade in the Product Cycle," *Quarterly Journal of Economics*, Vol. 80 (May 1966), pp. 192–200.

[29]For the development of the bargaining school, see Theodore H. Moran, "Multinational Corporations and Dependency: A Dialogue for Dependentistas and Non-dependentistas," in James A. Caparaso, ed., *Dependence and Dependency in the Global System*, special issue of *International Organization*, Vol. 32 (Winter 1978), pp. 81–82; and Joseph M. Grieco, *Between Dependency and Autonomy: India's Experience with the International Computer Industry* (Berkeley: University of California Press, 1984), pp. 172–73.

[30]Raymond Vernon, *Sovereignty at Bay: The Multinational Spread of U.S. Enterprises* (New York: Basic Books, 1971), p. 48.

[31]Theodore H. Moran, *Multinational Corporations and the Politics of Dependence: Copper in Chile* (Princeton, N.J.: Princeton University Press, 1974), p. 160.

[32]Frederick Knickerbocker, *Oligopolistic Reaction and the Multinational Enterprise* (Boston Mass.: Graduate School of Business Administration, Harvard University, 1973). See also Vernon, "International Investment," op. cit., p. 200; and C. Fred Bergsten, Thomas Horst, and Theodore H. Moran, *American Multinationals and American Interests* (Washington, D.C.: The Brookings Institution, 1978), p. 374.

[33]Moran, *Multinational Corporations and the Politics of Dependence: Copper in Chile*, op. cit., p. 164.

[34]Alfred Stepan, *The State and Society: Peru in Comparative Perspective* (Princeton: Princeton University Press, 1978), p. 235.

[35]For the evolution of Vernon's thinking, compare *Sovereignty at Bay*, op. cit., p. 256, with *Storm Over the Multinationals: The Real Issues* (Cambridge, Mass.: Harvard University Press, 1977), pp. 171–72. See also Bergsten, Horst, and Moran, *American Multi-*

*nationals*, op. cit., pp. 376–81; and Grieco, *Between Dependency and Autonomy*, op. cit., pp. 151– 56.

[36]Douglas C. Bennett and Kenneth E. Sharpe, "Agenda Setting and Bargaining Power: The Mexican State versus the International Automobile Industry," *World Politics*, Vol. 32 (October 1979), p. 86.

[37]Gary Gereffi, *The Pharmaceutical Industry and Dependency in the Third World* (Princeton, N.J.: Princeton University Press, 1983), pp. 16–61.

[38]Gary Gereffi and Richard S. Newfarmer, "International Oligopoly and Uneven Development: Some Lessons from Industrial Case Studies," in Richard S. Newfarmer, ed., *Profits, Progress and Poverty: Case Studies of International Industries in Latin America* (Notre Dame, Ind.: University of Notre Dame Press, 1985), p. 432.

[39]Ibid.; see also Peter Evans, *Dependent Development: The Alliance of Multinational, State, and Local Capital in Brazil* (Princeton, N.J.: Princeton University Press, 1978); and Douglas C. Bennett and Kenneth E. Sharpe, "The State as Banker and Entrepreneur," *Comparative Politics*, Vol. 12 (January 1980), pp. 169–70.

[40]Gereffi and Newfarmer, "International Oligopoly," p. 432.

[41]Evans, *Dependent Development*, op. cit., p. 276.

[42]Gereffi and Newfarmer, "International Oligopoly," op. cit., p. 434.

[43]Johnson, "Efficiency and Welfare Implications," op. cit., (fn. 13), p. 53.

[44]Volker Bornschier, Christopher Chase-Dunn, and R. Rubinson, "Cross National Evidence of the Effects of Foreign Investment and Aid on Economic Growth and Inequality: A Survey of Findings and a Re-analysis," *American Journal of Sociology*, Vol. 84 (November 1978), pp. 651–83; and Volker Bornschier and Jean-Pierre Hoby, "Economic Policy and Multinational Corporations in Development: The Measurable Impacts in Cross-National Perspective," *Social Problems*, Vol. 28 (April 1981), pp. 363–77.

[45]Bornschier and Hoby, "Economic Policy," p. 365 and p. 366, respectively.

[46]Bornschier, Chase-Dunn, and Rubinson, "Cross-National Evidence," op. cit., p. 678–79; p. 674.

[47]Michael B. Dolan and Brian W. Tomlin, "First World-Third World Linkages: External Relations and Economic Development," *International Organization*, Vol. 34 (Winter 1980), pp. 51–53.

[48]Richard E. Caves, *Multinational Enterprise and Economic Analysis* (Cambridge: Cambridge University Press, 1982), p. 276.

[49]Robert W. Jackman, "Dependence on Foreign Investment and Economic Growth in the Third World," *World Politics*, Vol. 34 (January 1982), pp. 187–93 and p. 195, respectively.

[50]John M. Rothgeb, Jr., "The Effects of Foreign Investment on Overall and Sectoral Growth in Third World States," *Journal of Peace Research*, Vol. 21, No. 1 (1984), pp. 11–12.

[51]Bornschier, Chase-Dunn, and Rubinson, "Cross National Evidence," op. cit., pp. 654–65. See also Christopher Chase-Dunn, "The Effects of International Economic Dependence on Development and Inequality: A Cross-National Study," *American Sociological Review*, Vol. 40 (December 1975), pp. 720–38.

[52]Vincent A. Mahler, "Mining, Agriculture, and Manufacturing: The Impact of Foreign Investment on Social Distribution in Third World Countries," *Comparative Political Studies*, Vol. 14 (October 1981), pp. 267–97.

[53]Dolan and Tomlin, "First World-Third World Linkages," op. cit., pp. 57–58; p. 59.

[54]Constantine V. Vaitsos, *Intercountry Income Distribution and Transnational Enterprises* (Oxford, U.K.: Clarendon Press, 1974), pp. 42–65.

[55]Richard S. Newfarmer, "International Oligopoly in the Electrical Industry," in Newfarmer, *Profits, Progress and Poverty*, op. cit., pp. 126–27.

[56]Vaitsos, *Intercountry Income Distribution*, op. cit., pp. 128–30. A similar analysis is offered by Miquel Wionczek, "Notes on Technology Transfer through Multinational Enterprises," *Economic Development and Cultural Change*, Vol. 7 (April 1976), pp. 147–54.

[57]Daniel Chudnovsky, "The Changing Remittance Behavior of United States Manufacturing Firms in Latin America," *World Development*, Vol. 10 (June 1982), pp. 514–16.

[58]Gerald K. Helleiner, "International Technology Issues: Southern Needs and Northern Responses," in Jagdish N. Bhagwati, ed., *The New International Economic Order: The North-South Debate* (Cambridge, Mass: MIT Press, 1977), p. 306; Sanjaya Lall and Paul Streeten, *Foreign Investment, Transnationals, and Developing Countries* (Boulder, Colo.: Westview Press, 1977), p. 71.

[59]Richard Newfarmer, "An Introduction to the Issues," in Newfarmer, *Profits, Progress and Poverty*, op. cit., pp. 42–44.

[60]Louis T. Wells, "Economic Man and Engineering Man: Choice in a Low-Wage Country," *Public Policy*, Vol. 21 (Summer 1973), pp. 330–31.

[61]Bergsten, Horst, and Moran, *American Multinationals*, op. cit., p. 366.

[62]Gustav Ranis and Chi Schive, "Direct Foreign Investment in Taiwan's Development," in Walter Galenson, ed., *Foreign Trade and Investment: Economic Development in the Newly Industrializing Asian Countries* (Madison: University of Wisconsin Press, 1985), pp. 106, 115.

[63]Susumu Watanabe, "Multinational Enterprises, Employment, and Technology Adaptations," *International Labour Review*, Vol. 120 (November-December 1981), pp. 695–96.

[64]Muller, "Multinational Corporation," op. cit., p. 133.

[65]International Labour Office, *Employment Effects of Multinationals in Developing Countries* (Geneva: ILO, 1981), p. 23.

[66]Patricio Meller and Alejandra Mizala, "U.S. Multinationals and Latin American Manufacturing Employment Absorption," *World Development*, Vol. 10 (February 1982), pp. 119, 122.

[67]Linda Lim and Pang Eng Fong, *Technology Choice and Employment Creation: A Case Study of Three Multinational Enterprises in Singapore* (Geneva: International Labour Office, 1981); Centre for Transnational Corporations, *Transnational Corporation Linkages in Developing Countries: The Case of Backward Linkages Via Subcontracting* (New York: United Nations, 1981), pp. 2, 9–10, 29–31, 33, 49–50.

[68]Sanjaya Lall, "Transfer Pricing and Developing Countries: Some Problems of Investigation," *World Development*, Vol. 7 (January 1979), pp. 59–71.

[69]Rhys Jenkins, "The Export Performance of Multinational Corporations in Mexican Industry," *Journal of Development Studies*, Vol. 15 (April 1979), pp. 97–104.

[70]Sanjaya Lall and Sharif Mohammed, "Foreign Ownership and Manufacturing Export Performance in the Large Corporate Sector of India," *Journal of Development Studies*, Vol. 20 (October 1983), pp. 63–64.

[71]Newfarmer, "Introduction to the Issues," op. cit., p. 47.

[72]Armand Mattelart, *Transnationals and the Third World: The Struggle for Culture* (South Hadley, Mass.: Bergin and Garvey, 1983), pp. 29–79.

[73]United Nations Educational, Scientific, and Cultural Organization (UNESCO), *Transnational Corporations and Endogenous Development: Effects on Culture, Communications, Education, Science and Technology* (Paris: UNESCO, 1982), p. 127.

[74]Michael B. Bader, "Breast-Feeding: The Role of Multinational Corporations in Latin America," in Krishna Kumar, ed., *Transnational Enterprises: Their Impact on Third World Societies and Cultures* (Boulder, Colo.: Westview Press, 1980), pp. 249–74; Mattelart, *The Struggle for Culture*, op. cit., pp. 90–3.

[75]Fernando Reyes Matta, "The Information Bedazzlement of Latin America," in Kumar, *Transnational Enterprises*, op. cit.

[76]Colin Leys, *Underdevelopment in Kenya: The Political Economy of Neo-Colonialism* (Berkeley: University of California Press, 1975), pp. 144–45.

[77]Stephen J. Kobrin, "Multinational Corporations, Sociocultural Dependence, and Industrialization: Need Satisfaction or Want Creation," *Journal of Developing Areas*, Vol. 13 (January 1979), pp. 114–15.

[78]A very helpful overview of these political issues was presented by H. Jeffrey Leonard, "Multinational Corporations and Politics in Developing Countries," *World Politics*, Vol. 32 (April 1980), pp. 454–83.

[79]Biersteker, *Distortion or Development*, op. cit., pp. 137–50.

[80]Leys, *Underdevelopment in Kenya*, op. cit., pp. 137–50.

[81]Gereffi, *Pharmaceutical Industry*, op. cit., pp. 136–52.

[82]Franklin B. Weinstein, "Multinational Corporations and the Third World: The Case of Japan and Southeast Asia," *International Organization*, Vol. 30 (Summer 1976), pp. 373-404; Thomas J. Biersteker, "The Illusion of State Power: Transnational Corporations and the Neutralization of Host-Country Legislation," *Journal of Peace Research*, Vol. 17 No. 3 (1980), pp. 207–22; Lynn Krieger Mytelka, *Regional Development in a Global Economy: The Multinational Corporation, Technology, and Andean Integration* (New Haven, Conn.: Yale University Press, 1979), pp. 29–38, 62–112.

[83]Bennett and Sharpe, "Agenda Setting," op. cit., pp. 78, 80–81; and Gereffi, *Pharmaceutical Industry*, op. cit., pp. 90–94.

[84]Adalberto J. Pinelo, *The Multinational Corporation as a Force in Latin American Politics: A Case Study of the International Petroleum Company in Peru* (New York: Praeger, 1973).

[85]Charles T. Godspell, *American Corporations and Peruvian Politics* (Cambridge, Mass.: Harvard University Press, 1974), pp. 131–32.

[86]Moran, *Multinational Corporations and the Politics of Dependence: Copper in Chile,,* op. cit., pp. 172–224.

[87]Grieco, *Between Dependency and Autonomy*, op. cit., pp. 132–35

[88]Albert O. Hirschman, *A Bias for Hope: Essays on Development and Latin America* (New Haven, Conn: Yale University Press, 1971), p. 231.

[89]See Ronald Reagan, "International Investment Policy," *Weekly Compilation of Presidential Documents*, Vol. 19 (September 12, 1983), pp. 1214–19.

# Chapter 2

# Evaluating Foreign Investment

## Dennis J. Encarnation and Louis T. Wells, Jr.

Few developing countries permit multinational enterprises to locate investments inside their borders unencumbered by public policies and government agencies designed to screen would-be investors. Although the effectiveness of specific policies in shaping investment decisions is hotly debated (see Chapter 6), few doubt that the business-government negotiation process is critical to the final decisions.[1] Yet one cannot help wondering whether such negotiations with foreign investors are necessary at all. The rationale for negotiating is typically based on policy makers' implicit assumptions about the effects of foreign investment on economic development. And these assumptions, in turn, are generally based on a great deal of faith, or, less frequently, policy makers have been informed by a development literature that offers little unambiguous guidance (see Chapter 1 in this volume).

To date, the empirical evidence for determining the impact of foreign investment on economic development remains rather weak. Nevertheless, what little is known, reinforced by new evidence reported in this chapter, supports the implicit assumptions of most government policy makers in developing countries: The portfolio of would-be foreign investments can best be characterized as a "mixed bag" in the prevailing policy environment. That is, in countries with limited domestic markets, barriers to trade, and subsidized inputs, the incidence of economically harmful proposals submitted by prospective investors is likely to be high—comprising a sizable minority of import-substituting projects.

To many Western-trained economists, the disjuncture between public and private interests that leads to harmful investment proposals suggests the need for wide-ranging policy reforms—what the World Bank calls "structural adjustment." But for policy makers in many developing countries, the implications are quite different: Since thoroughgoing reforms are unlikely to be practical in the near future, a "second-best" solution must be devised to screen the high percentage of harmful foreign investment proposals. Recognizing this, government officials, international organizations, academic researchers, and consultants galore have made innumerable proposals concerning how governments should negotiate with foreign investors.[2] Yet the conventional advice, regardless of its source, frequently has gone unimplemented or, when implemented, has turned out to lead to results quite different from those intended. The patterns of variation are not random; as indicated later in this chapter, they are the result of identifiable variables.

## Why Screen Foreign Investment?

In the development literature, the multinational enterprise has been attacked by some as a hindrance to development, while it has been praised by others as an important engine to pull countries out of their poverty. Given their multifarious origins, earlier studies have not attempted to assess the economic impacts of foreign-owned projects through the use of a single, consistent set of measures.

This weakness has been partially overcome in two studies of particular usefulness to policy makers, studies that used variations of social cost-benefit analysis to measure the overall effect of foreign investment on economic development. One was done for the U. N. Conference on Trade and Development (UNCTAD) in the early 1970s by Sanjaya Lall and Paul Streeten, two critics of the role of multinationals in development.[3] At roughly the same time, Grant Reuber completed a study under the auspices of the Organisation for Economic Co-operation and Development (OECD).[4] Although the ideological predispositions of the two studies differed, as did their methodologies and data, the results were surprisingly consistent: Both concluded that upwards of 30 per cent of proposed import-substituting projects were harmful for the domestic economy. Understanding the reasons for this conclusion is critical to policy makers charged with screening foreign investment proposals.

Lall and Streeten examined 133 foreign-owned and locally owned projects operating in six countries. For 88 of these firms, they were able to calculate national-income effects, using a social cost-benefit methodology. For two-thirds of the 88, the effect of foreign investment on national income was positive; for the other one-third, negative. This pattern did not vary by the foreign or domestic ownership of the project.

Although the lack of a statistically significant difference between foreign and locally owned projects may initially seem surprising, it is easily understood if one considers the principal reason for the private profitability of socially unattractive projects. High rates of protection from import competition facilitated high private rates of return but not high social rates of return regardless of whether the investor was foreign or local. Indeed, the competitiveness of sales had the greatest impact on the Lall and Streeten calculation of social rates of return.[5]

The OECD study arrived at similar conclusions, although Reuber used a different methodology and data base than Lall and Streeten. The study examined 45 foreign-owned projects from a sample covering 30 host countries. Instead of using a conventional social cost-benefit model to evaluate the impact of each project on generating national income, he compared (among other calculations) the production costs of the subsidiaries to the production costs of their parent operations. The results were a crude approximation of social cost-benefit calculations that rely on market price assumptions.[6] (That is, Reuber's results approximate those of a social cost-benefit analysis that assumes that all inputs are charged at local market prices, and that all outputs are valued at world market prices.) Using this simpler method, Reuber concluded that over one-quarter of the subsidiaries had production costs that were equal to or lower than those of the parent operations; the remainder—nearly three-quarters of the 45 subsidiaries he examined—had higher production costs.

Reuber subsequently separated projects according to whether their output was destined largely for the domestic market of the host country or for export. For the 14 export projects he identified, the relationship just mentioned was reversed: that is, over three-quarters of the 14 had production costs that were equal to or lower than the production costs of the parent operations; less than one-quarter had higher costs. As for the 31 projects that were not export-oriented, Reuber calculated that the host country could have imported equivalent products at a 30-per-cent savings over local production. In other words, export-oriented projects had lower production costs and, by inference, higher social profitability than the average projects that were import-substituting. Again, like Lall and Streeten, Reuber concluded that the competitiveness of sales had a major impact on production costs. For import-substituting projects, protection from import competition put little pressure on managers to cut production costs; the absence of such protection in export markets brought a subsidiary's production costs more in line with those of the parent company.

In conclusion, in both the UNCTAD and OECD studies, government policies shaping the market for a project's output were important determinants of the social profitability of that project. And among these policies, tariffs figured prominently. But no attention was paid to other policies shaping the input markets of these projects. This topic would await later research building on these two studies.

## New Data, Same Conclusions

In a more recent single-country study, we have attempted to improve on the data and methodology employed in the pioneering work commissioned by UNCTAD and OECD. Like Lall and Streeten, we used a more standard social cost-benefit analysis, but modeled it on the methods of Roemer and Stern.[7] We defined the benefits of a proposed project to be its contribution to national income—the value of goods and services produced by that project for domestic consumption or investment, plus additional earnings generated by exports. In calculating the domestic value of goods and services subsequently consumed or invested, we substituted world market prices for the sales prices assumed by the prospective investors. We assumed export sales consummated at world market prices.

While the *benefits* of a proposed project show up in increased consumption, investment, and exports, its *costs* to the national economy consist of the resources used. These include domestic labor, local capital, and locally purchased goods and services, plus a range of foreign-exchange costs—imported raw materials, components, and machinery, as well as the foreign share of dividends, royalties, interest, debt repayment, and technology fees. Where there were reasons to suspect that market prices underestimated or overestimated the value of local resources used by the project, we substituted shadow prices for those reported by the would-be investor. In this way, our study departed from the UNCTAD and OECD studies. The shadow prices were intended to reflect the opportunity cost of the resources to the national economy. Thus, if energy could be exported for more than the project paid under government price policies, the shadow price would be above the market price. If labor would be unemployed in the absence of the project, its shadow price would be lower than its market price. In various calculations, we used shadow prices for labor, energy, foreign exchange, and domestic capital.

We did not, however, attempt to estimate any impact that a project might have on other host-country concerns, aside from its direct contribution to the national product. For example, we did not estimate any economic effects external to the project itself. These might include a range of costs to society, including pollution from a manufacturing plant or loss of potential investment by local producers restrained by fear of foreign competition. The external economic effects might also include benefits—such as training workers who eventually apply their newfound skills elsewhere in the economy, or signaling other would-be investors to follow suit. We also did not estimate a wide range of social effects—effects on local consumption, income distribution, or defense procurement, to mention just a few. These and other effects not captured by our indicators could make some seemingly attractive projects unattractive. And some projects that do not contribute directly to national product might become attractive if these other criteria were taken into account.

Although we recognize the potential importance of these other criteria, we suspect that the direct, positive impact on the national product is the contribution most sought by countries when they accept foreign investment. Of course, this appraisal of a project's benefits should take into account the foregone alternative uses of domestic resources used directly by the project. Below, we assume that domestic capital, if employed alternatively, would yield at least a 10-per-cent return to society, and that future benefits should be discounted at the same rate. Given this criterion, if the social rate of return of the project is less than 10 per cent, the host country's screening board should reject the project in the belief that a better, alternative use can be made of local project inputs.

As reported below, our findings showed few projects yielding rates of return close to this cutoff point. For the vast majority, either very positive or very negative returns were the prospect. Therefore, we doubt that project externalities and the other criteria for project evaluation noted would result in dramatic shifts in our overall assessment of beneficial and costly projects—even though these other criteria might alter the rank-ordering of projects.

An additional benefit of our methodology was the relative ease of gathering requisite data from local sources. The calculation of shadow prices, for example, reflected the informed opinion of local analysts. We collected all other data from application forms submitted by prospective foreign investors to the investment screening board of a large developing country. A sample of fifty foreign manufacturing firms was drawn from the pool of all foreign investment proposals completed and submitted to that board during a recent five-year period. These applications generally contained ten-year forecasts of income statements and balance sheets for the proposed projects. Using standard financial techniques, we extended the forecasts to twenty years to include any later benefits that might accrue to the country as infant industries matured. Forty-two of the would-be investors sought to supply the domestic market of the country, where they invested in industries typically protected by the government against import competition. In these cases, the investment screening board asked prospective investors to estimate the costs of imports equivalent to their proposed production. The remaining eight projects proposed to sell most—and typically all— of their output to export markets.

Since private investors submitted estimates for projects not yet in existence, we had no way of independently verifying the accuracy of their figures. Some investors may have submitted biased figures to make their projects look better. For example, an investor may have understated the project's capital requirements or overstated the value of foreign exchange saved through the local manufacture of goods previously imported. If so, the results summarized below underestimate the social costs of these projects. The reporting bias could also push in the opposite direction, given the peculiarities of local government policies. The host country's investment board granted exemptions from import duty on capital equipment according to a list of equipment needs submitted by the investor; fearing that the total list would not be approved, or seeking profits from duty-free imports, an investor might have hedged and overstated the project's capital requirements. Even if the board approved the entire sum, the items subsequently imported duty-free could be sold at a premium in the local economy. Undoubtedly, both sets of biases existed, but there was little indication that they were systematic or recurrent. Indeed, each of the checks we used could discern no such pattern.[8]

Like Reuber, and like Lall and Streeten, we found that a majority (ranging from 55 to 75 per cent, depending on our assumptions) of the proposed projects would increase the host country's national income (see Table 1). And like our predecessors, we also found that a sizable minority of proposed investments, if accepted, would have a deleterious effect on that country's national product. That is, anywhere from 25 to 45 per cent of the projects proposed to use resources in ways that yielded fewer goods and services for the host country than those resources cost the country. This sizable minority therefore would be unattractive to the host country even though they would be profitable to private investors.

# Table 1. Social Cost-Benefit Analysis of 50 Proposed Projects

| Assumptions of Model | Distribution of 50 Projects by Social Rate of Return | | |
|---|---|---|---|
| | Percentage of Projects with SRR of Less than 10% | (of which, % negative) | Percentage of Projects with SRR of 10% or more |
| **No Tariff on Foreign Inputs[a]:** | | | |
| Market prices reported by investor[b] | 40% | (85%) | 60% |
| Market prices except labor[c] | 36 | (94) | 64 |
| Market prices except energy[d] | 44 | (91) | 56 |
| Market prices except labor, energy, and foreign exchange costs[c,d,e] | 32 | (81) | 68 |
| **20% Tariff on Foreign Inputs[f]:** | | | |
| Market prices reported by investor[b] | 28 | (100) | 72 |
| Market prices except labor, energy, and foreign exchange costs[c,d,e] | 26 | (85) | 74 |

[a] Assumes that prices for imported inputs as reported by the investor did not include 20 per cent duty imposed by government.

[b] Assumes that prices paid by the investor for all inputs reflected the value of the input to the economy; that is, market prices equal shadow prices.

[c] Assumes that the shadow price of labor was 70 per cent of its market price; that is, some 30 per cent of the project's wage bill went to workers who would be unemployed or underemployed in the project's absence; for all other inputs, market prices equal shadow prices.

[d] Assumes that the shadow price of energy was twice its market price; that is, energy used by the project could be sold on world market at a price 100 per cent higher than its domestic price; for all other inputs, market prices equal shadow prices.

[e] Assumes that the shadow foreign-exchange rate relative to the U.S. dollar was 120 per cent of the official rate; that is, the effective foreign-country cost of the project was greater than reported because the host country's currency relative to the dollar was overvalued by 20 per cent; for all other inputs, market prices equal shadow prices.

[f] Assumes that prices for imported inputs as reported by the investor included a 20-per cent duty; the recalculated price of imported inputs equal 80 per cent of the reported price.

Table 1 shows that the proportion of unattractive projects was higher among projects that were sizable consumers of government-subsidized energy. As noted, such large foreign-exchange costs may reflect the prices of imported raw materials, components, and machinery, as well as the foreign share and timing of dividends, royalties, interest, debt repayments, and technology fees. Only small increases were recorded in the proportion of attractive projects when we assumed that 30 per cent of the wage bill went to workers who otherwise would have been unemployed or underemployed in the absence of the project. Similarly, only small shifts occurred when social rates of return for energy costs and foreign exchange were substituted for market rates.

Differences between social profitability and private profitability were not, however, limited to different views of the costs of energy, raw materials, labor, and other inputs. Much more important were the results of government policies affecting prices in output markets. As noted earlier, the competitiveness of sales had the greatest impact on Lall and Streeten's calculation of social rates of return: The greater the protection from import competition, the lower the social rate of return. Reinforcing this conclusion, Reuber found that export-oriented projects had lower average production costs and, by inference, higher social rates of return than did import-substituting projects protected by tariffs.

Both sets of conclusions find support in our findings summarized in Table 2. Moving from industries with low rates of protection to those with higher rates, the proportion of would-be projects deleterious to the host economy correspondingly increased; indeed, the rank-order correlation was perfect. (There was, by comparison, no consistent relationship between tariff protection and other government incentives, such as tax holidays.) Put simply, investors in protected industries could build plants that did not make a contribution (net) to the local economy, but that did generate adequate private rates of return to make them attractive to the firm. Conversely, where protection was low, most projects were beneficial to the economy as well as to the investor. The extreme case was made up of export projects (typically 100 per cent exports); all eight firms here had to compete without any protection on the world market, and all eight were beneficial to the host-country economy.

### Policy Implications

These findings are significant for government policy makers in host countries. The rewards for eliminating bad projects appear to be quite large: Of the projects that were unattractive when measured

## Table 2. Protectionism and Social Profitability

| Industry | Tariff Rate on Competing Imports | | Percentage of Projects with Social Rate of Return of Less than 10% |
|---|---|---|---|
| | Nominal[a] | Effective[b] | |
| Export-Oriented[d] | 0% | 0% or less | 0% |
| Import-Substituting,[e] of which: | | | |
| Chemicals[f] | about 10% | 26% | 30 |
| Pharmaceuticals | 20–25% | 150 | 33 |
| Textiles | 50–100% | 191 | 50 |
| Autos | about 100% | 717 | 70 |

[a] Derived from government sources.

[b] Derived from a World Bank report on effective protection in the country.

[c] Assumes that prices paid by the investor for all inputs reflected the value of the input to the economy; that is, market prices equal shadow prices. Also assumes that prices for imported inputs included a 20-per cent duty; the recalculated price of imported inputs equals 80 per cent of the reported price. See Table 1, Market prices reported by investor.

[d] Includes all projects that export a majority of their output; most exported 100 per cent of their output.

[e] Includes industries with three or more projects selling the majority of their output in the domestic market.

[f] Excludes pharmaceuticals.

by their contribution to national product, most yielded negative returns to the economy on the resources that they used.

The elimination of these 'bad' projects could be achieved in either of two ways. First, policies can be changed so that the price signals given the investor for project inputs and outputs match their relevant social costs. Alternatively, the host country can administratively screen out or reshape through negotiations the projects that are likely to be harmful to the economy.

The most important step to bring market prices in line with social prices would be for the country to lower its effective rates of protection. If the products of investors, local or foreign, had to compete with imports, virtually all socially unattractive projects in our sample also would have been unattractive to private investors. Less government protection from imports might be a necessary but not a sufficient step to bring private and social returns into line. Taking further steps would be especially important if the internal prices of labor, energy, foreign exchange, and other inputs departed even more significantly from social values than they did in the country we studied. In such instances, major subsidies for energy and other resources would have to be eliminated before investors themselves would reject socially 'bad' projects. But the data for the country that we studied strongly suggested that lower protection alone would go a long way toward leading investors to be interested only in socially attractive projects in most developing countries.

Western economists, including those at the World Bank, would generally consider the reduction of effective protection, changes in the pricing of domestic resources, and increased effective domestic competition (in both product and resource markets) to be the first-best solution to the problem of eliminating unattractive investments. Yet despite such recommendations, few countries with high rates of protection are likely to eliminate tariffs and other trade barriers quickly. And few find it politically easy to eliminate generous subsidies. Consequently, policy makers in developing countries are left with admittedly second-best solutions: administrative screening of proposals to eliminate those likely to be harmful to the economy, negotiating with other foreign investors to bring social rates of return above a minimum cutoff, and simultaneously promoting investments that have adequate social rates of return.

## Screening, Negotiating, and Promoting Foreign Investment

Although this second-best approach may be easier to implement than the first-best, establishing an effective mechanism for screening, negotiating, and promoting foreign investment nevertheless has proved exceedingly difficult. The task poses frustrating choices for policy makers in host countries.

First, policy makers must decide how centralized to make the negotiating process. There are a number of possibilities, each with advantages and disadvantages. For example, some government organizations that might be particularly effective in negotiating with investors for the most favorable terms and in screening unattractive proposals are likely to discourage would-be investors. Few countries have established a single organization that was effective both in screening out 'bad' proposals and in promoting foreign investment.

In a separate study of the organizations used by a number of governments to evaluate proposals, negotiate with foreigners, and promote investment, we found considerable variation in the organizational choices of governments across countries, across industries, and over time.[9] The same country was likely to use different approaches for different industries at any one time; its approach for the same industry might well change over time; and different countries may adopt similar approaches to deal with investors in the same industries. These patterns of choice were not random; they were influenced primarily by three identifiable variables discussed later in this chapter: a country's general development strategy and the role of foreign investment in that strategy, the salience of a particular industry in the development plans of that country, and the degree of competition that the country faced in attracting particular kinds of investors.

## The Choices

In our in-depth study of the practices of the Philippines, Singapore, India, and Indonesia (and a quick review of those of several other countries), we observed four basic ways of handling the tasks of promoting foreign investment, screening subsequent foreign investment proposals, and negotiating the terms under which projects would be accepted.

The first option, unusual for developing countries, is a 'policy approach.' Countries following this strategy do not conduct individual negotiations with investors over important issues. Rather, they determine in advance general policies that specify, at least for the majority of investors, the industries in which they would be accepted or excluded and the terms under which they could operate. Such policies may be lenient toward foreign investment, excluding few potential projects; or they may be very restrictive, virtually closing the country to foreign investment. Hong Kong and the U.S. federal government illustrate the first type; Burma is an example of the second.

For Western economists who prefer 'getting the prices right' as the first-best solution, a simplified 'policy approach' that reduces government discretion may seem like the best of the second-best, especially if it encourages foreign investment. Among the benefits of non-negotiation is the greater predictability of the outcome for both government and investor, compared with the inevitably more ambiguous negotiations associated with selective policies. Consequently, the potential costs for the firm considering entry are likely to be low. But in the presence of price distortions resulting from tariffs, subsidies, and limited competition, a very 'open door' policy will result in the entry of those investments identified earlier as not socially profitable. Moreover, a government's fear of these social costs may generate simple exclusionary rules that keep out many investments that would be beneficial to the country. Short of adopting simple rules that either promote or discourage investment indiscriminately, project-by-project screening may be necessary if the host country is to extract all the potential social benefits from each prospective investment.

Once a government adopts public policies that require negotiations with prospective foreign investors, its approach to negotiating with these investors is likely to fall along a continuum that has a decentralized approach at one extreme and a centralized one at the other—options two and three, respectively. Under a decentralized regime, a foreign investor typically must conduct a series of difficult negotiations dispersed across several ministries, agencies, and enterprises whose operations and interests would be affected by the investment—for example, the ministries of industry, trade, or finance; the central bank; and perhaps a state enterprise in the sector. Virtually all developing countries have adopted this approach at some point—and for many it still continues in some industries. At the other end of the continuum, authority to negotiate with an investor is concentrated in one organization that has the full authority to accept or reject an applicant and to conclude the terms that will govern the investor's project in the country. Between centralized and decentralized structures lie various coordinating mechanisms; these mechanisms comprise a fourth option.

### Advantages and Disadvantages

The extremes of this continuum offer quite different advantages and disadvantages to the host country (see Table 3).

A *decentralized* approach, for example, is attractive for several reasons. First, enterprises can muster the technical expertise necessary to evaluate proposals for a specific industry. Tax expertise is likely to be concentrated in the finance ministry; knowledge of labor laws and issues, in the labor ministry; technical skills for the relevant industry, in the ministry of industries; and so on. Second, these government units are likely to be the same agencies that will eventually administer the terms of any agreements reached. Having them conduct the relevant part of the negotiations is likely to generate terms that can be effectively administered with available resources. Further, if the administrators are the negotiators, there is a reasonable chance of learning from past successes and mistakes. Indeed, when the same people are regularly assigned to foreign investment negotiations, technical skills and in some cases length of employment enable such specialized units to learn and retain lessons that may enhance the government's negotiating skills in the future.

At the same time, a decentralized approach may cause serious problems. First, the involved agencies and ministries are likely to have little technical knowledge or limited experience with the industry or with foreign investors generally. For example, they may insist on performance requirements that discourage an otherwise desirable investor, without even caring about or understanding the full implications of their demands. Second, diffuse units operating autonomously also have little ability to evaluate overall net benefits in light of larger policy issues. For example, a ministry of labor is likely to support a project that generates employment, whatever the cost in terms of foreign exchange or foregone tax revenues; as a consequence, too little or too much may be offered to the potential investor. Moreover, an individual government unit has no incentive or mechanism to consider the wider implications of its actions on potential foreign investors in other industries; as a result, inappropriate precedents may be established.

Finally, a decentralized approach is likely to be costly to the foreign investor. The period of negotiation is likely to be longer and the results unpredictable at the outset. Potential investors with only marginal interests are likely to go elsewhere. In fact, the pool of investors applying to a country with a decentralized process might well be smaller than for a similar country that is quicker and promises investors more predictable outcomes. In the countries we studied, it was the effect on investors that led governments to abandon the decentralized process for a more centralized approach.

*Centralized* bodies are of two distinct types, each with benefits and disadvantages. Both have the objective of reducing the high costs to potential foreign investors otherwise associated with decentralized approaches.

One type of centralized body can be found in Singapore and a few other countries, where negotiations with the vast majority of foreign investors have been brought together under one autonomous body. This approach directly addresses the problem of greatest concern to most countries that have abandoned a decentralized approach: Negotiate quickly and have a predictable pattern of outcomes. It also offers other advantages. An autonomous body that covers a wide range of negotiations can consider the overall impact of a project on the country, and it can weigh the total package of incentives and performance requirements to determine what is needed to attract a desired investor. Moreover, it is very likely to give careful consideration to issues of precedent in its negotiations and decisions.

Still, such a centralized body has its problems. It leads to a separation of negotiation from implementation, which usually remains the problem of the relevant technical ministries. The distance between negotiator and administrator can lead to terms that

**Table 3. Strengths and Weaknesses of Patterns and Structures of Decision Making**

| Patterns and Structures | Strengths/Benefits | Weaknesses/Costs |
|---|---|---|
| **Abstention:** <br> No structures or procedures | Predictability for investors <br> No administrative costs <br> Quick response time | Unrestricted entry: entry of firms inconsistent with national interest <br> Autarky: excludes socially beneficial investments |
| **Decentralization:** <br> Government functional agencies; State-owned enterprises | Can muster technical expertise for specific industry <br> Results in high organizational learning on part of government <br> Agencies that negotiate often the same that implement policies | Little evaluation of overall net benefits; focus on technical feasibility <br> Little consideration of larger policy issues <br> Little consideration of impact of decisions on other investors <br> Little promotion of national investment opportunities <br> High negotiating costs for investors <br> Disjunction between policy as negotiated and policy as implemented, since implementors are multiple |

| | | |
|---|---|---|
| **Coordination:** | | |
| Permanent interagency board | Reduces investor's negotiating costs<br>Reduces inter-ministerial conflict<br>Improves monitoring of international environment<br>Considers larger policy issues and their impact on other investors<br>Offers greater promotion of investment opportunities | Little in-depth industry knowledge<br>Disjuncture between policy as negotiated and policy as implemented, since implementation occurs outside the new structure |
| Ad hoc interagency committees | Offers all advantages of permanent board listed above<br>Masters industry expertise | Little consideration of impact on other investors or larger policy issues<br>Little organizational learning<br>Little promotion of investment opportunities |
| **Delegation:** | | |
| Industry-specific agencies and state-owned enterprises | Reduces investor's negotiating costs<br>Policy negotiated is policy implemented<br>Greater promotion of investment and greater scanning of environment<br>Improved organizational learning | Ignores interests of other agencies and their constituencies<br>Ignores larger policy issues and their impact on other investors |
| Broadly defined development authorities | Offers all advantages of the industry-specific agencies and state-owned enterprises listed above<br>Considers larger policy issues and impact on other investors | Ignores interest of other agencies and their constituencies<br>Little in-depth industry knowledge<br>Loss of personnel to industry |

Source: Dennis J. Encarnation and Louis T. Wells, Jr., "Sovereignty en Garde: Negotiating with Foreign Investors," *International Organization*, Vol. 39 (Winter 1985), pp. 76–77.

may well be difficult to administer. Moreover, the breadth of the task assigned to a broad autonomous unit almost assures that it will not have in-depth expertise in industry-specific issues.

To overcome the latter problem, some governments have established a separate type of centralized body with specialized expertise that covers only a single industry or a single type of investment. For example, oil agreements may be negotiated by a particular state enterprise; or agreements with potential exporters may be the sole responsibility of an export-processing-zone authority. Like the autonomous unit with authority for a wide range of industries, this more specialized agency is also likely to conduct quick and reasonably predictable negotiations. But unlike its more broadly defined counterpart, industry-specific organizations rarely take into account the impacts of their agreements on the other investment negotiations outside their area of authority. This creates problems. State oil companies, for example, are unlikely to worry about the impact of their petroleum agreements on discussions with mining or manufacturing firms. Moreover, the single-industry organization is likely to ignore other larger policy issues, including the net national benefit of the investment.

Finally, both types of centralized organizations also impose a major *political* cost on the host country. Establishing such organizations requires the government to "disenfranchise" agencies that expressed interest in the outcome of negotiations and sought to participate. Centralization means, for example, that tax matters are decided outside the ministry of finance; foreign exchange issues, outside the central bank; and so on. It is for this reason that broad-based, autonomous agencies for foreign investment are so unusual.

Unwilling to incur the political costs associated with the imposition of centralized structures, and displeased with the operation of decentralized approaches, many countries have tried to combine some of the advantages of each. In particular, they have attempted to coordinate the activities of the various government agencies involved earlier in a decentralized negotiation process, without going to the extremes of centralization.

This intermediate step also takes at least two forms. Most common is the investment coordinating board, which is run jointly by a number of ministries whose interests are typically affected by foreign investment. Like other organizational responses to foreign investment, coordinating boards have had their advantages and disadvantages. Unlike industry-specific bodies, however, they provide a mechanism for examining the overall benefits and costs of proposed projects and for weighing the total package of incentives and performance requirements. Moreover, coordinating boards consider the precedents that are generated by individual negotiations. Particularly important, when they work well, they reduce the costs of negotiation for the investor.

Rarely, however, do coordinating bodies work as well as intended. First, they typically develop little expertise in particular industries or policy areas. Even worse, powerful ministries often refuse to cooperate in the coordination effort. Those ministries may not honor the agreements reached by the coordinating board, or they may slow down the negotiating process by sending low-level personnel or no one at all to meetings. Wise investors then learn to negotiate with the separate ministries regardless of the descriptions of the power of the boards. Those who have depended on the coordinating board often have found their agreements not honored; the experience of such investors further damages the host country's investment climate.

In an effort to overcome these weaknesses of interministerial boards, governments sometimes take another approach to coordination. They form special ad hoc coordinating committees to deal with particular investments. Except for their duration, these project-specific committees are quite similar to industry-specific centralized bodies. Politically, ad hoc bodies seek to minimize a ministry's possible effort to sabotage negotiations through co-optation; administratively, they endeavor to assemble a special team with in-depth knowledge of the industry involved. Like their centralized counterparts, such committees generally pay little attention to matters of precedent and overall policy; even worse, they may rely little on institutional learning.

### Factors Affecting the Choices

In the developing countries where we studied negotiating practices, the choices made followed quite regular patterns influenced by three sets of variables: the host country's development strategy and general stance on foreign investment, the importance of the particular industry, and the degree of competition among host countries for a particular kind of investment.

First, a country's general development strategy and thereby its attitude toward foreign investment determined the approach that would govern its negotiations with most would-be investors. Governments that were not eager to attract foreign investment tended to choose more decentralized approaches. Governments that desired more foreign investment tended to establish more centralized organizations; this typically meant some kind of coordinating body. In choosing, each country had to weigh the political cost incurred by centralizing the negotiation process against the high costs that decentralized processes imposed on potential investors. Only those with a strong desire for more investment were willing to pay the political costs of disenfranchising ministries otherwise involved in more decentralized negotiations.

This relationship between strategy and structure also exists within a single country. Changes in attitude toward foreign investment frequently preceded changes in screening processes. Indonesia, for example, required investors to negotiate with a large number of government agencies in the Sukarno days, when it was particularly suspicious of the supposed benefits from foreign investment. Under the Suharto regime, however, attitudes changed. Eager to attract foreign investment, the government moved toward coordinating the negotiation process. Complaints about the effectiveness of coordinating efforts led to an increase in the role of the coordinating board in the mid-1970s. And by the 1980s, the desire to promote exports led to consideration of a centralized, autonomous authority to handle investments entering a proposed export-processing-zone.

Whatever strategies countries choose for negotiating with the majority of investors, they tend to make special arrangements when the industry is particularly important or salient—a second variable influencing the choice of negotiating structures. In the cases of such industries, governments have been unwilling to live with the possibility that a decentralized approach might result in a poor agreement, or none at all. And they have not been willing to tolerate the lack of industry expertise that typically characterizes a broad coordinating board or investment authority. The most suitable approach for countries facing a particularly salient project has been to vest power to negotiate in a specialized state enterprise or to create a special ad hoc coordinating committee if no relevant state firm existed. Either approach offers the prospect of speedy negotiations, the possibility of weighing the incentives and performance requirements as a package, and, most important, the potential for bringing a good deal of industry expertise to the negotiations.

There were other special circumstances in which the countries we examined decided not to use their usual negotiating approach. Special arrangements were generally established when the competition among countries for particular kinds of investors was particularly intense—the third and final set of conditions influencing the choice of negotiating structures. Examples commonly involved export-oriented projects. Although a country, especially one with a large domestic market, could attract foreign investors for the local market by offering protection from import competition, this most effective incentive was not available for firms that wanted to set up facilities for export. Such companies can locate their plants in any of a number of countries that offer cheap production resources. In most cases, they need only inexpensive labor, sufficient infrastructure, good transportation, and communication facilities. Many countries viewed this kind of investment as attractive; indeed, our own research (see Table 1) shows that this investment consistently increased national income.

Given this common perception, the competition for these 'footloose' investors was usually quite intense. Fearful of losing the battle for such investors, many countries have centralized negotiations for such firms in one unit. The goal of centralization is to create an organization that can act quickly and decisively, thereby increasing the attractiveness of the country to investors. Accordingly, in many countries, such as the Philippines and India, potential investors for export plants have had the option of investing in export processing zones. Such zones generally not only offer infrastructure, but also are run by an organization that is fully vested with authority to reach agreements quickly.

### The Operation of Screening Bodies

The first problem facing policy makers in developing countries has been to choose from this organizational portfolio. Most countries have established a portfolio of approaches that reflects the various types of investment under consideration. Thus Indonesia in the 1970s negotiated with most investors through the BKPM, a coordinating board that represented ministries such as trade, industry, and finance. At the same time, however, a state enterprise, Pertamina, had almost full effective authority to negotiate oil and gas agreements. Simultaneously, negotiations for a large petrochemical project were handled by an ad hoc committee with representation from several government agencies, including Pertamina and the Ministry of Industries. Moreover, some consideration was being given to the creation of new export-processing zones where, like other countries in the region, the authority for negotiation might be centralized in an organization solely responsible for the operation of the zone. Indonesia's experience is not unique; our research saw this pattern replicated in various ways in, for example, India and the Philippines. The next problem has been to balance the accomplishment of one or more of these often competing objectives: attracting potential investors, screening their proposals, negotiating entry terms, and administering the agreements just negotiated. Some observers would add an additional task: determining when the terms under which investors operate should be renegotiated.

None of the countries we examined resolved adequately the apparent dilemma posed by the dual objectives of first attracting potential investors and subsequently reviewing their proposals to screen out projects that are not socially attractive. Most organizations placed almost all of their emphasis on one or the other of these two functions, but never the two together. The Economic Development Board (EDB) of Singapore, for example, put most of its effort into promotion. EDB rewarded personnel according to their success in attracting investment. Those same employees typically moved into the private sector after a short tenure with EDB. In contrast, the BKPM in Indonesia devoted little of its resources to investment promotion. Screening appeared to be its principal function, evidenced by its long application form and lengthy approval procedures.

Even when screening appeared to be the major function, the effectiveness of that screening was often in doubt. This was especially true in the large developing country where we performed the social cost-benefit analyses summarized earlier. There, the head of the country's investment board expressed his unwillingness to perform relevant social cost-benefit analysis on investor proposals because the possibility of rejecting bad proposals by using this methodology would have a negative impact on the number of potential investors that would subsequently apply to the board. The dilemma had especially unfortunate consequences in this particular case. The board did little to attract investment. At the same time, it did not screen out bad proposals. In our own analysis, we were unable to find any relationship between a proposed project's contribution to national income and its acceptance or rejection by the investment board. In other words, the board neither screened projects nor promoted investment effectively. Even where investment boards screened proposals more effectively, there typically was not a close relationship between the terms negotiated and those implemented. We have encountered frequent discrepancies between the seeming intent of an agreement negotiated by one organization and the implementation of that agreement by another body. For example, ministries of finance occasionally did not honor tariff exemptions granted by investment authorities. In other cases, tax authorities later renegotiated tax terms to make them more or less favorable to the investor than those that had been negotiated with the investment authority. These differences usually arose during the implementation stage, when practical problems of administering the original terms began to appear, when ministries needed to collect more revenue, or (we occasionally suspected) when unofficial payments were passed to particular officials. Regardless of its cause, this disjuncture between terms negotiated and terms implemented would have rendered meaningless earlier cost-benefit analyses.

# Policy Implications for Developing Countries

What do the experiences that we studied suggest for other developing countries concerned with foreign investment? The results
clearly show that most developing countries cannot have confidence
that projects that are attractive to foreign investors are attractive to
the country. Some assurance of a match between private and national interests exists only if: 1) prices that face the investor are
good guides to the opportunity costs of inputs used by the project,
and 2) prices of the output of the project are close to those that
indicate the social value of the product. In the projects we studied,
failure to satisfy one or both of these conditions resulted in investment proposals that were privately, but not socially, attractive. In
the absence of broad policy reforms that lead to accurate price
guidelines for managers—what the World Bank calls structural
adjustment—the government must seriously consider careful
screening of proposals on their economic merits.

Existing research, all on market economies, says a great deal
about where the emphasis should be placed in the screening process. When the proposals are for projects that would serve a domestic market that is protected from import competition, careful evaluation is most necessary to assess price distortions in output
markets. On the other hand, such an evaluation is less essential
when projects are to manufacture for export markets—all the better since competition among countries for this investment demands
quick and predictable decisions.

Unfortunately, this generalization about export projects has an
important caveat. One cannot be so sanguine about the effects of
export projects in an economy where many domestic prices are
administered rather than determined by market competition. We
know of no research that evaluates a sample of proposals or projects
in countries with a large number of administered prices for domestic resources, but some anecdotal evidence suggests that in such
environments even export projects can easily be wasteful of national resources. One case is of an onion-drying plant that would
import onions to a free-trade zone, dry them with fuel oil that was
priced below export value, and sell the dried onions overseas at
world market prices. A study of the proposed project indicated that
the host country would be better off exporting the oil (or importing
less oil) and rejecting the drying plant. A comparable assessment of
a metal smelter in a non-OPEC oil-producing country concluded
that the nation would have earned more foreign exchange by exporting the fuel oil and the ore concentrate than it did by processing
the ore locally in an inefficient (by world standards) plant. Similar
results might obtain in a sawmill that cuts logs that could not

otherwise be exported because of a ban, or that faces high export taxes. These examples suggest that screening may be necessary even for export projects in countries with administered prices that depart considerably from opportunity costs, or where export taxes affect input costs. And, as Table 1 shows, such distortions in prices must also be considered for domestically oriented projects.

Although the potential benefits of screening foreign investment are clear for a country with import protection and with price distortions in the internal market, the experience of other countries suggests that those benefits are in fact quite difficult to achieve. First, the screening process is not easy. Of all the organizations that we studied, none actually performed careful economic cost/benefit calculations. The reasons were numerous. Scarcity of skilled personnel was certainly one factor. Another was the difficulty in assembling adequate data. Moreover, the failure was, on occasion, blamed on the supposed incompatibility of screening and investment promotion.

The problems in undertaking economic analysis suggest that efforts should be made to concentrate analytical skills on those areas of investment where economic and private profits are most likely to differ. If screening on a project-by-project basis is itself a second-best solution, the difficulties associated with implementation point to a third-best solution. One approach, sub-optimal from a theoretical point of view but perhaps necessary as a practical matter, is to make crude classifications of types of investment proposals. This enables the screening bodies to devote scarce resources to the most likely trouble areas. Such a system might, for example, separate out export projects for a very simple, quick test. In the country we studied, a simple test of the ratio of energy used (underpriced to the investor) to labor employed (overpriced to the investor) could be used. A ratio above a certain figure would identify proposals needing special attention. Since the vast majority of projects with lower ratios would be beneficial, they could be approved virtually automatically.

Similarly, proposals for serving the local market might be divided into industries categorized according to priority and to effective protection. Scarce analytical resources might be devoted first to high-priority sectors, with special attention subsequently paid to those industries with high rates of effective protection. Model terms might be prepared to improve predictability for would-be investors. Some poor projects might slip through such a screening process, but the increased speed of analysis would be likely to generate more proposals for consideration. Proposals for low-priority sectors might have to wait for evaluation and negotiation until time is available. Some potential investment might, of course, be lost due to slow processing; but the losses might well be unimportant if the sectors were indeed low-priority.

Another set of lessons for host governments derives from the difficulties posed by organizational issues. As discussed earlier, if negotiations were decentralized, they were particularly likely to be ineffective and to discourage potential investment. On the other hand, centralization came at a high political cost. Only when the stakes seemed particularly high were governments willing to disenfranchise ministries in order to centralize the negotiation function. Because of lack of political commitment at the top, coordination of negotiations was often ineffective and in some cases quickly deteriorated into decentralized negotiations. Coordination can work only if a government is actually willing to remove authority from departments with legitmate interests in the outcome of negotiations with potential investors. The experiences of various developing countries indicate where the problems lie. Understanding the likely sources of problems in different structures is an important step in designing an effective organization and an evaluation mechanism.

The studies reported here also have major implications for U.S. policy. Many recent statements by U.S. policy makers have urged developing countries to reduce their barriers to foreign investment, so that they might benefit from the 'magic of the market.' Such exhortations are viewed with amusement by many officials in developing countries, who understand, at least intuitively, the complexity of the issues. Others, less trustful of American intentions, react more sharply, believing that the goals of the United States must simply be to generate more profits for U.S. multinationals.

Moreover, existing research—reinforced by new evidence reported here—suggests that the caution shown in developing countries toward U.S. pressure is quite appropriate. The issues surrounding foreign investment are indeed much more complex than U.S. policy statements recognize. Indeed, some barriers to foreign investment may be sensible—as long as overall economic policies do lead to a disjuncture between private and social rates of return.

Before developing countries grant an unambiguous welcome to foreign investors, major policy reforms must be implemented. Most important among these, our work shows, is a dramatic reduction in the barriers to trade erected by developing countries. In addition, for some of these countries, restructuring prices of energy, capital, and other inputs may be necessary. Reforms such as these are also often the subject of recommendations by U.S. officials and by the World Bank; but in most countries, these reforms will have to *precede* more open policies toward foreign investment.

Such 'structural adjustment' is very difficult to achieve. Entrenched domestic interests benefit from current policies, as do foreign firms whose investments were made under protectionist regimes. And some of the policies now under attack nevertheless serve quite legitimate goals. Further, many policy makers in developing countries do not share any deep ideological commitment to the benefits of market competition. Change will come; in fact, more market-oriented policies are increasingly being adopted in many developing countries *without* U.S. pressure. But that adjustment will inevitably be gradual and erratic. Such change may even be slowed by strong U.S. pressure and by the resulting suspicion that adjustment is really designed to serve U.S. commercial interests. If internal change is inevitably slow, and foreign pressure perhaps counterproductive, what can the United States and the World Bank do?

First, until reform has occurred, assistance to improve the results of screening processes is likely to be more valuable than exhortations for their removal.

Second, steps to recognize and reduce inconsistencies in the general policies that are being recommended will probably make implementation more likely. Although some inconsistencies are inevitable, especially in democracies, they seriously impede efforts to encourage structural adjustment. For example, in industrial democracies, protectionist policies co-exist with liberal prescriptions for other countries. But protectionism in the United States, Europe, and Japan only lends support to the defenders of comparable controls in developing countries. For example, every restriction on textile exports from the developing countries imposed by members of the Organisation for Economic Co-operation and Development (OECD) is often cited as evidence that the industrial countries are preaching to others what they are incapable of doing for themselves.

Indiscriminate attacks by industrial democracies on subsidies and performance requirements (e.g., minimum exports) in the developing countries are also viewed as inconsistent with an emphasis on the outcome of free markets. After all, many of those subsidies and performance requirements were originally established to offset market distortions introduced in both developing and industrial countries. Export certificates, for example, may be designed to offset the higher prices of locally procured inputs that result from the import protection received by local suppliers in developing countries. Although the United States is likely to claim that these certificates are simply subsidies that should be subjected to countervailing duties, developing countries may view them as mechanisms for putting the exporting firm in the cost position it would face if it were free to purchase its inputs on the world market.

Comparable incentives in developing countries also may be used to offset the market distortions introduced by industrial democracies. For example, several OECD members impose a higher tariff on plywood than on log imports; to overcome such market distortions, developing countries also grant subsidies to timber firms already required by these countries to turn their products into plywood. In other words, supporters of subsidies and performance requirements in developing countries may see such measures as leading to better approximations of free market outcomes than would obtain in their absence.

Finally, U.S. and World Bank exhortations to developing countries that they should both attract more foreign investment and lower import protection are already viewed by some as inconsistent. In Chapter 6 in this volume, Stephen Guisinger supports the view that such exhortations are indeed inconsistent: commodity incentives—that is, tariffs and quotas—have been by far the most effective incentive for attracting foreign investment to manufacture for the local market (the most frequent type of foreign investment).[10]

If developing countries do lower their import barriers, the result, at least over the medium term, is almost certain to be a reduction in foreign investment—and probably in domestic investment as well. The investment that follows such structural adjustment will certainly contribute more to economic development than much of what occurred under protectionist policies. Nevertheless, the medium-term fall in foreign (and domestic) investment will be real and will further strengthen the political forces arguing against liberalization.

In the United States and the World Bank, as well as in developing countries, a realistic recognition of the complex links between market distortions (both commodity and factor) and foreign investment (both volume and quality) may lessen the chances of an eventual defeat of policy reform.

## Notes

[1] When managers of foreign firms are asked to rank-order the factors that were important to their investment decision, one consistent conclusion emerges, irrespective of host country or manufacturing industry: Political and administrative concerns are ranked as more important than government incentives. These general concerns figure prominently in managers' appraisals of the overall "investment climate" of a host country. For a summary of and addition to this research, see Stephen J. Kobrin, *Managing Political Risk Assessment* (Berkeley: University of California Press, 1982), pp. 114–20.

[2] See, for example, United Nations, Department of Economic and Social Affairs, *The Impact of Multinational Corporations on Development and International Relations* (New York: 1974), p. 38ff.

[3] Sanjaya Lall and Paul Streeten, *Foreign Investment, Transnationals and Developing Countries* (Boulder, Colo.: Westview Press, 1977).

4 Grant L. Reuber, *Private Foreign Investment in Development* (Oxford: Clarendon Press, 1973).

5 Lall and Streeten, *Foreign Investment,* op. cit., p. 174.

6 For summary table, see Reuber, *Private Foreign Investment,* op. cit., p. 179.

7 Michael Roemer and Joseph J. Stern, *The Appraisal of Development Projects* (New York: Praeger, 1975). There are differences between this and other methods, such as the so-called Little and Mirrlees approach; see I.M.D. Little and James A. Mirrlees, *Project Appraisal and Planning for Development* (New York: Basic Books, 1974). The variations can yield different rank-orderings for projects but do not yield different cutoffs for selecting projects. Moreover, these differences in analytical techniques are far less important than biases in the data analyzed.

8 For example, overstating a project's capital requirements would lower the projected return for the private investor. Consequently, by separating the sample into two sets of firms—one for which the income statements indicated a relatively high rate of return and another where the projected private return was low—we could test to see whether there was a difference in reporting. This test yielded no indication of such a reporting bias.

9 See Dennis J. Encarnation and Louis T. Wells, Jr., "Sovereignty en Garde: Negotiating with Foreign Investors," *International Organization,* Vol. 39 (Winter 1985), pp. 47–78; Dennis J. Encarnation and Louis T. Wells, Jr., "Competitive Strategies in Global Industries: A View from the Host Country," in Michael Porter, ed., *Competitive Strategies in Global Industries* (Boston: Harvard Business School Press, forthcoming).

10 According to Guisinger (see Chapter 6), factor incentives (e.g., tax holidays) influenced the location decision of only two projects manufacturing for the local market. In contrast, commodity incentives affected the decisions in twenty-three cases. This pattern is reversed for export-oriented projects, where import protection can provide assistance to the investor, and where the investor is free to shop among possible locations, since the local market is unimportant. In spite of the publicity given to export projects, the vast majority of investments in developing countries are made to serve the local market.

# Chapter 3

# Foreign Investment in Low-Income Developing Countries

Vincent Cable and Bishakha Mukherjee

At first sight, the arguments for seeking to attract foreign direct investment (FDI) to low-income developing countries are even greater than for other developing countries. The need for an easily deliverable package of technology, management skills, and know-how is more apparent. The balance-of-payments constraints facing most of these countries are extremely severe, especially in Africa, making foreign investment attractive as a means of assisting their balances of payments both through the injection of capital initially and through the generation of foreign-exchange earnings in the long term.

Yet analysis and experience suggest that—other things being equal—low-income developing countries have particular difficulties in attracting foreign investment. The International Monetary Fund (IMF) acknowledges that:

> Countries with small internal markets, few natural resources, a relatively underdeveloped infrastructure and limited possibilities for manufactured exports may not be able to attract substantial direct investment even with liberal regulations and generous incentives. Such countries are also generally not able to borrow significantly on commercial terms, and must rely primarily on concessional borrowing.[1]

One major implication of this is that while loan financing and FDI can be substitute forms of financial flow,[2] at least to some extent, this does not apply to aid and foreign investment, which are more

**Table 1. Stock of Private Investment in Low-Income and Other Developing Countries: A Comparison**

| Low-Income Countries | Year | Stock of Investment ($ millions) | GNP ($ millions) | Stock of Investment as a portion of GNP (%) | Per Capita Income ($) |
|---|---|---|---|---|---|
| Central African Republic | 1981 | 130 | 820 | 15 | 320 |
| Gambia | 1983 | 30 | 200 | 15 | 260 |
| Kenya | 1983 | 840 | 5,710 | 15 | 340 |
| Niger | 1981 | 105 | 1,880 | 6 | 330 |
| Sierra Leone | 1982 | 90 | 1,250 | 7 | 390 |
| Sudan | 1981 | 540 | 7,300 | 7 | 380 |
| Tanzania | 1978 | 170 | 3,890 | 4 | 230 |
| Bangladesh | 1978 | 80 | 7,650 | 1 | 90 |
| India | 1978 | 2,500 | 116,000 | 2 | 180 |
| Pakistan | 1983 | 1,120 | 31,600 | 4 | 390 |
| Sri Lanka | 1983 | 310 | 5,060 | 6 | 330 |
| **Middle-Income Countries** | | | | | |
| Botswana | 1983 | 710 | 780 | 91 | 930 |
| Egypt | 1982 | 3,390 | 30,100 | 11 | 690 |
| Ivory Coast | 1981 | 890 | 10,200 | 9 | 1,200 |
| Liberia | 1978 | 1,230 | 780 | 158 | 460 |
| Lesotho | 1982 | 70 | 710 | 10 | 510 |
| Mauritius | 1983 | 35 | 1,140 | 3 | 1,160 |
| Nigeria | 1978 | 3,950 | 45,400 | 9 | 560 |
| Senegal | 1978 | 340 | 1,840 | 19 | 340 |
| Tunisia | 1983 | 1,390 | 8,090 | 17 | 1,300 |

| | | | | | |
|---|---|---|---|---|---|
| Zambia | 1981 | 455 | 3,480 | 13 | 600 |
| Zimbabwe | 1982 | 1,750 | 6,375 | 27 | 850 |
| Indonesia | 1982 | 6,530 | 88,500 | 7 | 580 |
| Philippines | 1983 | 2,700 | 34,000 | 8 | 760 |
| Thailand | 1983 | 1,520 | 39,200 | 4 | 820 |
| Jamaica | 1982 | 875 | 2,925 | 31 | 1,330 |
| Guyana | 1982 | 115 | 520 | 22 | 590 |
| Colombia | 1983 | 2,510 | 37,000 | 7 | 1,450 |
| Ecuador | 1982 | 890 | 10,100 | 9 | 1,350 |
| Peru | 1983 | 2,470 | 16,500 | 15 | 1,000 |

**High-Income Countries**

| | | | | | |
|---|---|---|---|---|---|
| Fiji | 1983 | 360 | 1,140 | 32 | 1,820 |
| Hong Kong | 1978 | 2,100 | 14,000 | 15 | 3,040 |
| Republic of Korea | 1982 | 1,490 | 75,100 | 2 | 1,910 |
| Malaysia | 1983 | 8,310 | 27,500 | 30 | 1,840 |
| Singapore | 1983 | 9,465 | 16,300 | 58 | 6,500 |
| Barbados | 1982 | 200 | 760 | 26 | 2,900 |
| Trinidad and Tobago | 1981 | 1,835 | 6,800 | 27 | 5,670 |
| Argentina | 1981 | 5,340 | 118,100 | 5 | 2,500 |
| Brazil | 1982 | 22,100 | 282,000 | 8 | 2,240 |
| Chile | 1983 | 2,745 | 17,400 | 16 | 1,890 |
| Mexico | 1983 | 13,400 | 136,000 | 10 | 1,900 |
| Uruguay | 1983 | 880 | 7,690 | 11 | 2,650 |
| Venezuela | 1982 | 4,200 | 48,800 | 9 | 4,140 |

Note: Since consistent data are not available for all countries, the figures for each country are for different years. The investment stock data in particular are subject to a wide margin of error and are crude approximations only.

Source: Based on OECD, "Geographical Distribution of Financial Flows to Developing Countries 1980/83"; and World Bank, GNP/GNP per capita tables.

meaningfully seen as complementary. Aid flows can create the infrastructure within which FDI can operate, and they can alleviate the external financing constraints that often lead to policies inimical to FDI. The call for increased FDI in Africa recently made by the World Bank and by the Economic Commission for Africa is clearly for *additional* concessional flows, rather than as an alternative for them.[3] In this context, this chapter examines the prospects for FDI in low-income countries and the scope for policy action by either host countries or capital-exporting countries.

Foreign direct investment is concentrated in a small number of the more advanced, middle-income developing countries. Low-income nations attract proportionately less investment than others. There are, however, serious data problems in analyzing the distribution of FDI between countries. Statistics on the *stock*—and to a lesser extent the *flow*—of foreign investment are notoriously deficient; in the low-income developing countries with poorly developed statistical services, the errors are compounded.[4] Moreover, the concept of "low-income developing countries" is ambiguous. The World Bank's per capita income definition includes in this category both China and India, which, although they may have some experience relevant to the problems of small, poor states in Africa, have a degree of industrial and administrative sophistication—as well as market size—of a wholly different order.

As David Goldsbrough shows in Chapter 7, five countries (Brazil, Indonesia, Malaysia, Mexico, and Singapore) accounted for about half of FDI flows during the period 1973–1984. In contrast, countries with per capita incomes below $500—with two-thirds of the population of all developing countries and one-fifth of the gross national product (GNP)—accounted for only 14 per cent of the stock of foreign investment (of which 10 per cent was concentrated in Egypt, India, Indonesia, and Pakistan). As for the flow of new funds, countries with per capita incomes of less than $500 in 1980 accounted for less than 10 per cent in 1981–82; those with per capita incomes above $1,500 received some 75 per cent. Such income concentration is in part self-reinforcing, since reinvested profits are a major source of new investment (more than half of the measured flow of new investment) and since rapid and successful development is in itself both a source of new reinvestable surplus and an attraction to new inflows.

## Factors Influencing the Demand for FDI

There is much evidence that low-income developing countries are—like other developing countries—attempting to increase the inflow of FDI by relaxing restrictions and offering greater inducements.[5] Several factors underlie this increased demand for FDI. One is undoubtedly a greater recognition of the role of the private sector in general. Another relates to judgments about the relative speed and effectiveness of technology transfer by foreign investment relative to other modes. But the external financing crisis facing many developing countries has made financial considerations even more important.

## Substitution Among External Financial Flows

The imbalance between debt and equity in overall external financing is one important factor that has led to increased demand for foreign direct investment. In many countries, excessive borrowing has contributed to high servicing costs and to rigidity in external repayment commitments unrelated to foreign-exchange earning capacity. Low-income countries—especially those in Sub-Saharan Africa (as discussed later in this chapter)—also face a particularly serious debt problem; thirteen countries with per capita incomes of $500 or less were among the thirty-two countries requiring debt rescheduling from early 1983 to mid-1984. Can FDI provide a substantial alternative to debt-creating flows for low-income countries? There are several reasons for believing that it will be difficult to change the relative proportions, at least in the short term.

First, the main source of long-term capital for low-income developing countries is concessional aid, or official development assistance (ODA). For forty-six low-income countries, the net flow of FDI was $500 million as against $10 billion in ODA. Thus foreign direct investment can hardly be considered an *alternative* to ODA. While ODA may be debt-creating to the extent it encompasses concessional loans rather than grants, long-term low-interest loans create a paper debt without necessarily creating serious servicing problems (e.g., India's external debt of $20 billion is higher than that of some major debtors). Where problems do arise, a mechanism is available through retroactive terms adjustment to soften servicing implications. (The further waiving of debt service for low-income developing countries could probably increase net flows to them by over 30 per cent.) Debt problems have emerged at least in part because ODA receipts to low-income countries have fallen in real terms, precipitating a shift to non-concessional lending. It is in this area that questions of substitution arise. Moreover, ODA has typically financed public-sector projects in physical infrastructure, urban development, social services, rural development, and small-scale industries. Most of these activities cannot be financed by, but can help stimulate, foreign direct investment.

Second, there is other evidence of complementarity rather than "substitutability" between loan and equity finance in both a positive and negative sense. Factors which make for a positive investment climate also tend to enhance creditworthiness. Country credit ratings and investment risk assessments tend to follow similar criteria. (For example, among low-income countries, India, China, Sri Lanka, and Kenya would rank quite high on both counts.)

Third, experience suggests that substitutability between loan and equity finance is often more apparent than real. The equity component of FDI may itself be rather small. Even under its standard IMF definition (let alone the wider definition that includes new forms), foreign direct investment includes borrowing from parent companies and affiliates. G. K. Helleiner has described a survey of foreign direct investment projects in which half of the new capital led to debt obligations; he has also pointed to the more general tendency of multinationals to act as intermediaries in international capital markets, thereby generating external debt.[6] In this connection, a major contributing factor is the preference of many multinational companies for less risky, non-equity financing in their subsidiaries in developing countries. Even in Sri Lanka—one of the few low-income developing countries that have been successful in attracting substantial investor interest in recent years—a noteworthy feature of the export-processing zone projects has been the substantial role played by long-term loans (chiefly long-term suppliers' credits) in financing investment in fixed assets. Thus, the capital inflow in equity form is often far smaller than the recorded FDI and is accompanied by substantial contractual debt obligations.

### Foreign Investment as a Source of Export Growth

The external financing crisis affecting many developing countries has also made them receptive to foreign direct investment because of the role it can play in improving trade—especially export—performance. Two preliminary observations should be made. First, the role of foreign investment (and the advantages and disadvantages of different forms) varies considerably for manufactured exports, raw materials, and services (such as tourism). Although we shall refer to each of these categories, our emphasis here is on manufactures. Second, the experience of middle-income countries that have pursued successful strategies of outward-oriented development, based in particular on manufactured exports, is very divergent. Some, like the Republic of Korea, have little direct foreign investment involvement in the export sector; others, such as Singapore and Taiwan, have much more. Moreover, there is contradictory evidence as to whether FDI is "trade-creating," with considerable differences among both host and capital-exporting countries.[8]

For several reasons, some governments are taking an increasingly positive view of the role of foreign direct investment in the export sector. Multinationals have an advantage over indigenous firms due to their scale, specific market knowledge, established distribution chains, capacity for managing and organizing production, and experience in creating markets for all kinds of goods (and services), especially for non-standardized goods requiring marketing expertise. Experience, confirmed by research, also suggests that multinational companies are better able to circumvent protectionist restrictions.[9] For low-income developing countries with little exporting experience, the involvement of multinationals is, on these grounds, attractive.

In addition, alternative arrangements, such as international subcontracting (as in clothing and consumer electronics), have acted as a partial substitute for traditional FDI in some cases. Haiti's rapid emergence as a "least developed" exporter of manufactures based on subcontracting points to both the drawbacks and attractions of this approach.[10] Non-equity arrangements have done nothing to reduce exporters' dependence on foreign firms (whose control is exercised through quality and specification standards and through marketing under a brand name). Moreover, such arrangements have at the same time removed the need for a fixed investment in—and tangible physical commitment to—the host country. There has also been some critical reappraisal of non-equity investment arrangements, such as management contacts unrelated to performance, in other export activities, including mining and tourism, since these, too, have done little to reduce external control while they have removed substantial risk for the private investor. Thus direct investment, in contrast, now appears to be a relatively more satisfactory vehicle in many cases.

The experience of several low-income developing countries points to the role that foreign investment can play in export growth. The export growth experienced in Sri Lanka since 1978 can be very largely attributed to non-traditional products originating in FDI enterprises (three-quarters of the investment in export-processing zones is foreign in origin). Even governments that have restricted foreign investment in general are now giving priority to FDI in the export sector. Kenya's 1981 guidelines for investors, for example, indicate a higher priority for new private investment in resource-based, export-oriented industries, and in export-oriented industries based on imported inputs. And the spread of export-processing zones in several African countries and in India has the same basic motivation. Thus, within the general move toward liberalization affecting foreign investment, there is a tilt toward export-oriented enterprises, especially in manufacturing. This selectivity—expressed, for example, in performance requirements—has begun to arouse some concern among both companies and capital-exporting countries. For companies, such a tilt suggests a direction of capital toward relatively high-risk and possibly low-profit activity; for industrial-country governments, it implies a presumption that they will adjust by accepting competing goods produced in overseas subsidiaries of multinationals. Thus a broad consensus on the desirability of more foreign direct investment has to be qualified to the extent that host countries and investors may approach it with quite different and possibly conflicting expectations.

## Factors Influencing the Supply of Foreign Investment

Several factors particular to low-income countries may render the supply of foreign direct investment inelastic with respect to general or specific inducements. First, market size is relatively small for a given population and absolutely small for all low-income developing countries except China and India. Yet surveys show that the foremost influence on foreign investment in developing countries is the wish to obtain access to a large domestic market. Some low-income countries try to enhance their appeal in this respect by offering highly protected domestic markets to investors (Kenya is an example), but, as Dennis Encarnation and Louis Wells point out in Chapter 2, the economic costs of this strategy may be very high. Another option is to try to create a secure regional market. Where this has occurred, foreign investors have been prominent in industries exporting to such markets. However, the experiences of most integration arrangements inspire little confidence that trade can be kept free and that non-convertible currency transactions can be settled satisfactorily.

Second, the low local wages that attract "off-shore" manufacturing exporters to the poorer developing countries may well be offset by other factors: poor infrastructure and communications; high transport costs on exports and imported inputs; low productivity due to lack of skills or education, repair and maintenance problems for machinery; and political or financial instability. The continuing success of comparatively high-wage locations like Singapore and Barbados and the relative lack of success of Sub-Saharan Africa in attracting export-oriented investment illustrate the magnitude of this particular problem. Providing concessional aid to develop physical and human infrastructures that complement foreign investment is one way of helping low-income developing countries to realize their competitive potential.

Third, the resource base is likely to be small relative to the population except in those cases where mineral resources are under-explored. Well-structured support by international agencies for geological survey efforts as well as an imaginative approach to commercial prospecting would help in this respect. (One major unexploited resource in which foreign investors could play a key role is fisheries. For this to proceed satisfactorily, however, substantial government support is needed in the form of survey work and fisheries protection. The natural resource of good tourist facilities can also be exploited in some low-income developing countries, but it is often inhibited by under-developed infrastructure.)

Fourth, the necessary, complementary, private capital from domestic sources may be deficient. There is, however, a great difference in this respect between major low-income countries, especially India, whose domestic savings and investment ratios are among the world's highest, and low-income African nations where the savings ratio fell from 14.3 per cent of gross domestic product (GDP) in 1973 to 5.4 per cent in 1983.

## Host-Country Policies

Given these formidable constraints, what can host countries do? How do host governments influence the climate for investment? What particular policy instruments are crucial? What realistic possibilities are there for using various inducements to attract new flows to countries whose size, location, resources, and history are not otherwise attractive to investors? Clearly, investments are based on profit potential; and judgments on profitability grounds are likely to relate to particular projects, industries, and types of companies. Yet it *is* possible to influence profit potential through both general and specific policies.

### General Business Climate and Investor Confidence

There is abundant evidence that the policies that have had the greatest impact both in attracting FDI and in ensuring high social returns are not special incentives but the principal economic policies of host countries. The Organisation for Economic Co-operation and Development (OECD) summarizes this well: "Experience has shown that measures undertaken by home and host governments to improve the flow of foreign direct investment or to direct it to specific sectors and locations influence investment decisions only marginally. Such incentives cannot substitute for the 'fundamentals': the investment climate, political security and profit opportunities."[11] This, then, leaves the question of how countries can attract FDI when these fundamentals are unsatisfactory for reasons largely beyond government control. The countries may be poor and small, or have little resource endowment, or have a legacy of political instability.

Many countries also have serious external financing difficulties. In Africa, in particular, rising debt and arrears in debt service are associated with a need for additional external finance as well as for adjustment; conditions have been created—with respect to exchange rates and controls, pricing policies, interest rates, investment policies, and the efficiency of public enterprises—that are inimical to foreign direct investment. Investors are concerned both about financial stability and (at least those interested in domestic markets) about growth. Yet the experience of International Monetary Fund programs in Africa suggests that while progress on financial stability has been achieved in a majority of cases, growth performance has been poor.[12] Moreover, although it is intuitively sensible to believe, as the Fund argues, that restoring financial stability can generate confidence that will encourage foreign investors, there is little evidence of this occurring in the absence of well-established economic recovery. Until this occurs, what other steps can developing countries take?

### Foreign-Exchange Controls

Freedom to remit profits and dividends and to repatriate capital is an essential element in an attractive climate for foreign investment. Several developing countries have achieved a virtuous circle of expanding exports and capital inflows that reinforces the external strength of the economy and makes it yet more attractive to new inflows of capital. Many low-income developing countries do not, however, inhabit such a virtuous circle; instead, they embark upon policies designed to attract foreign investment in order to escape from a balance-of-payments crisis or a long-term external financing constraint. In some cases—especially where there was colonial settlement—a large stock of private foreign or domestically owned capital is available, which, given the freedom, would be exported. The starting point, therefore, is likely to be a history of exchange restrictions and controls. A not atypical situation is that of Kenya, which wishes to attract foreign investment and recognizes basic freedom to remit capital and dividends, but which maintains various forms of exchange control.

Exchange-control regulations affect companies in several ways:

as limits on the importation of goods necessary for production; as restrictions on the repatriation of capital (regulations may permit repatriation of capital up to book value, plus reinvestment of after-tax profits, but this understates the market value, especially after inflation); and as curbs on local currency borrowing. These restrictions often inhibit the redeployment of "blocked" funds into productive investment—because of limits on their use, including the lack of freedom to remit profits. Moreover, as a general rule, there will be little new foreign investment and little expansion of existing investments without considerable host-country freedom to enjoy the returns in foreign exchange. For governments unable to embark on comprehensive exchange liberalization for foreign investors, old or new, there are technical solutions that can, at least for major projects, reconcile investor and host-country interests. One example (in an otherwise unpromising context) is a Ghanaian investment by Consolidated Goldfields in a project backed by the International Finance Corporation. The company has an existing investment from which remittances are blocked; but rather than disinvest, Consolidated Goldfields has contributed, through loans, to an expansion program against an assurance that it can retain, "off-shore," 45 per cent of its foreign-exchange earnings.

### Tax Incentives Schemes

Many developing countries have introduced generous fiscal incentives for inward investment. Typically these include tax holidays, supported by accelerated depreciation allowances and investment allowances or subsidies. A substantial body of evidence and theory has now been amassed that casts a great deal of doubt on the value of such incentives.[13] Why then do most developing countries pursue such policies? And what rational policy options are there for low-income countries seeking to attract foreign investment and caught up in competitive bidding for it?

Part of the answer is that the conventional wisdom may underestimate the importance of incentives—at least for individual host countries. A cross-country, cross-industry study by Stephen Guisinger suggests that host-country policies, including incentives, are weighted more heavily by investors than has usually been thought (see Chapter 6). Within the distinct 'markets' for foreign investment that we have referred to earlier—involving domestic markets of host countries, regional markets, and world markets—there is active and effective competition among host countries.

Incentives are seen by investors as secondary—but if incentives are widely available, then it seems unwise not to offer them. The Commonwealth country studies suggest that both host countries and companies do attach some importance to tax regimes and incentives, especially when pursuing export-oriented investment. The best way to minimize the costs of such competition (as has been done in the Southern African Development Co-ordination Conference (SADCC) countries or in the Caribbean, where there are regional associations) is for coordinated incentive policies to reduce the extent of competitive bidding for investment.[14]

It is in the mining and petroleum sectors that the tax regime is particularly crucial, since, in the case of large projects, tax revenue can be an important component of overall government revenue. A difficult policy judgment must be made in permitting companies a reward for the high risk of exploration and extraction that is sufficient to induce investment while ensuring that society maximizes the long-term flow of revenue. There is a growing recognition in many developing countries of the need for a regime that strikes a sensible balance between objectives: avoiding devices that increase the risk of loss, such as high, flat-rate royalties or export taxes, and concentrating instead on measures that tax revealed profitability. Taxation over and above normal company income tax is levied only after the achievement of a specified rate of return on project outlays. Such a system now operates in Equatorial Guinea, Gambia, Guinea Bissau, Liberia, Madagascar, Senegal, Sierra Leone, Somalia, and Tanzania, as well as in better established major mineral producers such as Papua New Guinea. It does, however, make considerable demands on the supervisory capacity of host-country officials.

### Restrictions and Procedures

Many countries impose limitations on the operations of foreign companies—on the foreign equity share in certain sectors, for example—that act as a deterrent to inflows. Whatever restrictions exist, evidence strongly indicates that the speed and simplicity of official clearance is crucial in forming favorable business perceptions. However, it also has to be recognized that an effective mechanism for screening and negotiating foreign investment is exceedingly difficult to establish. Several countries are now overhauling their procedures and incentives in response to private investor concern about over-regulation, as well as creating a unitary investment promotion and advisory center—following the model of similar institutions in Indonesia and Papua New Guinea. The necessity of streamlining controls is perhaps most acute in countries where there is a framework of planning and regulation—since delays in decision making may become more of a deterrent than the regulations themselves. (See Chapter 2 in this volume.)

### Trade Policy and Special Zones

Many countries are now seeking to adjust to more open regimes with the aim of achieving greater export growth. But for some, with complex protectionist regimes in place, a "second-best" solution is a free-trade zone.[15] Such zones can also serve as a focus for infrastructure development of a kind considered necessary for export-oriented foreign investment. The infrastructure itself can become (as in China) a basis for both private and official financing.

For example, the Sri Lankan authorities have treated foreign-owned, export-oriented investments on an enclave basis while maintaining a separate regime for other foreign investments. Foreign enterprises exporting their output and using external funds are permitted duty-free importation, exemption from exchange control, and generous tax-holiday provisions. After six years of the first zone's existence, established and committed projects had an employment potential of 50,000 and provided 10.5 per cent of Sri Lanka's exports. The approach has been criticized, however, especially for its low net foreign exchange, allowing for remittances as well as imported inputs (20 to 25 per cent of the gross figure).[16] As with other schemes of this kind, success in building backward linkages may be limited. And the success of the zone, like other attempts to attract "footloose" foreign investment, hinges on confidence, which is very vulnerable to changing perceptions of stability.

The experience of Sub-Saharan countries embarking on this course is less encouraging.[17] The Dakar Zone is the only such functioning unit in Sub-Saharan Africa. Although it offers generous incentives (complete company tax exemption until the end of the century) and good infrastructure, it has contributed little to the growth of Senegal's export base. After ten years, only seven companies, employing just over 1,000 people, were operating there. The explanation is that the market for export-oriented investment is highly competitive and that a West African location—with relatively high transport and labor costs (even though wages are low) and limited prospects for sales in regional markets—has small pulling power.

In striking contrast, Mauritius, despite a locational disadvantage and relatively high wages, has an Export Processing Zone that has been remarkably successful. Yet its success only highlights the problems likely to be faced by low-income newcomers in attracting new investment to such zones. Very little of the capital comes from equity financing by multinationals. (Only a third of the investment is equity-financed; of that, half is from Mauritius sources, a third from Hong Kong textile sources seeking a quota-free base, and most of the rest is from overseas Mauritians.) Moreover, difficulties with protectionist barriers overseas and depressed world markets are increasing, and there has been a sharp rise in firm closures; the government has been obliged to extend its ten-year tax holiday incentive to keep in production firms that were established a decade ago but that no longer generate high returns. The same difficulties are being experienced by Bangladesh, one least developed country trying to attract export-oriented investment to its free-trade zones.

In view of these problems and the poor record of extending similar arrangements to Sub-Saharan Africa, it is difficult to envision such schemes providing a major incentive for foreign investors in low-income developing countries. One incentive that can be offered by countries with a large domestic market is some degree of access to that market, with or without full payment of duty. This option is being considered by China and India and illustrates a central point in this discussion: Purely export-oriented investment is, by itself, likely to be difficult to attract.

## Special Problems of Low-Income Countries

The discussion thus far has tried to generalize about a category of countries that is quite heterogeneous. A particular distinction should be made, however, between most of the countries of Sub-Saharan Africa; the very small low-income states (such as Gambia, Kiribati, and the Maldives); and the major low-income developing countries in Asia (China and India). A few specific points can be made in relation to policy for each of the main groups.

### The Crisis-Hit Economies: Sub-Saharan Africa

A major problem for policy makers in many low-income countries is how to attract foreign investment against a background of very adverse economic circumstances and, in particular, a serious foreign-exchange situation.

Even where liberalization of foreign-exchange transactions is not practical, techniques can be developed to ensure that foreign-exchange shortages do not inhibit the flow of remittances or prevent investors from acquiring inputs necessary for normal operations: Foreign exchange can be made freely available, at least for export projects; off-shore escrow accounts can be used to manage foreign-exchange business; and lines of credit can be advanced from central banks to obtain spare parts and other necessary imported inputs. These are, however, merely expedients to deal with a deeper problem whose resolution lies in a combination of structural adjustment (particularly in correcting over-valued exchange rates), the resumption of normal trade credit lines where these have been disrupted, and additional long-term external flows of all kinds.

Although a substantial additional inflow of foreign investment into these low-income countries is unlikely in the short run, investment in mining (especially gold and possibly iron ore) and petroleum offer significant potential. Since Africa is relatively under-explored for these resources, the prospects for more investments are reasonably promising. One precedent is that of Tanzania, which has, in unpropitious circumstances, harnessed both concessional capital and substantial investment by foreign oil companies.[18] The main factors behind Tanzania's approach are a stable agreement providing assurance to the investors, clear ground rules, and a tax regime that varies automatically according to economic circumstances and therefore leaves no uncertainty as to what constitutes profitability. The government has maintained sovereign control over its resources while leaving operational matters to the investor.

In Ghana, the successful renegotiation of the Volta Aluminium Company Agreements in the last few years also suggests how a country with a history of instability and economic crisis can nonetheless use skillful negotiation to obtain beneficial terms from foreign investors in major resource-based projects.[19] The experience of a substantial number of low-income and other developing countries indicates that foreign investment can be successfully negotiated for resource-based projects where multinationals are encouraged to retain majority equity and where taxes are clearly defined and based on revealed profitability.

In relation to potential capital inflows more generally, the major source is likely to be reinvested profits by established multinational corporations or new capital flows from them. The scope for a rapid growth of capital flows from new sources is less encouraging in the short run. Perceptions will alter only gradually, as successful experiences multiply. But new foreign investors can be introduced in other ways:[20]

• *The existence of a serious unresolved problem of external indebtedness provides some scope for debt equity conversion.* This could, for example, provide one mechanism for dealing with blocked private-sector trade credits as part of debt-restructuring arrangements.

• *Foreign investors can be involved as investors in company restructuring arrangements, especially consequent upon the privatization of state-managed and state-owned agencies.* Care is required in this area, however. Both the economics and the politics of 'privatization' are complex. Companies making a loss are not in general likely to be attractive to foreign investors, except at knock-down prices, and there would be domestic resistance to selling more viable enterprises, especially where this approach creates monopolies.

• *Planned foreign collaboration of a non-equity kind can be given more of the character of direct investment.* Management and service contracts can be negotiated with fees fixed on a sliding scale to reflect performance or to incorporate a direct equity element. Greater equity participation can also be sought from plant and process equipment manufacturers in lieu of suppliers' credit.

### Small Low-Income States

Small low-income countries have characteristics that make foreign investment more important, but also more problematic.[21] In very small countries, indigenous development of technology and large-scale commercial operations are likely to be very limited, making foreign investment indispensable. Also, limited domestic markets mean that economies are very open and highly dependent on trade and thus on exporting enterprises that can achieve access to foreign markets. But for foreign investors, the absence of a domestic market means a prospect of only relatively high-risk export activities. Infrastructure and public administration, which are subject to economies of scale, are likely to be costly or deficient. For small island states, remoteness—and therefore high transport costs—is an additional problem. Yet some small states such as Singapore or Barbados—no longer low-income countries—have built up a substantial stock of foreign investment as part of a long period of successful development.

Most low-income countries need not only to attract foreign investment, but also to enhance their capacity to bargain and negotiate. Small states are at a particular disadvantage in this respect. For them, an agreed multilateral code would be particularly valuable. In the absence of such an agreement, there is a good deal of scope for technical assistance to negotiate contractual arrangements. Foreign investment can, however, serve a major objective of policy by helping to reduce economic vulnerability through diversification. Among the areas for which foreign investment is likely to be sought by these countries are manufactured exports, tourism, and fishing.

Despite the problems in manufactured exports, several low-income developing countries have succeeded in attracting manufacturing exporters. For example, the Maldives has a small garment assembly in operation, based on investments from Far Eastern entrepreneurs seeking low-cost, quota-free locations. But the most easily established industry (garment assembly) is vulnerable to quota action in industrial countries—even on very small volumes—as the Maldives has discovered in the United States.

For countries with an attractive location, tourism offers potential for foreign investment; in this case, country size and remoteness are not obvious deterrents—indeed, they may be the reverse. The development of foreign hotel chains is not, however, typically associated with foreign direct investment. One survey shows that fewer than 20 per cent of the hotels in developing countries are owned or partially owned by multinational investors; in two-thirds of the hotels, the form of association is a management contract with a state or with private local enterprises.[22] Although foreign enterprises may well bring important qualities to bear—management and organizational expertise, training facilities, knowledge (e.g., links with airlines)—they will not necessarily shoulder the project risks unless contracts are specifically designed to ensure that fees bear a direct relationship to net earnings by the local economy.

Since the adoption of the 200-mile Exclusive Economic Zones, most small island states have large, under-exploited fisheries resources. Multinationals may play an important role in linking the exploitation of specific fish stocks with the packaging and quality needs of distant markets.[23] Typically, collaboration involves little more than license fees, but it may be extended to a more comprehensive joint venture including processing. Small low-income countries often need assistance in negotiation to ensure that license fees are remunerative and that risks are shared with investors.

### Populous Low-Income Countries

With their large size, more varied natural resources, and much greater technological and industrial sophistication, China and India have a greater 'pull' on foreign investors than other low-income countries. At the same time, however, they view foreign investment as less crucial. Both governments have identified specific roles for foreign investment in transferring technology not otherwise available and in increasing exports. Neither goal is likely to be congruent with the aims of most investors, who are more interested in gaining access to large domestic markets, especially to supply goods and services requiring standardized technology. The experience of China and India demonstrates the difficulties of achieving a satisfactory trade-off between the goals of multinationals and host countries.

Against this background, the record of foreign investment has been mixed in both countries. In China, the Special Economic Zones were to be the mainspring for foreign participation. However, the expected rush to create industrial parks for the export of manufactured goods, with their embodied high-technology transfers, has not materialized.[24] The major growth has been in the simpler forms of trade compensation and processing agreements involving little technological transfer. Backward linkages have been limited. The Special Economic Zones in China were also planned to be export bases. Instead, investors have sought—and gained—greater access for their products to the domestic market. The zones will require substantial infrastructural construction before they can offer modernized, streamlined facilities for export. Other inhibiting factors have had an effect: Many of the investment incentives are nonoperative due to the unrealistic thresholds set by the Chinese authorities for multinationals to become eligible for benefits; the capacity to absorb foreign technology is often low; and there have been disagreements over legal regulations and profit repatriation. The Chinese have recently taken steps to liberalize their requirements—for example, by adjusting downward many of the earlier high-technology expectations. India, like China, has tried to be selective. But unlike China, it has been pursuing a consistent foreign investment policy over a long period. (Another important difference, of course, is the strength of its indigenous private sector.) However, despite the selectivity exercised (or perhaps because of it), foreign collaborations have not resulted in the importation of substantial new technology, and technology gaps are now widely acknowledged.[25] India's free trade zones and its 100 per-cent Export-Oriented Units have been largely unsuccessful in attracting foreign interest, and their role in the country's foreign trade remains marginal.[26] One major reason for the almost negligible foreign presence in the only multiproduct zone (Kandla) is the lack of access to the domestic market; the government allows only 25 per cent of a company's production to be sold to the domestic market, and only against valid import licenses. Relatively underdeveloped infrastructural facilities are another deterrent.

In response to these problems, the Indian government has established four additional free-trade zones and is taking steps to ensure that the new zones have well-developed infrastructural facilities and better incentives. And recent reforms in industrial policy encourage foreign companies to play a "supportive" role in some key areas, particularly electronics and vehicles. The government has, however, repeatedly warned business not to expect too much movement in the area of foreign investment policy. Like its predecessors, it is concerned that indiscriminate foreign investment will lead to "inappropriate" technology and products—and also that most foreign investment that is designed to meet domestic demand

risk insurance. Others seem to be discouraged from seeking guarantees by what they regard as excessive bureaucratic procedures inherent in the schemes. Furthermore, many elements of uncertainty concerning host-country policies and circumstances are not readily covered by insurance. Reinterpretation of the details of contractual arrangements, for example, is far more complex and difficult to consider or protect against in advance than such obvious measures as expropriation, exchange controls, or civil disturbances.

In this context, interest has been growing in a system of multilateral investment insurance that could plug some of the gaps in the national coverage and operate with smaller premiums because of a greater diversity of risk. The availability of a multilateral scheme offering improved coverage for investments in developing countries that have so far received modest amounts of foreign direct investment and are perceived as at high risk would contribute to reduced concentration of FDI among very few host countries. The proposed Multilateral Investment Guarantee Agency (MIGA) is designed to perform this role.

### Codes of Conduct

The particular predicament of many low-income countries is that while they welcome foreign investment in principle, their small size and lack of bargaining power frequently lead to actual or feared abuses by a dominant multinational corporation. Concern about the disproportion in bargaining power between small and weak states and large multinational companies provides a continuing rationale for a code of conduct covering the behavior of multinationals.

But little progress has been made on this issue. Developing countries have wanted the code to have the force of a treaty, whereas the industrial, OECD countries take the view that a code should contain broad principles or guidelines, not legally enforceable rules. In the current political climate in major countries, which is generally hostile to business regulation, there seems little prospect of the former concept prevailing. Nonetheless, if an agreed code were to emerge, it would undoubtedly assist in improving the political climate for foreign investment in low-income developing countries on a long-term basis and alleviate the suspicion that still surrounds it in many countries.

### Catalytic Agencies

Because of the difficulties that many low-income developing countries have in attracting foreign investment, agencies such as the International Finance Corporation (IFC) and the Commonwealth

Development Corporation (CDC) can play an important role in mobilizing foreign direct investment. They can also offer policy advice and assistance in negotiations with prospective foreign partners to achieve an equitable sharing of risks and benefits.

The IFC had financed (as of June 1984) 777 projects in eighty-four countries, representing total investment costs of $27 billion (excluding the multiplier factor of associated foreign direct investment). Of this total, roughly $820 million, or 15 per cent, was accounted for by low-income developing countries ($287 million by India and China) under the current World Bank definition.[27] The proportion is not high, but it is higher than that of total FDI going to low-income developing countries. The recent capital increase for IFC and the reorientation of its program toward the poorer developing countries should strengthen its capacity to promote FDI in these areas. In the case of the Commonwealth Development Corporation, which has total lending investments of $850 million, over 80 per cent of new commitments is accounted for by "the poorer countries."[28] Special features of CDC operations have been a focus on low-income Commonwealth Asian and African countries and an emphasis on export agriculture linking FDI in "nuclear" estates with family smallholder development. In the United States, the Overseas Private Investment Corporation (OPIC) claims that "over half" of its projects (both direct financing and insurance) are in "the poorest countries."[29]

An important supporting role lies in ensuring not only that foreign private businesses are involved in development but also that corporate financial instruments are used so as to spread risk among the participating bodies. This would involve encouraging fixed-price turnkey contracts (which shift part of the risk to the contractors); technology royalty agreements with a greater share of risk to the licensor where technologies are unproven; linkage of interest rates on loans to project profitability or commodity prices; and performance-related management contracts.[30]

## Conclusions

Governments of low-income (as well as other) developing countries are increasingly aware of the potential value of foreign investment. There is, however, a danger of exaggerated expectations of what foreign investment can achieve, particularly of its role in easing a severe foreign-exchange position through net inflows. Significantly, the IMF has now revised its forecasts for the growth of FDI downward to 3 per cent a year (much as during the 1970s), reflecting modest hope in what can be accomplished with changes in host-country policies and with international schemes.

The limited natural resource endowments and home markets of many low-income countries, especially the poorest among them, tend to make these countries particularly unattractive to foreign investors. Even where foreign investors are drawn to viable projects, experience suggests that they will often prefer loan financing and various forms of non-equity arrangements, in which risks are perceived to be lower.

Despite these limited prospects, interesting possibilities for foreign investment do exist even in the poorest countries where certain natural resources are underexplored or unexploited; where the private sector is now more warmly welcomed; and where a greater component of risk capital can be attained from foreign collaboration. Especially with supporting assistance from international agencies, foreign investors should be able to be satisfactorily involved on a somewhat larger scale.

The same external financing crisis that has given impetus to more liberal foreign-investment policies in many low-income countries has also engendered more of a commitment to export-oriented development. There have been hopes that foreign investment can help low-income developing countries achieve more rapid export growth—as it appears to have done in some East Asian newly industrializing countries. But African attempts to attract export-oriented investment (particularly in export-processing zones) demonstrate the considerable difficulties involved. A major influence on whether or not this type of development can achieve any momentum will be the absence of protectionist barriers in major consuming countries.

Even within the contraints of an unfavorable environment, host governments can create conditions more conducive to inflows of foreign capital. But the evidence suggests that in low-income developing countries, as elsewhere, special incentives are a good deal less important than "fundamentals" such as expectations of growth, policies generally conducive to the development of the private sector, and the absence of controls on foreign-exchange transactions and prices. There is no short-term agenda for low-income countries seeking to attract foreign investment into crisis-plagued economies. Action on these recommendations can only be taken as part of a successful, long-run strategy of adjustment.

# Notes

Note: This paper expresses the personal opinions of the authors and does not represent the official view of the Commonwealth Secretariat. The paper draws on studies prepared as part of the Secretariat's program to assist member countries with policy development in foreign investment. These studies include the papers, and proceedings of the Commonwealth Secretariat's seminars on foreign investment policies and prospects in Africa, and in Asia and the Pacific, as well as a study of foreign investment in developing countries edited by Vincent Cable and B. Persaud (Croom-Helm, forthcoming).

[1] David Goldsbrough, *Foreign Private Investment in Developing Countries*, Occasional Paper No. 33 (Washington, D.C.: International Monetary Fund, 1985), p. 9.

[2] This argument is more fully developed in Chapter 7 of this volume.

[3] World Bank, *Toward Sustained Development in Sub-Saharan Africa* (Washington, D.C.: 1984), p. 48; African Development Bank and Economic Commission for Africa, *Economic Report on Africa, 1984* (Abidjan and Addis Ababa: 1984), para. 81.

[4] The principal problems arise from the fact that the main source of flow data (the IMF) has to apply a flexible concept of foreign control in defining direct investment: It is taken by some countries to mean as little as 10 per cent foreign ownership; in others, much more. The IMF definition takes in indirect as well as direct capital contributions, such as net loans from companies to their subsidiaries and reinvested profits, though country coverage is often inconsistent. There are often problems, too, in converting data from domestic to foreign currency when some transactions (reinvested profits) are conducted in the former and others in the latter. When the stock of capital is measured, the problems are greatly compounded by discrepancies in the treatment of assets and liabilities as well as by the inherent limitations of book-value measures.

[5] United Nations Centre on Transnational Corporations, *Transnational Corporations in World Development* (New York: 1985).

[6] See UNCTAD, "The Role of Foreign Investment in Development Finance: Current Issues," TD/B/C/196, Geneva, 1984.

[7] G. K. Helleiner, *Direct Foreign Investment and Manufacturing for Export in Developing Countries: A Review of the Issues* (London: Commonwealth Secretariat, unpublished, 1984).

[8] Hal Hill and Brian Johns, "The Role of Direct Foreign Investment in Developing East Asian Countries," *Weltwirtschaftliches Archiv* (Review of World Economics), Kiel (1985), pp. 355–81.

[9] G. K. Helleiner, "Transnational Enterprises and the New Political Economy of U.S. Trade Policy," *Oxford Economic Papers*, Vol. 29, No. 1 (March 1977).

[10] V. N. Balasubramanyam, "Incentives and Disincentives for Foreign Direct Investment in Less Developed Countries," *Weltwirtschaftliches Archiv* (Review of World Economics), Kiel (1984), p. 720–735.

[11] Organisation for Economic Co-operation and Development, *Investing in Developing Countries* (Paris: 1983), p. 14.

[12] J. B. Zulu and S. M. Nsouli, *Adjustment Programs in Africa: The Recent Experience*, Occasional Paper No. 34 (Washington, D.C.: International Monetary Fund, 1985).

[13] David Lim, "Fiscal Incentives and Direct Foreign Investment in LDCs," *The Journal of Development Studies*, Vol. 19 (1983), pp. 207–212.

[14] This point is emphasized in case studies of countries that have been successful in attracting foreign investment—such as Singapore, Malaysia, and Barbados. See, for example, Commonwealth Secretariat, *Papers and Proceedings of the Seminar on Foreign Investment Policies and Prospects in Asia and Pacific* (London: forthcoming)

[15] Antoine Basile and Dimitri Germidis: *Investing in Free Export Processing Zones* (Paris: Organisation for Economic Co-operation and Development, 1984).

[16] Data from Central Bank of Ceylon and Greater Colombo Economic Commission, *Annual Reports*, (various years)

[17] Jean Currie, "Comparison of Export Oriented Investment: Senegal, Ghana and Mauritius," in Commonwealth Secretariat, *Papers and Proceedings of Seminar on Foreign Investment Policies and Prospects in Africa* (London: 1985).

[18] C. Goss and R. Nellist, "Attracting Overseas Capital in the Search for Petroleum: Tanzania's Success Story to Date," in Commonwealth Secretariat, *Seminar on Africa*, op. cit.

[19] R. Sims, "Renegotiation of the Volta Aluminium Agreements: Lessons in Negotiating with Multinational Companies," in Commonwealth Secretariat, *Papers and Proceedings of Seminar on Foreign Investment in Africa*, op. cit.

[20] R. Sims, "Renegotiation of the Volta Aluminum Agreements," op. cit.

[21] *Vulnerability: Small States in the Global Society*, Report of a Commonwealth Consultative Group (London: Commonwealth Secretariat, 1985).

[22]John H. Dunning and Matthew McQueen, "The Eclectic Theory of International Production: A Case Study of the International Hotel Industry," *Managerial and Decision Economics*, Vol. 2, No. 4 (1981), pp. 197–203.

[23]David P. Rutenberg, "Multinational Food and Fish Corporations," in Alan M. Rugman, ed., *New Theories of the Multinational Enterprise* (London: Croom Helm, 1982).

[24]M. W. Oborne, *Zones of the People's Republic of China: Resume of Research Findings* (Paris: Organisation for Economic Co-operation and Development, 1985); and Jean Currie, "The Role of Foreign Investment in China," and Commonwealth Secretariat, *Papers and Proceedings of the Seminar on Foreign Investment in Asia and the Pacific,* op. cit.

[25]Sanjaya Lall, "India," *World Development*, Vol. 12, Nos. 5/6 (1984), pp. 535-65.

[26]R. Kumar, *Export Processing Zones in India: An Evaluation*, and M. Ramadhyani, *100% Export Oriented Units: Performance and Prospects* (New Delhi: Indian Council for Research on International Economic Relations, 1985).

[27]Data from International Finance Corporation, *Annual Report*, various years.

[28]Data from Commonwealth Development Corporation, *Annual Report*, various years.

[29]The President's Task Force on International Private Enterprise, *Report to the President* (Washington, D.C.: 1984).

[30]Giovanni Vacchelli, "The Changing Role for Investment Finance in Developing World Projects," Paper presented to the Conference on Business Transactions with Developing Countries: Managing and Financing International Trade and Transnational Investment, Cambridge Business Conferences, 1985.

# Chapter 4

# Multinational Corporations and Third World Agriculture

David J. Glover

The involvement of multinational corporations (MNCs) in Third World agriculture has a long history. Since colonial times, firms such as Lonrho, Firestone, and United Fruit have exported primary commodities from their plantations in Asia, Africa, and Latin America, shaping the economies of the host countries in a very direct fashion. Today, the involvement of MNCs takes myriad forms, many of which do not directly involve those firms in agricultural production. The indirect effects of multinational firms on Third World agriculture are significant, however, and are of heightened interest because of concern about food policy in developing countries, particularly in Sub-Saharan Africa.

This chapter provides an overview of both the direct and indirect roles of MNCs—pointing out some of the potential benefits and limitations of multinational involvement. The focus on 'involvement' rather than 'investment' is deliberate; many marketing arrangements and management contracts do not include any investment of capital or bearing of risk by the MNC. They do, however, allow the firm considerable control over the production process. Furthermore, the decisions implemented through such arrangements appear to reflect not simply local circumstances but also the firms' global corporate strategies. (The characteristics and implications of these arrangements in non-agricultural spheres are discussed in Chapter 5 of this volume.) The degree to which such strategies are consistent with Third World development goals is analyzed in the latter part of this chapter, although the scope of the question precludes definitive answers or even a full consideration of all of its aspects.

This chapter begins with a brief indication of the breadth and magnitude of multinational involvement in agriculture and then describes some of the mechanisms through which multinational firms interact with Third World agriculture. The chapter examines the impact of each of these mechanisms on host countries and concludes with some implications for U.S. policy.

## Multinationals and Agriculture

"Agribusiness" is a term that is rarely defined but whose meaning is nonetheless reasonably clear. It refers to those activities of private corporations (usually but not necessarily based in industrial countries, and sometimes in collaboration with governments or international agencies) that impinge on the production of agricultural commodities and livestock. The activities can include production, processing, domestic marketing, international commodity trading, futures trading, sales of inputs or farm machinery, technical assistance, and management.

The amount of private foreign direct investment in agricultural production in developing countries is probably quite small in relation to the output produced on land owned by host-country citizens, firms, or governments. However, the involvement of foreign firms in activities indirectly related to agriculture is widespread.

Data that give a more precise picture of the direct or indirect role of multinationals unfortunately are not readily available. The most complete statistics pertain to *food-processing* firms.[1] About 22 per cent of the food-processing activities of the 189 leading firms takes place outside the home country; of the foreign activities, about one-quarter are in developing countries. The United Nations Centre on Transnational Corporations (UNCTC) has identified about 800 investments by MNCs in this field in the Third World. U.S. firms tend to invest in Latin America, and European firms in Africa and Asia, although Nestlé is found throughout the developing world. Furthermore, foreign investment in agro-based industries, as in other fields, is highly concentrated. The UNCTC found that the larger and richer developing countries have attracted the greatest number of MNC affiliates and that the fifteen countries with the largest food-processing industries were host to an average of eighteen such MNCs. Brazil and Mexico host affiliates of more than forty foreign-based investors.[2]

Of the sixty-five largest *food-industry* firms, two-thirds are U.S.-based. The two largest, however, are European (Unilever and

Nestlé).[3] These two also have the highest proportion of their subsidiaries in developing countries. In general, firms active in the food industry are among the most highly diversified. "Of the 51 food processors with $2 billion or more in total revenues, all but six are engaged in at least one line of business altogether unrelated to the food industry," the UNCTC reports.[4]

## Modes of MNC and Host-Country Interaction

The means by which MNCs interact with agricultural producers can be classified into three groups: plantations, in which the MNC itself is the producer, using hired labor; arm's-length, non-contractual transactions in which the firm either buys from or sells to producers, directly or through state agencies but without contractual ties; and other forms of involvement that lie between these two extremes.

*Plantations.* In spite of a general tendency toward other forms of involvement, MNC-owned plantations remain important in the production of a number of commodities, both traditional and nontraditional. In general, these are commodities in which there are significant economies of scale in production.

Three MNCs (United Fruit, Castle & Cooke, and Del Monte) control about half of the bananas traded internationally.[5] Most of the fruit comes from four Central American countries; from 57 to 78 per cent of exports in each country is produced on company plantations, with the remainder coming from local producers under contract ("associate producers").[6] Plantation ownership entails three advantages for these firms: leverage in negotiating prices with associate producers, facilities for conducting long-term agronomic research, and a core supply of top-quality fruit. This third advantage allows the firm to handle supply-and-demand fluctuations in world markets; company plantations can operate near capacity year-round, while contract and open-market purchases vary to meet fluctuations.

The same firms have reacted to saturated banana markets and declining price prospects by diversifying into palm oil production, generally by converting unproductive Central American plantations and occasionally by purchasing new land. Since the fruit must be processed promptly after harvest, the companies have set up crushing plants and refineries nearby. Some have also set up pineapple plantations in Central America, Kenya, and the Philippines. Diversification into palm oil probably reflects the worldwide boom in planting to meet growing demand in industrial and developing countries for fried and processed foods. Pineapple production in the Third World reflects less an expanding market than a shift from high-wage production in Hawaii. Marketing techniques and channels used for bananas can also be applied to pineapples, and both palm oil and pineapples permit some transfer of a firm's expertise in managing large-scale tree crop plantations in the tropics.

The most important single producer of palm oil, however, is Unilever, the largest agribusiness firm in the world. It is involved in a wide range of activities related to palm oil, including processing, trading, and manufacture of consumer goods; the company owns 90,000 hectares of plantation land in Asia and Africa.[7]

Sugar cane is probably the crop in which MNCs have moved farthest from plantation ownership to new forms of involvement. There are, however, marked differences among companies. While Booker McConnell and Tate & Lyle have done the most in terms of management contracts and consultancies, Lonrho maintains important plantations in Malawi, Mauritius, South Africa, and Swaziland.

Although Latin America shows a marked tendency toward contract farming in the production of specialty fruits and vegetables, flowers, and the like, Africa does not. Perhaps because of differences in host-country policies, or perhaps because of a lack of suitable growers, MNCs have frequently set up plantations to produce these crops. The most famous example was Bud Senegal, a subsidiary of Castle & Cooke, which air-freighted green beans from the African country to Europe in the early 1970s. When prices did not meet expectations, the operation came to an abrupt end. Brooke Bond exports flowers and vegetables to Europe from its plantations in Kenya.[8]

A recent survey of MNCs in Latin American agriculture found only two countries in which such firms had recently established plantations—for timber and cattle in Brazil, and for oil palm in Ecuador.[9] In both cases, the tracts of land were located in frontier areas bordering the Amazon Basin. In the Brazilian case, the government offered incentives to induce the firms to open up these zones.

*Non-Contractual Transactions.* Among the activities of multinationals that indirectly affect the nature of Third World agriculture are the following: processing; commodity and futures trading; shipping; and sales of seeds, fertilizer, chemicals, farm machinery, processed foods, and beverages. Even a product that uses few local agricultural inputs (e.g., bread or soft drinks) can affect local agriculture, since increased consumption of such products will reduce the demand for local substitutes (e.g., maize or fruit juices).

A UNCTC study that looked only at the food industries identified nine systems in which MNCs were active as international traders (and, in many cases, in other capacities as well): meat, dairy, fisheries, fruit and vegetables, grains, oils, sugar and bottled beverages, commodity beverages, and spices.[10] The study found genuine arm's-length trading by MNCs (i.e., to unrelated firms) was characteristic of grains, oils, commodity beverages, and spices; intra-firm trade typified transactions in fruits and vegetables. In the other systems, the forms of involvement fell somewhere in between.

*Other Forms of Involvement.* Multinationals are involved in developing-country agriculture through a number of mechanisms that fall between direct production and arm's-length transactions. By entering into production contracts with growers and various kinds of multipartite agreements with growers and local governments, many MNCs exert considerable influence over the conduct of agricultural production without owning land or engaging in production themselves. Many case studies indicate that these contractual relationships have become the preferred means of operation for a great many MNCs.[11]

The simplest of these relationships is *contract farming*, in which the firms process and/or export the produce of local farmers, having acquired it through contracts that pre-set the price, quantity, and quality to be purchased. This planning allows the firm to keep a processing plant operating at capacity or an export marketing operation tied in with seasonal patterns of demand. Often the firm provides technical assistance, inputs, credit, equipment rentals, and other services. This system reduces uncertainty and provides other advantages to both parties. The company does not have to own land or manage a hired labor force, and growers obtain access to markets and services that might otherwise be unavailable.

The industry in which contract farming is quantitatively most important is bananas, where the three dominant firms purchase about one-third of their supplies from associate producers. The latter are generally local plantation owners who employ large labor forces. United Brands and Castle & Cooke have bought bananas from associate producers for nearly a hundred years, and the proportion of exports provided by these producers has increased—accelerating since the mid-1950s in response to economic nationalism. (There appears to be little likelihood, however, that the MNCs will withdraw from production altogether.)

Contract farming is also heavily used in fruit and vegetable production, particularly in Central America; and smaller growers, cooperatives, and individual peasants have been involved. Most frequently, this entails the export of high-value items such as asparagus, cucumbers, melons, or strawberries, with the firm providing quality control, brand names, and marketing channels.

MNCs may have a number of motives for purchasing through contracts.[12] Avoiding conflict over landownership and labor issues is probably most significant. Cost advantages may also be possible. For crops requiring much labor and careful attention, smallholder production may be more efficient than plantations; in cases where it is not (e.g., bananas), local plantation owners may be able to achieve lower costs than MNCs by paying lower wages. Local firms are less conspicuous than foreign ones and can often pay workers less and deal more harshly with unions.

Another possible advantage of contract farming is that local growers may find it easier than MNCs to get the local government (or indirectly, international aid agencies) to provide credit for operating capital or rehabilitation of plantations. If these sources provide loans at sufficiently low interest rates, the cost of operating or restoring the farms can be kept down, allowing the firm to avoid financial risks. Local purchasing also lessens the risk of expropriation by locating fewer assets within the host country. Contract farming may promote good public relations and present a progressive image by involving local producers. It can also make the companies' wages and social benefits look good in comparison with those paid by local growers. Finally, contract farming may contribute to the formation of alliances with local businessmen who may defend the MNC's interests on certain issues.

In many cases, other actors participate in contract farming schemes, providing some of the services otherwise offered by MNCs. The most common participants in such *multipartite arrangements* are the host-country government and/or international aid or lending agencies such as the U.S. Agency for International Development (AID), the World Bank, or the Commonwealth Development Corporation (CDC). The CDC has been particularly active in this type of scheme. In one common arrangement, a national development bank rather than the MNC provides growers with credit for the purchase of fertilizer, seeds, and the like. At harvest time, the firm pays growers the contract price, but takes off the top a sum that goes to the bank to repay its loan to the grower. In this system, MNCs avoid the problems of assessing creditworthiness and prosecuting defaulters. In some cases, government agencies provide inputs or technical assistance. At the extreme, the MNC has little or no equity in the operation and receives fees through a management contract. In other cases, joint ventures have been established with the MNC, the government, and the growers all holding shares. Multipartite schemes are common in sugar in East and Southern Africa, in fruits and vegetables in Central America, and in cotton in Francophone Africa (involving the Compagnie Française de Développement de Textiles).

The banana multinationals generally have closely followed the classic contract farming model, providing growers with an integrated package of services and inputs (some produced by the MNC's affiliates). Financing is usually the only function delegated to government. The sugar multinationals have gone farthest toward management contracts and consultancies. Each of the three major MNCs (Booker McConnell, Tate & Lyle, and Lonrho) currently has management contracts with governments in Africa. The best known is the Mumias outgrower sugar scheme in Kenya; the largest to date is Kenana in Sudan (with an infrastructure cost of $613 million).[13]

The remuneration system in the Mumias scheme is a common one. Booker McConnell's affiliate, Booker Agriculture International, receives three types of income: a fixed fee to cover expatriate salaries and related overheads, a commission on sales of sugar (the project's output is marketed in Kenya), and a small share of net profits.[14] This remuneration structure is designed to encourage both output and efficiency.

It should be noted that the difference between the typical arrangements for bananas and those for sugar is in the number of functions performed by the firms and the form of remuneration they receive. In both cases the firm or project authority performs or supervises a great many production tasks (e.g., fumigation, irrigation, aerial spraying, and—for sugar—frequently harvesting and weeding). In bananas, the firm performs these functions and deducts the costs from the price paid to associate producers. In sugar, more functions are carried out by the project authority, and the firm receives various fees. In other crops, the grower's relationship with the firm or project authority is less intense, and more tasks are done by family or hired labor.

## Implications for Host-Country Welfare

*Plantations.* There is little doubt that the partial withdrawal of MNCs from plantation production is more than anything a response to political pressure from host countries, including actual and threatened nationalizations. Foreign ownership of large tracts of land is simply unacceptable to most developing-country governments today. Aside from nationalist sentiments, more specific criticisms have been leveled at the plantation system. The practice of holding large areas of unused land was particularly characteristic of the banana companies, as part of a strategy for combating Panama disease; for many years, the only way to control this form of soil infestation was to flood an affected area, rotating banana cultivation from one tract to another while the land was being treated. The introduction of new banana varieties has eliminated this problem, however, and much less unused land is owned by the companies today.

Although some critics claim that monoculture leads to soil depletion, this does not appear to have been the case in the banana industry. Many MNC plantations have produced Cavendish bananas for thirty years and have maintained consistent and even accelerating increases in yield per hectare right up to the present day.

Plantations have been perceived as exploiting cheap labor in developing countries, given that wages are generally only a fraction of those paid to agricultural workers in industrial countries. In the Central American banana industry, however, plantation wages are generally two to three times the local average in agriculture. Another criticism leveled at the plantation system is that the relatively high wages paid by MNCs create a labor aristocracy whose relative prosperity exacerbates social inequality and whose values undermine working-class solidarity. Each of these arguments has such a high normative content that objective evaluation is difficult.

The most telling criticism of plantations is their enclave nature. Indeed, the linkage effects of banana production are slight; very few inputs are of local origin, and much of the value added occurs *after* the product leaves the exporting country. This is characteristic of export banana production per se, however, since the linkage effects of plantations and associate producers are virtually the same.[15] Thus the shift to greater local participation in production has not altered the enclave nature of the industry.

These criticisms are less significant for their intrinsic merit than for the negative investment climate they have created for plantation ownership. This climate, coupled with some positive advantages derived from delegating production, have led many MNCs to shift into the other forms of involvement discussed below.

*Non-Contractual Transactions.* Many of the welfare implications of arm's-length sales have been discussed in the context of the 1970s debate over the Third World's demands for the New International Economic Order. Three of these issues are worth mentioning briefly here. First, international trade in many agricultural commodities and inputs is dominated by a small number of firms. While some developing countries (e.g., Brazil and the Ivory Coast) exercise some countervailing market power, most do not. Dissatisfied with prices paid by these oligopsonies, many countries have collectively tried to implement agreements and producers' associations that would improve the level and stability of commodity prices. These schemes have not met with much success, in part because of resistance from developing-country governments, in part because of the adverse effects of the recession on prices. With demand in the North at a low level and a pressing need for export earnings in the South, it has been difficult to maintain any agreement that depends on output restrictions or stockpiles. No agreements have been proposed that would offset the market power of oligopolies in agricultural input markets.

Second, the advertising-intensive marketing strategies of multinational food-processing firms tend to alter tastes in developing countries. Nutritional questions aside, the taste changes often shift demand toward goods in which the host country does not have a comparative advantage in production (for example, wheat). Few multinational food processors have drawn on traditional crops like cassava, maize, or quinoa as the bases for their consumer food mixes.

Finally, the appropriateness of the technology embodied in MNC agro-inputs and machinery has been questioned. Chemicals banned from use in the North are routinely sold in many developing countries of the South, and equipment developed for use on large North American farms is marketed by MNCs in countries with very different endowments of land and labor. Lack of effort to develop technology to meet Third World needs appears to stem from two factors: the relatively small contribution of sales in developing countries to total earnings, and hence the small payoff from investment in "custom made" technologies; and the greater ease of appropriating income streams from complex technologies as opposed to simple, imitable ones.[16] In this area, a very specific but important policy measure that developed countries could implement would be to extend the ban on the domestic sale of harmful chemicals to a complete ban on their production.

*Other Forms of Involvement.* Contract farming brings MNCs and Third World farmers into direct contact, with the potential for both conflict and benefit. One of the dangers is that farmers will find themselves in a weak bargaining position vis-à-vis the MNCs because of inferior access to information or alternative markets—and thus be vulnerable to manipulation. Firms have been known to raise their quality standards when demand was low or production unexpectedly high in order to reduce the amount of produce they had to accept from contract growers. They have also been known to overcharge for inputs, delay payments, and otherwise manipulate the effective net product price.

Cases in which MNCs deal not with direct producers but with local plantation owners, who in turn hire workers, are probably the most worrisome. Wages, living conditions, and opportunities for union organization are almost invariably poorer on contract growers' farms than on company plantations. Under such conditions, contract farming could be considered a form of indirect exploitation in which MNCs can enjoy the benefits of labor repression without paying the political costs.

In other cases, however, particularly where MNCs deal directly with smallholders over crops in which the latter have some comparative advantage in production, benefits have accrued to local farmers. There have been impressive learning effects, particularly in the cultivation of new crops, the development of attentive and businesslike farming practices, and significant income increases made possible by access to relatively lucrative foreign markets. One case that has received several favorable reviews is that of ALCOSA, a firm that exports vegetables from Guatemala to the United States.[17]

In multipartite arrangements, the addition of the host-country government raises further issues. Does government involvement in tripartite arrangements improve the position of contract growers? The evidence is mixed. In Mexico, state participation permitted the inclusion of smallholders and cooperatives in a strawberry operation that MNCs had wanted to restrict to large- and medium-size growers.[18] In Honduras, in contrast, state intervention in a major banana operation was highly controversial. A 1,400-member, worker-managed enterprise, Isletas, produced bananas that were later exported by Standard Fruit. The bananas were sold to Standard through a state agency that also provided technical assistance at a fee. The agency, COHBANA, negotiated the producer price on behalf of Isletas but did not obtain prices appreciably higher than those paid to other associate producers. Furthermore, Isletas felt that the technical assistance it received from COHBANA was poor in quality and high in price compared with what Standard provides its own growers. To bypass this apparently useless intermediation, Isletas lobbied hard but without success for the right to deal directly with Standard.[19]

The implications of public financing of contract growers by state agencies are complex. For example, how is the grower's bargaining position affected by the government's financial participation? One might expect the government to favor a high producer price to facilitate recoupment of its loan. If this reduced the firms' profits, however, tax revenues would be reduced. Weighing the net effect of these two tendencies would require careful calculations. Furthermore, in a Honduran case involving sugar for the domestic market, three separate agencies were involved: the development bank, the tax authorities, and a price control agency that examined the firms' costs of production.[20] The price control agency's interest was in a low producer price, to keep wholesale prices politically acceptable.

The effects of public financing on net capital inflows are also difficult to assess. On the surface, it appears that public credit is being substituted for foreign capital, leaving less public credit for other rural development programs. The issue is particularly important in light of the current crisis. There is no guarantee, however, that MNCs would bring in capital from abroad, rather than borrow locally for investment funds, as they commonly do. In the latter case, the substitution would be between local public and local private capital. Furthermore, contract farming schemes are often attractive investments for international donor agencies. MNC involvement might be the selling point to bring in donor funds that would not otherwise be forthcoming. However, the effect of non-MNC financing does represent an unambiguous shifting of financial risk away from MNCs to Third World governments. In the typical case in which a developing country is less diversified than the multinational, portfolio theory indicates that a shifting of risk from the MNC to the developing-country government is socially inefficient.

Finally, multipartite arrangements raise a number of development management questions. The most successful schemes involving peasant farmers tend to be highly management-intensive. Considerable skill and manpower are required for the management of a processing plant; the coordination and supervision of planting, harvesting, and input delivery; and the accounting needed for hundreds of input and product payments. None of these is widely available in the Third World. It is possible that the management techniques used in these schemes could be learned and applied elsewhere in the economy. It is also possible that successful multipartite schemes may attract the best managers and extension agents away from relatively unrewarding employment in other national programs. These factors call into question the replicability of successful multipartite schemes. If management resources are to some extent fixed, expansion of these schemes would occur only at the expense of other programs.

*Other Implications: Foreign Involvement and the Food Question.* Foreign involvement in Third World agriculture of all types—plantations, arm's-length sales, and other forms—has been criticized for its export orientation. Since MNCs are generally involved in export crops, it is argued, they do not contribute to food self-sufficiency and may in fact undermine it by diverting land from the production of food crops. The argument should, however, be qualified in a number of respects.

1. Some of the crops produced by MNCs, notably sugar and oil palm, are destined for the local market, although quantities may also be exported.

2. Local conditions are sometimes more suitable for export crops than food crops. In such cases, there can be a significant welfare gain from trade. For example, a cooperative of former banana workers was formed in Honduras in the early 1960s to farm land formerly planted to bananas.[21] The coop experimented with many food crops, but found that they did not grow well in these soil and drainage conditions. On reverting to bananas (the export crop), the cooperative's income increased to levels far above those of food-crop producers.

3. The reject rate in fruit and vegetable export operations often exceeds 50 per cent. These rejects—often set aside merely for reasons of ripeness or size—can be sold in local markets for a fraction of the price paid by industrial-country consumers. The produce has equal nutritional value and can complement the traditional starchy diet of low-income Third World consumers.

4. The production of export crops and food crops can be complementary. Irrigation water in sugar schemes has been used to grow vegetables for local markets. Fertilizer applied one year for an export crop can have residual effects the following year for a rotation food crop.

5. Export crops do provide income for local producers, many of whom are smallholders. Control of foreign trade by multinationals may depress prices below the level they would reach in a freer market, but apparently it still provides prices that are attractive to some producers. In many cases, the biggest margins are taken not by MNCs, but by government marketing boards and state-managed corporations.

6. Finally, and related to the previous point, in specializing in export crops, MNCs are often responding rationally to the incen-

tives embodied in government pricing policies. If producer prices for food crops are kept to a level that is not remunerative, neither MNCs nor local farmers will produce them.

## Changes in Bargaining Power Over Time

It is doubtful that shifting responsibility for production and financing to local agents has significantly increased the welfare or bargaining power of Third World producers or governments. The picture is clearest in the banana industry, where both local participation and collective action by the governments of producer countries became increasingly important during the 1970s. In September 1974, the governments of Colombia, Costa Rica, Guatemala, Honduras, and Panama formed the Union of Banana Exporting Countries (UPEB, an acronym of the title in Spanish) to assist its members in obtaining better prices, either by bargaining with the multinationals or by entering new markets. In 1975, UPEB coordinated the imposition of a banana export tax that resulted in a considerable flow of revenue to the governments concerned. The initial gains have not been maintained, however, and have in many cases been reversed. In the face of falling prices, MNCs have: successfully bargained for substantial reductions of the tax level in most countries; shifted some of their procurement to Colombia, which did not impose a tax; and convincingly threatened to pull out of a major plantation in Costa Rica. Initial increases in producer prices have not been sustained in the face of weak consumer demand. As pointed out earlier, the associate-producer program has not increased the banana sector's linkages to the local economy, and the banana industry remains essentially an enclave activity.

It is difficult to say what the implications of contract farming will be for the bargaining power of growers, and there are few studies that examine changes over time. In cases like the banana industry, where a shift to contracting involves a shift to local plantation owners, there appears to be a deterioration in the bargaining power of direct producers (i.e., workers), as evidenced by the wages and working conditions they receive.

In smallholder contract farming, the situation is more complex. The existence of a single, highly visible protagonist seems to prompt growers to organize more than a situation in which farmers sell their produce in the open market. Firms often accept or even promote the formation of growers' associations, since such groups can be useful in organizing deliveries, marketing rejects, and other activities. As growers organize and as they gain greater knowledge of cultivation practices for new crops, decreasing their dependence on the firm, their bargaining power can be expected to increase.

Other elements of the contracting situation tend to impede grower organization. Frequently, several types of farmers (large and small, progressive and traditional) produce for the same company but have widely differing interests. Furthermore, no contract is perfectly contingent; each gives the firm considerable room to provide some growers with better conditions than others. (The assignment of desirable planting or delivery dates is an example.) This provides an incentive for growers to cultivate friendly, even personalistic relations with the company and to refrain from antagonizing the firm by joining a growers' association. The vulnerable position of many contract growers appears to arouse resentment at the same time that it inhibits risk-taking, with a net effect that varies from case to case. The most frequent outcome seems to be the formation of a growers' organization—but either one that is fragile and beset with internal splits, or one that is under the firm's control and serves mainly to enhance coordination between the firm and its growers.

## Implications for Developing-Country Policy Makers

To maximize the benefits available from foreign investment in agriculture, developing-country policy makers should attempt to match the form of investment chosen to the economic and technological conditions of the case in question. In agriculture, as in other sectors, new forms of involvement too often have been seen as a panacea. There is ample evidence, however, that in some cases the new forms shift risk to host-country producers. They may also result in reduced income for workers employed by the local partners of multinationals, compared with the income of those employed on MNC plantations. (The banana industry is a case in point.) Many sugar schemes involving contractual arrangements with local producers are to a large extent disguised plantations; the local producers have little real independence, but costly management systems must be put in place to coordinate their work. In this sense, these schemes combine the worst of both worlds.

A more promising approach would be to match the organizational form to the economic and technological imperatives of particular crops or markets. These imperatives can vary by region according to factor endowments. The crops in which smallholders can have a comparative advantage cut across categories such as export versus import substituting crops and food versus cash crops. In cases where small growers are high-cost producers, firms should not be compelled to buy from them. In such cases, plantations can play a useful role provided that other instruments, such as taxation, are used to distribute available benefits more widely within the economy. At the same time, smallholders should be supported in cases where they can be efficient but lack experience, credit, or other facilities that new forms of involvement can provide; this is true for many non-traditional crops such as fruit and vegetables.

Governments frequently control the wholesale or retail prices of basic foods such as sugar when these are sold in the domestic market. Policy makers should be aware that agro-industrial firms will react to price controls by trying to lower raw-material costs. In industries in which smallholders are high-cost producers, small-scale contract growers will bear the brunt of such price controls.

The welfare of contract growers often can be increased by the formation of growers' organizations. Some of the most successful contract farming or multipartite schemes have been those in which such organizations play a significant role, sometimes as shareholders or members of a board of directors. Growers' associations not only can act as bargaining groups, but also can play a coordinating and even management role. In the future, it may be possible to turn over some tasks, such as management or ownership of the processing plant, to farmers' groups. This can give growers a stake in the industry, increase their range of skills, and reduce management costs. Government can play an important role in permitting or promoting such associations.

Government involvement in multipartite schemes should aim to reinforce growers' bargaining power and promote competition. State-managed corporations that substitute public monopolies for private ones or that play an unproductive intermediary role do little to enhance growers' welfare.

Finally, policy makers might wish to explore the use of contract farming and multipartite arrangements for food production. It may well be that the production of low-priced food crops alone could not support the heavy management costs of these schemes; however, the greater incorporation of food crops within predominantly cash-crop schemes deserves further exploration. Another promising measure is local market development for export crops. Some of the fruits and vegetables intended for foreign markets are highly nutritious, and produce rejected for cosmetic reasons could be sold at low prices locally. Sometimes this does not occur because the product or the method of preparing it is unknown to local consumers (e.g., asparagus, and some types of melons).

## Implications for U.S. Policy

U.S. policy makers do not have a great deal of influence on the performance of agricultural multinationals abroad. Even host-country governments are limited in the degree to which they can influence MNC behavior, which responds to a significant degree to macro-economic conditions and global strategic considerations. There are, however, some areas in which U.S. policy does impinge on agricultural MNCs, and these deserve some attention.

As noted, new forms of involvement often include the financial participation of foreign aid agencies; AID has been quite active in multipartite schemes in Central America and elsewhere. In these cases, the agency should be able to exert some influence over the nature of the scheme. It might, for example, insist on a financial contribution from the MNC, assuming that the host country and AID find this desirable. However, at a time when many donors seem to have difficulty finding good projects in which to invest, reducing AID's financial contributions to agricultural schemes may not satisfy bureaucratic imperatives if increased spending on agriculture is an agency goal. More generally, AID might adopt some of the guidelines suggested in the preceding section in the projects it finances.

The second area in which the United States can exert some influence is trade policy. Tariff and non-tariff barriers impede the flow of many agricultural commodities, traditional and non-traditional, and tariff escalation in many cases inhibits a higher degree of local processing. One estimate has placed the potential benefits to developing countries in terms of increased Third World agricultural exports from global trade liberalization at U.S.$5 billion; examples of commodities for which Third World producers would benefit most from trade liberalization include sugar, tropical fruits and beverages, maize, tobacco, and vegetables.[22]

Barriers to imports of labor-intensive crops such as fruits and vegetables also contribute to illegal immigration to the United States. Since wages and working conditions in seasonal agricultural labor generally are not attractive to those with legal employment alternatives, many agricultural laborers come from Mexico and Central America to work the fields. The *maquiladora* schemes just south of the Mexican border (essentially export-processing zones) were explicitly designed to employ Mexican labor in Mexico.[23] To the extent that the reduction of illegal immigration is a U.S. policy goal, lowering barriers to fruit and vegetable imports also could make a contribution.

# Notes

Note: The views expressed are solely those of the author and not necessarily those of IDRC.

[1] United Nations Centre on Transnational Corporations (UNCTC), *Transnational Corporations in Food and Beverage Processing* (New York: United Nations, 1981), p. 11–16.

[2] Ibid., p. 14.

[3] G. Ghersi, *Les Cent Premiers Groupes Agro-Industriels Mondiaux* (Montpellier: Centre International des Hautes Études Agronomiques Méditerranéennes, 1980), p. 10 (cited in Mogens Buch-Hansen, "Agribusiness: The Latest Stage of Agricultural and Food Production Development," Working Paper 40, Roshilde University Centre, Denmark).

[4] UNCTC, *Transnational Corporations*, op. cit., p. 7.

[5] Organization of American States, *Sectoral Study of Transnational Enterprises in Latin America: The Banana Industry* (Washington, D.C.: OAS, 1975), p. 22.

[6] Frank Ellis, *A Study of Employment in the Banana Export Industry of Panama and Central America* (Geneva: International Labour Office, 1977), p. 15.

[7] Barbara Dinham and Colin Hines, *Agribusiness in Africa* (London: Earth Resources Research Ltd., 1983), p. 28

[8] Ibid., p. 104.

[9] Ruth Rama, *Nuevas Formas de Inversión Internacional en la Agricultura y la Agro-industria de America Latina* (Paris: OECD Development Centre, 1985), p. 70.

[10] UNCTC, *Transnational Corporations*, op. cit.

[11] Rama, *Nuevas Formas*, op. cit.

[12] David Glover, "Contract Farming and the Transnationals," Ph.D. thesis, University of Toronto, unpublished, 1983, p. 419.

[13] Dinham and Hines, *Agribusiness in Africa*, op. cit., p. 83.

[14] Ray Goldberg and Richard McGinty, *Agribusiness Management for Developing Countries* (Cambridge, Mass.: Ballinger, 1979), p. 551.

[15] Ellis, *Banana Export Industry*, op. cit.

[16] Stephen Magee, "Information and Multinational Corporations: An Appropriability Theory of Direct Foreign Investment," in J.N. Bhagwati, ed., *The New International Economic Order* (Cambridge, Mass.: MIT Press, 1977).

[17] Ken Kusterer et al., *The Social Impact of Agribusiness: ALCOSA in Guatemala* (Washington, D.C.: U.S. Agency for International Development, 1981).

[18] Rama, *Nuevas Formas*, op. cit., p. 70.

[19] Glover, "Contract Farming," op. cit., pp. 296–311.

[20] Ibid., p. 197.

[21] Ramon Salgado "Cooperativismo y Política Agraria en Honduras," Lic. thesis, Universidad de Costa Rica, unpublished, p. 113.

[22] Estimate referred to in Roger Young, "Canada and the South: The Case of Agriculture," Paper presented to the Conference on Canadian Agriculture in a Global Context, University of Waterloo, Canada, May 1985.

[23] Wolfgang Konig, *Towards an Evaluation of International Subcontracting: Maquiladoras in Mexico* (Washington, D.C.: U.N. Economic Commission on Latin America, 1975).

# Chapter 5

# New Forms of Investment in Developing Countries

Charles P. Oman

During the postwar period and into the 1960s, international investment primarily involved transactions whereby corporations based in one country acquired or created firms in other host countries. Today statistics on foreign direct investment reflect mainly this 'traditional' kind of foreign direct investment. What they fail to show, however, is a variety of 'new' forms of investment that have been gathering impetus since the late 1960s and that are now playing a more important role in North-South activities. This chapter looks at the patterns of these new forms of investment and illustrates them with specific examples from the extractive and manufacturing sectors. It examines some of the principal causes of new forms of investment and tries to weigh some of their consequences.[1]

The term "new forms of investment" (NFI) covers a broad, heterogeneous range of international business operations that all have a common denominator: For an investment project in a host country, a foreign company supplies goods, either tangible or intangible, which constitute assets, but it does not own the project itself. In other words, the foreign partner's equity share, if any, does not constitute ownership control, as it did in traditional investments. But this does not mean that the foreign company cannot exercise partial or total control over the project by other means.

Among the new forms of foreign investment are joint ventures in which foreign equity does not exceed 50 per cent, licensing agreements, management contracts, franchising, turnkey and "product-in-hand" contracts, production sharing and risk-service contracts, and international subcontracting (when the subcontracting firm is at least 50 per cent locally owned). Many of these business forms of course are not particularly new; examples of many of them predate the 1960s. Use of the adjective 'new'—it could be replaced with 'non-traditional'—is meant to focus attention on the new *importance* of these business forms as a whole, given their significant growth in recent years.

An important question here is whether all these business forms can legitimately be considered investments. From the point of view of the host-country participants, they almost invariably do represent investments. But from the perspective of the foreign firms supplying technology, equipment, or access to export markets, the answer can vary from one project to the next. Nor does the answer depend on the type of resources the firm supplies; rather, it rests on the nature of the firm's involvement in the project.

This distinction between what a given international business operation represents for the host country and for the foreign supplier of assets—an investment or a sales operation[2]—may seem academic; but it is in fact crucial: It sheds light on the underlying logic of conflicts and convergences of interest between the two parties. When a foreign company participates as an investor, it shares with its host-country partner an interest in maximizing the difference between the costs of producing the project's output on the one hand and the value of that output on the other. Often the two parties also share an interest in generating or defending the market share of the project's output and, if possible, in generating monopoly rents in that market. In short, they share an interest in the project's success as an investment, in its future ability to generate a surplus. Conflicts of interest between the two partners arise primarily over how profits or losses are shared. In some cases, conflict may also arise over the definition of the geographic boundaries of the market (for example, over whether or not the product is to be exported from the host country, as this could conflict with the company's international marketing strategy).

When, however, an investment project in a developing country basically represents a sales operation for the foreign company supplying the assets, the foreign company's interest lies primarily in *maximizing* the difference between the pre-negotiated price to be paid by the host-country partner for the assets (technology, equipment, and so on) and the cost to the foreign company of supplying those resources. The company's concern about the future surplus-generating capacity of the project is secondary at best.[3] The interest of the host-country participant is usually just the opposite: It wants to *minimize* the price-cost difference for resources supplied by the company and is concerned above all with the success of the project as an investment.

Returning to our definition, then, it is possible to distinguish between a broad and a narrow, more rigorous definition of the "new forms of investment" concept. The broad definition was sketched out above: NFI investment projects are ones that are at least 50 per cent locally owned, with some assets supplied by one or more foreign companies. For such a project to qualify as NFI in the narrower definition, the project should represent an investment not only for the host-country participant(s), but also for at least one of the participating foreign companies. The foreign company should regard the surplus-generating capacity of the project in the host country as a, if not the, source of income and profit. This implies both that the company has a direct interest in the project's economic viability as an investment and that it has some way to appropriate or control at least part of the surplus generated. The project then represents an investment for the foreign company irrespective of its equity participation. In this definition, the foreign company must perceive its contribution to the project as an asset not only for the project, but for itself.[4]

## New versus Traditional Foreign Direct Investment: The Trends

Are the new forms of investment superseding traditional foreign direct investment (FDI) in the developing countries? In the 1970s, NFI grew more quickly than traditional FDI, but will this trend be reversed in the 1980s? To what extent is NFI a substitute for, and to what extent does it complement, traditional FDI?

Overall, the evidence points to two broad tendencies. During the last decade, some developing countries promoted NFI over traditional FDI so as to enhance local control over industry and to circumvent the rent-extracting powers of multinational firms, seen as being embodied in FDI. Today they may feel as if they had jumped from the frying pan into the fire. When real interest rates were low in the first half of the 1970s, many developing countries no doubt found it easier and cheaper to pursue strategies of debt-financed growth, with greater reliance on NFI for access to non-financial assets when necessary. It was then frequently easier to negotiate with multinational firms over the terms of NFI. But by the 1980s, higher interest rates and a feeling that the international banking community and the International Monetary Fund have quasi-monopoly powers in the financial markets—as well as awareness of their continuing, heavy reliance on multinational firms for access to technology and export markets—made many developing countries change their minds. That is why many of these countries, including some of the more ardent promoters of NFI during the 1970s, are liberalizing their investment policies and trying to attract traditional FDI.

Even so, there is considerable evidence of a changing division of risks and responsibilities among the three principal groups of participants in North-South investment: multinational firms, international lenders, and host-country elites. It suggests that NFI will continue to gain importance—superseding traditional FDI in some cases and complementing it in others. In part, this reflects continued interest by some developing countries in acquiring only those components of the traditional FDI package (technology, management, marketing, and finance) that cannot be obtained locally. Such "unpackaging" and selective overseas acquisition of assets via NFI may be seen by some countries, including some of the more industrialized or heavily indebted developing countries, as a way to minimize the foreign-exchange costs of obtaining only those particular assets required for industrial restructuring or for sustaining local industrial capital formation. But more importantly, the changing international division of risks and responsibilities also reflects a tendency for some multinational companies to modify their views on the advantages and disadvantages of NFI over traditional FDI in developing countries.

Some companies, for example, are finding that they can earn attractive returns from certain tangible or intangible assets that they can supply without necessarily having to own or finance projects. By supplying assets via NFI, they can also, in some cases, benefit from increased leverage on those assets because, for example, local partners or international lenders absorb start-up costs and provide working capital. And, especially important, NFI often means reduced exposure to commercial and political risks that accompany traditional FDI.

There is also evidence that 'newcomer' multinationals and market-share 'followers' frequently use NFI to compete with the more established multinational firms. In some cases, they use it *offensively*—to penetrate or increase market shares in industries or countries where the 'majors' are reluctant either to share equity (and rents) or to relinquish the decision-making power and information that might dilute their particular competitive advantages (e.g., state-of-the-art technology, brand names, etc.). Newcomers and followers may offer host countries shared ownership or greater access to technology in return for preferred (or exclusive) access to local markets.

In other cases, newcomers and followers are using NFI more *defensively*—in a context of globalized oligopolistic rivalry in which their managerial and especially financial resources are stretched thin because of increased competitive pressures to take investment positions in numerous markets. By sharing technology, control, and profits with local partners, they can benefit from the latter's knowledge of local markets, access to local finance, and willingness to share or assume important risks. This phenomenon may have received added impetus during the 1970s because of rising capital costs and cash-flow problems that some firms experienced due to depressed demand conditions in their home markets. And whether they have resorted to NFI as a competitive tool in developing countries offensively or defensively, newcomers and followers have sometimes brought considerable pressure to bear on the majors to follow suit.

Moreover, as technologies diffuse and products mature and become increasingly price-competitive, even the majors and market-share leaders sometimes initiate the use of NFI as part of a strategy of divestment. For example, if a company perceives that its control over a particular technology is waning, it may decide to obtain additional, marginal returns from that technology by licensing it and using those returns to help finance movement into newer, higher-growth activities—often in its home market or in other industrial countries. Another example is the phenomenon of 'industrial restructuring' in Japan, where the government (MITI)—either because of changing comparative advantage or for environmental reasons—has joined forces with firms and large trading companies to transfer entire industries or industry segments to developing countries by using the new forms of investment.[5]

Still, industry leaders often resort to NFI only in fairly protected and isolated markets; the new forms generally are considered marketing tools in countries where local production by the joint venture, licensee, or purchaser of a turnkey plant stands little chance of competing internationally with the the company's 'core' activities. This may be because the company will not supply its most advanced technology or because of relatively high production costs in the host economy, for example, due to inefficiencies of small-scale production behind tariff barriers. Industry 'majors' that do incorporate production from developing-country affiliates into their global networks, on the other hand, still tend to rely heavily on traditional FDI for such affiliates.

Thus the ultimate importance of NFI relative to FDI in coming years is likely to be determined less by unilateral developing-country government decisions on whether to increase their efforts to attract traditional FDI or to emphasize selective acquisition of assets through NFI, than it is by the dynamics of inter-firm competition—and by the interaction between those dynamics and host-government policies. And even though those dynamics reflect patterns of technological innovation and of supply and demand that are global in scale, they tend to be industry-specific. Hence, it is important to look at investment trends at the level of sectors and industries.

Overall, the evidence points to an emerging international, inter-actor division of risks and responsibilities, the principal characteristics of which can be summarized as follows:

- *Multinational firms* will tend to concentrate their efforts in industry segments where barriers to entry and hence value-added and profitability ratios are highest, while at the same time seeking to maintain or increase flexibility. They will thus generally focus on such strategic activities as technological innovation, marketing, and certain key aspects of management. These activities could increasingly become their primary bases of control and profits in a world economy characterized by the growing internationalization of production and inter-firm competition, coupled with rapid technological change and considerable instability in world product and financial markets. In other words, multinational companies may increasingly become intermediaries for both the input (technology and management) and output (world market) sides of industry in developing countries, while shifting a greater share of the investment risk associated with the investment process onto international lenders and, perhaps even more so, onto their host-country partners.
- *International lenders*—notably multinational banks, but also public national and multilateral financial institutions—may continue to play a leading role in channeling financial capital to developing countries in need of liquidity, particularly those with the industrial or primary-products export potential needed to service their debt. Financial institutions will thus continue to assume or will be delegated control over the financial dimension of the international investment process in developing countries. Within the financial community, however, the division of risks and responsibilities will vary from project to project and period to period, with private banks playing a clearly predominant role in some cases, and national or multi-

lateral financial agencies playing an increasingly important role (via co-financing, export credits, or mixed credits, for example) in others.

- *Host-country elites* in the private and public sectors may increasingly retain legal ownership of the investment projects in their countries and assume, or be delegated, certain managerial responsibilities. In addition, they may take on important risks and increase their share of returns.

### Risk and Responsibility Sharing in the Primary Sector

It is in the primary products sector that one finds the strongest empirical evidence to support the argument that traditional FDI is being superseded by NFI. In *petroleum extraction*, the shift to NFI began to gain momentum in the 1950s and was virtually complete in Third World petroleum-producing countries by the late 1970s. In the major capital-surplus petroleum-exporting countries, service contracts are commonly used, often in conjunction with joint ventures. In contrast, petroleum-producing countries that do not have large financial surpluses (many of which are major borrowers) often use the production-sharing formula. In the first group of countries, the inter-actor division of risks and responsibilities is often bilateral, between the host country and the multinational petroleum company. But in the second group, the financial dimension often involves international lending institutions. Mexico's PEMEX and Brazil's PETROBRAS, for example, received huge loans to finance exploration, production, and refining during the 1970s. Less spectacular but also important were loans to state oil companies in Algeria, Indonesia, Nigeria, and Peru. In both groups of countries, however, there is ample evidence that multinational petroleum companies are concentrating on supplying technology, certain key managerial functions, and international marketing, while the host countries assume ownership of the investment projects along with some important managerial responsibilities.

In *metals mining*, the shift toward NFI became clear in the late 1960s, and the desire for national sovereignty over mineral resources led many developing countries to put ownership of mining operations in the hands of state or private local enterprises. Management contracts in which the managing company's remuneration is based at least in part on profits or production levels are not uncommon in new projects, and they are sometimes combined with minority equity participation by the managing company. Turnkey contracts, which typically call for the contractor to conduct a feasibility study, to provide technology and know-how, and to carry out or supervise the design, engineering, and construction as well as supply capital equipment, have been widely used in minerals-processing projects. They are less frequent in minerals extraction itself, although they have been used in some mining projects that required major infrastructure investments. The most typical contracts since the late 1960s, however, have been between major developing-country state mining companies and international contractors (for example, a specialized engineering or construction company), in which the latter receives a fixed fee or percentage of total costs and assumes little risk associated with or control over the mining project.

In sharp contrast to petroleum, the rapidly rising investment costs in metals mining have been accompanied since the early 1970s by fluctuating and, on average, depressed output prices on the world market. One result is that relatively few new mining projects are being brought to fruition. Another is that, following a period of increased restrictions on FDI in the late 1960s and early 1970s, a number of mineral-producing countries have switched back to active promotion of traditional FDI. But the multinational mining companies have shown considerable reluctance to undertake major equity investments in developing countries. Those which are still active increasingly operate as mobilizers of international loan capital from public and private sources, as innovators and suppliers of production and processing technology, as project managers, and, above all, as providers of access to world-market outlets.[6] Engineering companies that often worked as contractors to these multinationals are now contracted directly by state mining companies in developing countries.

Although traditional FDI has not been as completely displaced by NFI in mining as it has been in petroleum extraction, the evidence nevertheless points to major changes in the international inter-actor division of risks and responsibilities, with the host countries assuming major risks and costs. And the requirements of finance capital are such that "the attitudes of lenders, be they international agencies, banks, or export credit insurers, are likely to be of critical importance and may well seriously limit the freedom of maneuver of the host countries and mining enterprises as they reach for new models of mining agreements for the remainder of this century."[7]

As for international investment in *agriculture* (see Chapter 4 in this volume), there has been considerable movement away from traditional FDI in the plantation system to NFI, particularly contract growing, both in traditional export products (sugar, bananas, and meat) and in primary products supplied to foreign-owned food processing firms whose output is largely sold locally (a trend discussed later in this chapter).

### The Manufacturing Sector

The evidence on NFI in manufacturing as a whole is less clear-cut than in the primary sector, both as regards the extent to which it is superseding traditional FDI and the extent to which a new inter-actor division of risks and responsibilities is emerging. These new forms of investment obviously have gained considerable importance over the last ten to fifteen years, but what stands out most in the manufacturing sector is the great diversity among host countries both in the importance of NFI as a group relative to traditional FDI and in their importance in gross domestic capital formation in industry.[8]

This wide diversity among host countries clearly reflects differences in host governments' policies on foreign ownership of investment. But it also indicates a complex interaction of other factors whose combined importance, especially in recent years, may well outweigh that of host governments' FDI policies. These factors include foreign firms' perceptions of: the size and growth potential of a country's market, its political stability, its bureaucracy and the nature of relations between government and the private sector, its long-run development strategy, its macro-economic and industrial policies, and the availability of local managerial talent and skilled labor.

If one controls for such country-specific factors (and company-specific views of them), a few sector-wide patterns nevertheless seem to emerge. First, other things being equal, the NFI are more likely to be found in investment projects whose output is destined for the host-country's local or regional market than in export-oriented projects. Second, NFI are more frequent in projects using relatively stable or mature technologies than in those using 'high' or rapidly changing technologies. Third, like traditional FDI, NFI tend to concentrate in host countries' principal growth industries or in high value-added segments within industries.

This last observation of course reflects the rent-seeking nature of foreign investment. But it also points to an important corollary: NFI in projects with promising growth and surplus-generating potential more often represent *investments* for the foreign participants (that is, they correspond to our narrower definition of the term), whereas projects whose growth potential appears limited or doubtful more often correspond to *sales* operations for foreign participants.

Because NFI patterns differ greatly among host countries and because many projects use NFI in conjunction with traditional FDI, it is important to analyze North-South NFI trends on an industry-by-industry basis.

*Petrochemicals.* Until recently, petrochemicals were produced almost exclusively by the industrial (OECD) countries; but today a spectacular change is taking place, to a large extent via NFI in developing countries. Whereas in 1970 only 2–3 per cent of world capacity in ethylene was found in developing countries, by 1982 that share had surpassed 8 per cent, and by 1990 it is expected to reach 20–22 per cent. Similar patterns can be seen in the cases of the five major thermoplastics.

Since the mid-1970s, a large proportion of this expansion in developing countries' production capacity has been on the basis of fifty-fifty or minority foreign-owned joint ventures, technology licensing agreements, and turnkey contracts. The foreign companies involved in these new forms of investment are some of the world's leading petrochemical producers, including the largest chemical companies as well as the chemical divisions of major petroleum firms.

In Latin America, the transition from a rather limited development of petrochemicals production in the 1950s and 1960s, when foreign investment was primarily via traditional FDI, to the emergence of large-scale, state-led petrochemical programs during the last fifteen years has been accompanied by a marked shift to NFI—primarily joint ventures, but also licensing and turnkey contracts. In Argentina and Brazil, this shift was triggered by the general lack of interest on the part of the petrochemical multinationals in further developing local capacity through traditional FDI. In Mexico, U.S. companies might have been interested, but the Mexican government's extension of PEMEX's monopoly to basic and secondary petrochemicals in 1960 hindered such a move.

A notable feature of the big petrochemical joint ventures established during the 1970s in Brazil and Mexico (now the major producers in Latin America) and in Asia is the foreign firms' contribution of technology in return for equity shares. In Mexico, despite legislation in 1970 that restricted foreign ownership to 40 per cent and despite a sluggish economy since 1982, the local market remains a major attraction to foreign investors—especially to U.S. firms and some large European companies (BASF, Bayer, ICI)—in downstream production. In Brazil, most production is also for the local market, although foreign partners are now being asked to promote exports and to help develop high value-added products as well.

Another important feature is the extent to which the NFI in Brazil and Mexico have led to major advances not only in substituting local for foreign hardware and detail engineering services, but also in local appropriation of skills and know-how in state-of-the-art process design engineering and in research and development. This trend is reflected, for example, in Brazil's third and most recent major NFI agreement signed in 1977 with Technip (France) and KTI (the Netherlands). These firms agreed to supply all the technical engineering data, including the technology to obtain and update those data, along with technical assistance and training of local technicians. In fact, Brazil now supplies some other developing countries with petrochemical technology and production know-how.

In Asia, several developing countries—India, the Republic of Korea, Taiwan, and the member countries of the Association of Southeast Asian Nations (ASEAN)—have significant petrochemical capacities, and the People's Republic of China is expected to have substantial capacity by the end of the decade. India's production dates back to the 1950s. Its 1963 petrochemical development plan, prepared with the help of the French Petroleum Institute, aimed for a pattern where basic production would be in local hands and downstream production would be in those of joint ventures. But India's experience has been less successful than Mexico's, and there is no clear division of responsibilities between sectors. Some traditional FDI still exists; some NFI came in, largely during the 1960s (mostly joint ventures with U.S. and European firms); and production is almost exclusively for a not very dynamic domestic market.

In the Republic of Korea, state-led development of the industry by private firms has resulted in considerable use of joint ventures and licensing, mostly involving U.S. and Japanese partners in downstream products, with ethylene now totally in Korean hands. Korea's first complex was completed in 1973, and a world-scale complex came onstream in 1979; the former relied heavily on fifty-fifty joint ventures, whereas the latter involved fewer joint ventures and more domestic firms with licensing agreements. Downstream production appears to be moving into Korean hands as well: Some foreign partners, such as Dow, have been bought out; and technology has been acquired through arm's-length licensing, as happened in 1984 with Union Carbide.

In Taiwan, the pattern is not unlike that of Korea, with the notable difference that all the foreign partners in Taiwan are U.S. 'majors'—perhaps reflecting U.S. political motivations to help develop the Taiwanese industry. Korea's Lucky Group and Taiwan's Formosa Plastics Corporations have become important suppliers of technology to other developing countries. In 1983, Saudi Arabia's SABIC chose Lucky to be its joint-venture partner in its largest polyvinyl chloride plant, and the Taiwan company as its partner in the urea plant.

In the ASEAN region, Japanese firms are involved in petrochemical joint ventures in most countries but, apart from Singapore, this is largely through turnkey and licensing contracts, with little capital contribution. In Singapore, by contrast, the Japanese have played a leading role since the late 1970s in setting up a world-scale complex in which the Singapore government is a 50-per cent shareholder. (Phillips and Shell are participants in two downstream facilities.) The project was designed to produce for export to the ASEAN region as well as for the Japanese home market as part of Japan's vertical integration/relocation strategy. Now, however, Japanese commitments to import from Saudi Arabia are highlighting problems of excess supply.

The creation of major petrochemical capacities in the Middle East is undoubtedly the most striking recent development for the industry worldwide and for the OECD countries in particular. Saudi Arabia alone has eleven major production facilities, all of which are fifty-fifty 'first-generation' joint ventures between Saudi Basic Industries Corporation (SABIC) and one or more multinational firms (primarily Japanese and U.S. ones, with the latter being mostly petroleum companies). In every instance, SABIC and the foreign partner each put up 15 per cent of the project's capital needs as equity, 60 per cent is provided by the Saudi Public Investment Fund in the form of long-term low-interest loans, and the remaining 10 per cent is raised from commercial banks; a ten-year tax holiday is also provided. Technology has not been capitalized as part of the foreign partner's equity share, but is the object of separate contracts, and usually third-party technology has been chosen. Thus it is obviously the foreign firms' ability to penetrate OECD petrochemical markets that constitutes their key 'immaterial asset'; it also explains both the highly favorable financial and fiscal arrangements provided by the host country and the difference between the foreign firms' 15-per cent contribution to financial needs and their 50-per cent equity shares.

By and large, the major petroleum and chemical companies' decisions to meet the demands of various Third World countries to help develop their local petrochemical capacities and to use NFI to do so reflect strategies these companies came up with in response to important changes in the industry starting in the early 1970s. One such change was the shift from rapid growth and high profitability during the 1950–1970 period to a maturation of the industry in the OECD area, with a slackening of growth potential and profits. Another major change came with the two successive oil-price hikes, which greatly increased the share of naphtha feedstocks in total output costs. The latter has had a crucial impact on profitability as well as on cost structures. In virtually every OECD country except the United States, which has oil and natural gas resources, the petrochemical industry that developed prior to 1973 has been caught between the need to pass on cost increases to safeguard financial viability and the difficulty of doing so because of depressed demand conditions.

The pattern of petrochemical investments in the developing countries points up the fact that 'newcomers'—which in this industry include the Japanese petrochemical firms and U.S. petroleum companies—often use the new forms of investment to gain favored access to new markets and to force some of the 'majors' to follow suit. The substitution of NFI for traditional FDI now appears irreversible. Some of the major developing-country producers are apparently trying to do without foreign investment altogether, except when foreign partners can help penetrate OECD markets. It is also worth noting that South-South collaboration has been growing primarily through NFI. This movement may well be accentuated by China's large demands for technological and industrial NFI in this industry.

*The Auto Industry.* Traditional foreign direct investment clearly dominates investment in vehicle production in developing countries. (*Production* implies over 50-per cent local content, whereas *assembly* implies over 50 per cent of imported parts and components.) But such investment is heavily concentrated in only a few countries: Brazil, Mexico, and Argentina. There were a fair number of joint ventures and licensing agreements during the early years of auto production, notably in the 1960s, but even then traditional FDI accounted for a larger share of production. Since then, most majority locally owned producers based on NFI have folded or have been absorbed by majority or wholly foreign-owned subsidiaries.

The other major auto-producing developing countries today are India and Korea. Foreign investment in India has been limited mostly to licensing, and production has been largely confined to models quite outdated by international standards. Now, however, Japanese investments in minority joint ventures are growing rapidly. In Korea, two firms dominate production. Hyundai was a wholly Korean-owned producer, and is now 85-per cent Korean-owned. (Mitsubishi has taken a 15-per cent equity share in return for its contribution to finance and international marketing.) Hyundai's "Pony" automobile, developed with the collaboration of various foreign suppliers of design, technology, finance, etc., is now a competitor in world markets. Daewoo is in a fifty-fifty joint venture with General Motors (GM); the venture is not active in exports, and Daewoo took over management from GM in 1983.

Car assembly presents a very different picture. Minority joint ventures and licensing play an important role in numerous developing countries (including ASEAN members, the Andean countries, Iran, Nigeria, and several North African nations). The investment pattern in assembly operations suggests that: a) host-government restrictions on foreign ownership are a major factor behind NFI; b) auto companies that are market-share followers often use NFI offensively to gain favored access to local markets (pressuring the leaders to follow suit in some cases); and/or defensively—to benefit from local partners' sharing risks and contributing to finance and marketing efforts; and c) the industry leaders tend to use NFI only when local production cannot compete internationally with the core activities of their international integrated production and marketing systems. NFI, notably joint ventures and licensing, are also somewhat more prevalent in the commercial-vehicle and component segments of the industry than in auto production per se.

The pattern of North-South investment in the auto industry reflects above all the high level of worldwide concentration in this industry; the very significant economies of scale in production (which are greater in passenger cars than in commercial vehicles); and the financial and technological advantages of subsidiaries of the major auto multinationals vis-à-vis majority locally owned firms that rely on NFI. It also reflects the importance that such industry leaders as GM and Ford attach to retaining full control and ownership of their affiliates, which operate within increasingly integrated worldwide production and marketing networks. Meanwhile, the Japanese majors continue to prefer to keep production at home. Korea's experience is thus unique among developing countries; and its success is far from assured, particularly given the relatively limited size of the country's domestic market.

*Electronics.* The electronics complex may be defined as covering three distinct segments: microelectronic components (semiconductors and integrated circuits), consumer electronics (radios, television, hi-fi equipment, electronic watches, hand calculators, and toys), and computers.

In *microelectronics*, increasing price competition, the relatively labor-intensive nature of the assembly and testing of semiconductors, and the relatively modest fixed-capital requirements led a number of major firms to set up assembly and testing operations in some Asian and Latin American countries in the early 1960s. But those operations, which produce virtually exclusively for OECD markets, involved mostly traditional FDI. In the late 1960s and especially in the 1970s, however, locally owned subcontracting companies were set up in a number of countries, including Hong Kong, the Philippines, and Taiwan. They were often established on the basis of contracts with smaller OECD-based firms that supplied equipment and technical and marketing assistance. Furthermore, in countries like Brazil, Korea, and Taiwan, recent efforts to increase semiconductor production capacities have given rise to a number of NFI arrangements. A few examples are the licensing agreements between the Brazilian firms, Itan and Docas, and several European firms; licensing between Korea's San Sung and the U.S. firm, Micron Technology; a joint venture between Gold Star (Korea) and AMI (United States); and licensing between Taiwan's state enterprise, ERSO, and RCA (United States).

In *consumer electronics*, licensing and joint ventures provided the basis for some developing-country producers, especially in East and Southeast Asia, to develop their production capacities. In the early years, assembly of radios and black-and-white television sets was the principal activity; but this led to greater local production of components, to the production of more sophisticated products, and finally, in countries like Korea and Taiwan, to the mastery of production techniques and technology by local firms. In the past few years, some of these firms have actually set up production subsidiaries in OECD countries: There are Korean subsidiaries in the United States and Portugal, and a Taiwanese color TV producer in the United Kingdom.

In *computers*, foreign investment in developing countries remains limited. This is particularly so in the case of large computers, in which what investment there is tends to be dominated by the traditional FDI of a few major companies. Efforts to promote the development of national production capacities, notably in Brazil, have given rise to licensing in mini- and micro-computers and in such peripherals as printers, screens, and disks. And it is principally market-share followers—like Sycor (United States), Logabax (France), Nixdorf (the Federal Republic of Germany), Fujitsu (Japan), and Ferrati (United Kingdom)—that have supplied production technology through NFI. On a much smaller scale, China, Korea, and Mexico have also begun to develop national computer industries, mainly through licensing and joint ventures.

In short, the pattern of NFI in the electronics complex points up the importance of rapid technological change, which explains why the majors are reluctant to share ownership or to license their most up-to-date technologies with developing-country producers. It also highlights the use of NFI by some 'followers,' primarily as an offensive tactic to gain access to potentially important markets in some newly industrializing countries. Such companies may also seek to amortize research and development expenditures through licensing activities in developing countries.

Future negotiations in this industry undoubtedly will focus on the issue of access to developing-country markets in exchange for access to rapidly changing production technology, particularly in microelectronics and computers.

*Textiles.* In the textile industry, international investment has played a less important role in the development of production capacity in developing countries than it has in other manufacturing industries of comparable importance. This is consistent with the observation that both traditional FDI and NFI tend to concentrate in host countries' major growth industries. The textile industry has not been a major growth industry for the Third World as a whole during the past two decades.

But in those developing countries where the industry has been a growth leader, foreign investment—and especially NFI—usually has been important. Such is clearly the case of the three leading exporters: Korea, Taiwan, and Hong Kong. It is also true in a number of emergent textile-producing countries, with the notable exception of India.

To understand the patterns of international investment in this industry, it is important to recall that the industry comprises three main segments: fibers (synthetic and natural), textile-mill products (fabrics), and end-use products (notably apparel). Also key is the role played by the international quota system in apparel trade under the Multi-Fibre Arrangement (MFA), which strongly influences the flow of textile production and technology from developed to developing countries, and within the Third World.

World production of synthetic fibers is dominated by a handful of OECD-based multinational chemical companies; the top twelve alone accounted for some 60 per cent of world output in 1980, for example. One result is that traditional FDI plays a bigger role than NFI in this segment, especially compared with the other two segments. Large capital costs, economies of scale, and patent protection constitute major barriers to entry; and relatively few developing countries have embarked upon synthetic fiber production. New forms of investment—especially by a few U.S. and European fiber producers (the latter are an integral part of their countries' larger, oligopolistic chemical industries)—have been important in some of the larger Latin American countries. Nevertheless, new forms of investment have helped develop fiber-production capacity in some Third World countries. The most active investors have been the Japanese fiber companies, which are part of vertically integrated textile groups; and they have done so primarily through joint ventures, licensing of know-how, and plant exports with technical assistance—particularly in Asia and to some extent in Latin America.

Compared with the fiber industry, the role of international investment in textile-mill products has been limited. This segment has been developed in many Third World countries on the basis of imported, often second-hand machinery. Only Japanese firms have been really active in this segment, and, again, their involvement has been largely through minority joint ventures, licensing, and plant exports with technical assistance. Many of the smaller Japanese firms have used NFI (and especially joint ventures) to relocate production capacity, often under the umbrella of the large *sogo shosha* (general trading companies) in conjunction with Japan's restructuring of its textile complex during the 1960s and early 1970s. It is worth noting that about two-thirds of the sales of Japanese textile affiliates in developing countries go to local markets, about a quarter to third-country markets, and less than a tenth to Japan.

But it is in the apparel industry, more than any other segment of the textile complex, that NFI has been of crucial importance—and traditional FDI, insignificant—in recent decades. Textile and clothing manufacturers as well as apparel retailers and buying groups in the OECD countries have played a major role in the development of apparel production for export from developing countries. These 'principals' supply designs and raw materials, organize shipping, provide advertising and brand names, and control distribution channels. Most of this is done through international subcontracting with locally owned firms. The contracts are normally short-term (about one year), which allows the principals to shift important risks and costs associated with demand fluctuations onto the subcontractors while retaining virtual control over operations.

Among the first to make extensive use of international subcontracting were Japan's trading companies, which set up agreements with local producers in Hong Kong, Taiwan, and Singapore. Starting in the late 1960s, they worked mostly for export to the U.S. market. Some of this activity has been taken over by U.S. buying groups, and it has been expanded considerably both by these groups and by U.S. textile and apparel manufacturers. Among the European firms, German manufacturers have been the most active in using Asian subcontractors. The main motivations have been labor-cost reductions in a context of slow demand growth and intense price competition (and, in Japan, rapid wage increases).

Whether or not this type of offshore apparel processing continues to grow will depend largely on the nature and speed of technological change in the clothing industry. One of the major transformations that industrial countries may be able to carry off is to reduce labor costs markedly while increasing production flexibility through robotization; apart from high-fashion apparel, they have no comparative advantage today. (If import pressures on textile and clothing manufactures are creating serious difficulties in some OECD countries, these problems should be attributed less to NFI in developing countries than to domestic restructuring difficulties—for example, in moving up-market or, as in the United States, in modernizing production.) Obviously, continued expansion will also depend on protectionist trends in the OECD region and the distribution of Multi-Fibre Arrangement quotas among developing countries.

It should also be noted that the MFA quotas, along with the high costs of new production technology and other barriers to international marketing, create major obstacles to developing countries aspiring to join the ranks of major textile and apparel exporters. The quota system has had a major influence on the spread of production to second-tier producing countries, a movement in which NFI have played a central role. But the consensus seems to be that most of the emergent producers, with the exception of China, are not likely to join the ranks of the major exporters in the foreseeable future.

*Food Processing.* Although traditional FDI predominates foreign investment in food-processing plants, the trend is clearly one of increasing use of NFI. Particularly important are joint ventures in which the foreign partner supplies more sophisticated product technology and, often, a brand name and advertising experience, and the local partner provides assured access to raw materials. Other NFI of growing importance in the industry include licensing and franchising, the latter especially in "fast foods."

The fact that the majors and market-share leaders in food processing still rely heavily on whole or majority ownership of their processing plants suggests that such firms are reluctant to share equity (and rents) or to relinquish decision-making power that might dilute their competitive advantages, notably in marketing and brand differentiation. But there is also considerable evidence that some newcomers and followers are using NFI offensively, to penetrate markets in competition with some of the majors. Sharing production technology and control with local partners, such firms benefit from the latter's knowledge of local markets and ability to share risks (as well as to ensure supplies of raw materials). They have thus sometimes exerted considerable pressure on competitors, including the majors, to follow suit.

These patterns in turn suggest that the future of NFI will depend largely on the dynamics of inter-firm rivalry, and especially on whether more newcomers and followers will want to expand through NFI. Although a relatively low level of concentration in the industry works in favor of such a trend, it is important to remember that most international investment is still in the OECD region, where the emphasis is on acquisitions and mergers.

Several observations confirm that the new forms of investment, like traditional FDI, tend to be concentrated in the high value-added segments of this industry. The branches in which both the majors and the newcomers have become the most involved are brand-name and differentiated processed foods as well as milk products, fruits, and vegetables. They are not usually in mass-consumption food products, as they tend to concentrate their activities in the higher-income markets. An important exception is, of course, beverages. Some foreign companies have used mass-marketing techniques to create mass-consumption markets for their drinks.

Another phenomenon is the use of new forms of investment, and notably contract growing—as discussed in Chapter 4—to shift the risks of primary production onto local growers, while keeping control over the high value-added segments of the food chain, processing and marketing.

Structural changes in developing countries also account for some increased use of NFI. In many countries, especially in Latin America, the process whereby modern elites have consolidated their power has been accompanied by, and indeed has sometimes depended on, import-substitution industrialization. This has usually created internal terms of trade that are unfavorable to agriculture. Consequently, there has been a massive migration to urban centers with an accompanying rise in urban food demand. It was in this context that the change in foreign-investment patterns in Latin American food production took place: From heavy reliance on traditional FDI in the production of mostly unprocessed export produce, there was a shift to contract-growing by food processors producing primarily for local urban markets.

## Implications of New Forms of Investment

There can be little doubt that many developing countries adopted policies in the late 1960s and early 1970s that were designed to increase national control over investment and returns on investment through NFI. But, as noted earlier, many of these countries now feel that they achieved only limited success at best. One reason, in their view, is that even with new forms of investment, they continue to depend on foreign firms for access to competitive technology and world markets. Another is a feeling of greater vulnerability to conditions in the international financial markets. A third may be that firms supplying assets through new forms of investment frequently approach these projects as sales rather than investment operations, which gives rise to the types of conflicts of interest cited in the discussion of the NFI concept.

Clearly, in a global investment scene characterized by changing economic conditions and investment strategies, the NFI offer important potential advantages to developing countries compared with traditional FDI, but greater risks as well. Among the advantages, the most important is undoubtedly the potential for increased host-country control over the process of capital formation, and for a larger share of returns from investment. There can be little question that NFI has favored such control in some cases: Witness the Japanese postwar experience, for example, as well as that of the Republic of Korea during the 1960s and 1970s.[9] In other cases, NFI have at least favored a higher host-country share of profits: Petroleum extraction is a case in point. Moreover, by combining the strengths and interests of host-country elites and the international business and finance communities, certain new forms of investment have broken ground in the development and capitalization of activities in the developing countries that were either new, or like petrochemicals, backward, like peasant agriculture.

Indeed, these new patterns could have significant implications: Given the vast development needs and growth potential of the Third World at a time when growth in the OECD region has slowed considerably by postwar standards, it would be reasonable to infer that by opening important new avenues of growth and longer-term business opportunities, NFI may hold important positive-sum-game implications for contributing to growth not only in host countries but in the global economy. In the extreme, it is conceivable that NFI may in the long run do for accumulation and growth internationally what the advent of the limited-liability joint stock corporation did a century ago in the national context of today's industrial economies. Like the corporation, NFI provide a legal and institutional framework in which entrepreneurs, owners of physical assets, and financiers can join forces, separate effective control from equity ownership, and divide risks and responsibilities.

The question, then, is to determine how a host country can take advantage of what NFI can potentially offer—and whether it might or might not do better with traditional FDI (perhaps in conjunction with improved fiscal policies). The evidence suggests that the an-

swer generally depends less on the host country's foreign-investment policies per se (although these should be reasonably stable
and transparent) than on the coherence and effectiveness of the
country's overall industrial and macro-economic policies. Much also
depends, of course, on the relative bargaining strength of local
elites vis-à-vis their international counterparts. This bargaining
strength in turn depends on such factors as the size and dynamism
of the local market and the level of development of local technological, managerial, and entrepreneurial capacity, and hence also
on the ability of local elites to take advantage of rivalry among
foreign firms.

But in assessing the potential advantages of new forms of
investment to developing countries, and, indeed, in explaining why
some countries favor such forms, it is important not to confuse often
nationalistic declarations with local reality. In some developing
countries, an important reason why local elites may favor NFI over
traditional FDI may be that they find it useful in competing with or
consolidating their economic and political power vis-à-vis other
groups at home. That is, new forms of investment may reflect and
reinforce two simultaneous movements: one of increased horizontal
integration by some local elites internationally (where NFI serve to
strengthen ties between them and the international business and
financial communities), and another of vertical hierarchization and
concentration of power within host countries. Viewed from the
broader national perspective, however, and particularly from that of
local groups excluded from direct participation in NFI, the new
forms may not hold any intrinsic advantages over traditional FDI.
Indeed, the rising pressure in some developing countries in favor of
NFI during the 1970s—a period of relatively rapid growth—may
have been as much or more a reflection of struggles among groups
to consolidate power as it was an expression of national interests
vis-à-vis foreign capital.

For some countries, those pressures may diminish during the
1980s—either because of the relative success of certain groups in
consolidating their positions of local power (some may even become
international investors in their own right[10]) or because today's
lower economic growth rates and debt problems leave them less
room to maneuver vis-à-vis the international business and financial communities. But in other developing countries, pressures for
NFI may remain strong for domestic political reasons if not for
clearly justifiable reasons of national economic interest. Both possibilities reflect the continuing, complex interaction among local
power structures, competition for control of the state and local
economic conditions, and the forms of foreign investment in developing countries.

Among the potential risks of NFI for host countries, perhaps the most important are those associated with the decision of whether to invest and with the choice of the size of the capacity to be installed. Under NFI, these decisions are frequently assumed by host-country firms or governments and are thus more likely to be de-linked from world market conditions and the supply of technology. Under traditional FDI, the risks and responsibilities associated with long-term investment decisions, supply of technology, financing, and marketing output are normally assumed by the multinational firm; its decisions are likely to be based on a careful and knowledgeable assessment of worldwide conditions of supply and demand. The local participant in an NFI venture rarely has an information and planning horizon as international in scope as a multinational, and its ability to keep abreast of technological innovation and changing world-market conditions is likely to be more limited. Decisions may be influenced more by local production potential, investment costs, the country's need for foreign exchange, or even local political considerations than by projected global supply and demand.

One result may be continued host-country dependence on foreign firms for access to new technology and world-market outlets, even though those firms may be less committed to the success of the investment project than they would be under traditional FDI. (They may even take measures to ensure that the NFI project cannot compete with their global system.) The danger is that the gains in local control or share of returns obtained by the host country may not be commensurate with the increase in risks assumed and the costs incurred. There have been cases of large NFI projects whose viability depended on exports (as, for example, in mining, steel, petrochemicals, or autos), but whose output could not be sold profitably on world markets. There also have been cases of NFI in highly cost-inefficient, local-market projects to which local elites were more economically and politically committed than they would be to a traditional FDI project. But their survival called for high output prices behind even higher import barriers and large public subsidies. Traditional FDI projects are not immune to such problems, of course, but the potential risks and costs to the host country may be considerably greater under NFI.

Exacerbated long-run disequilibria in global supply and demand trends, with a tendency toward over-production and over-capacity worldwide in some important industries, is also a danger for host countries—and for the global economy. This danger undoubtedly explains why some industrial firms approach certain investment projects in developing countries as sales operations rather than as investments.

It is of course conceivable that the long-term planning perspective relinquished by multinational firms in such projects may be assumed by international lenders, provided foreign loans are necessary. Such a possibility is consistent with studies of trends in offshore financial markets and multinational banking, which found that banks were making more credit-allocation decisions on a global scale, focusing on outcomes—"choosing winners and losers"—by firm and industry.[11] Indeed, the potential for global rationalization might even be enhanced by the lenders' participation under NFI, because in traditional FDI, oligopolistic inter-firm rivalry in some industries can have a destabilizing effect.

But the international financial community's potential power to contribute to a rationalization of productive investment on a global scale tends to be undermined by a number of factors. One is the limits that banks now place on lending to specific debtor countries, sometimes irrespective of the soundness of a particular project, because of the debtor country's overall debt level. Other factors include the pressure on banks to create relatively short-term assets and the relative instability of international financial markets (not to mention their capacity to devote large sums to short-term speculative-type activities). Nor do industrialized countries' national credit agencies, whose export credits and guarantees are often used in conjunction with large NFI projects, appear likely to resolve the problem of international investment rationalization. Indeed, their decisions are often heavily influenced by pressure to favor the competitive positions of firms from their own countries.

Thus, by opening up new avenues of lucrative investment and sales opportunities for foreign firms in developing countries, certain new forms of investment may be a response to short-term problems of host countries and foreign firms alike. But they risk creating or aggravating both financial and "real" disequilibria in host economies and internationally. And, insofar as new forms of investment not only reflect but also reinforce the tendency of firms to shorten their investment-planning horizons, these disequilibria may be accentuated. Such disequilibria can and in some cases already do pose serious problems for host and industrial countries, individually and collectively.

Such imbalances could in turn aggravate international trade and investment relations, notably but not exclusively, in the North-South context. This aggravation could lead—and, in some cases, has led—to increasing state intervention in world trade relations, financial markets, and even investment activities.[12] Intervention can take the form of inter-governmental investment treaties,[13] but it can also intensify protectionism, through actions including "anti-dumping" measures and "voluntary export restriction" agreements, not only between countries in the North and the South but also among industrial countries.

To put these global disequilibria and negative-sum-game scenarios into proper perspective, it is important to recall that the bulk of international investment by firms takes place, and increasingly so, in the industrial OECD countries. Although new forms of investment in developing countries offer potential advantages as well as risks to the host countries, their impact on the global economy could, at worst, be one of exacerbating difficulties in some industries. The origins of these difficulties clearly lie in the industrial countries. And that is where the solutions must be found.

## Notes

Note: The views expressed are those of the author and do not necessarily represent those of the Organisation for Economic Co-operation and Development.

[1] Many of the points discussed in this chapter are developed more fully in the author's forthcoming book, *New Forms of Investment in Developing Countries, Industry Studies* (Paris: OECD Development Centre, forthcoming). See also Charles Oman, "New Forms of International Investment in Developing Countries," OECD Centre Studies, No. 1 (Paris: OECD, 1984); and Charles Oman, ed.,"New Forms of Investment in Developing Countries: The National Perspective," OECD Development Centre Papers, No. 1 (Paris: OECD, 1984).

[2] A trade (sales) operation is an exchange transaction in which the seller (exporter) supplies a certain value of goods and/or services to the buyer (importer) in exchange for an *equivalent value*, but in a different form. Payment by the buyer is usually in money, but it may also be in other goods or services. Investment, on the other hand, implies the use of money and/or other goods (tangible or intangible) as assets, as capital, by one or more parties for the purpose of generating and appropriating *new value* ("value added") or a surplus of value over that embodied in the money/goods invested. For a fuller discussion of the conceptual distinction between "sales" and "investment," see Oman, "New Forms of International Investment," OECD Development Centre Studies, No. 1, op. cit.

[3] Companies whose principal activity is the supply of turnkey plants, for example, may, of course, take an interest in the project's success insofar as their reputation benefits from successful projects and suffers from unsuccessful ones. But their own balance sheet is not normally affected. Furthermore, firms whose core business is the same as that of the investment project may actually have an interest in making sure that the project does not compete with their business outside the host country; they thus have rather ambivalent interests, at best, regarding the commercial success of the investment project.

[4] For example, although the term "technology sale" is often used to describe licensing agreements, the term "sale" is generally inappropriate, since strictly speaking a sale implies the transfer of property rights from the seller to the buyer. Rather, the licensee is usually given carefully defined rights of access to and use of proprietary knowledge possessed, and retained, by the licensor. This is reflected in the fact that payments to the licensor frequently take the form of a percentage of sales or, occasionally, of profits. But even when the payment or "price" paid by the licensee is a lump sum, what the licensor is selling is in fact not the technology as such, but the firm's rights to future income—as the supplier of technological capital—from the licensee's operation. The licensor is "capitalizing" those rights. In either case (percentage on sales or lump sum), the technology plays the role of an asset, of capital, for the licensor, as well as for the licensee's operation. See also Oman, "New Forms of International Investment," op. cit.

[5] K. Kojima and T. Ozawa, *Japan's General Trading Companies: Merchants of Economic Development* (Paris: OECD Development Centre, 1985); T. Ozawa, "Japan's 'Revealed Preference' for the New Forms of Investment: A Stock-Taking Assessment," in Oman, "New Forms: The National Perspective," OECD Development Centre Papers, No. 1, op. cit.

[6] Some important copper companies, for example, have either disappeared completely (Anaconda was purchased by the oil company Arco and then taken out of the copper business) or have been absorbed into larger firms, where copper mining is only a minor activity (e.g., Kennecott, acquired by BP's subsidiary, Standard Oil Company of Ohio, and St. Joe Minerals, acquired by the construction-engineering firm Fluor).

[7] D. Suratgar, "International Project Finance and Security for Lenders," Paper presented to German Foundation for International Development Conference on International Mineral Resources Development—Emerging Legal and Institutional Arrangements, Berlin, August 1980, p. 1.

[8] Algeria, for example, has relied very heavily on NFI, and in particular on turnkey and "product-in-hand" contracts as a basis for industrial capital formation since independence. At the other end of the spectrum, Singapore shows little use of NFI. But compared with Korea, for example, both Algeria and Singapore rely heavily on foreign investment (NFI and/or traditional FDI) as a proportion of domestic capital formation. When Korea is compared with Brazil, it clearly has less foreign investment, but what it has is predominantly NFI. In both Brazil and Korea, joint ventures and technology licensing are the principal NFI. See Oman, "New Forms: The National Perspective," op. cit.

[9] See Bohn-Young Koo, "New Forms of Foreign Investment in Korea," in Oman, "New Forms: The National Perspective," op. cit.

[10] See Charles Oman, *New Forms of Investment By Developing Countries* (Paris: OECD Development Centre, forthcoming).

[11] See, for example, R. B. Cohen, "Structural Change in International Banking and Its Implications for the U.S. Economy," prepared for the Joint Economic Committee, U.S. Congress, Washington, D.C., December 1980.

[12] See, for example, Richard E. Feinberg, "LDC Debt and the Public-Sector Rescue," *Challenge*, Vol. 28, No. 3 (July/August 1985), pp. 27–34. The author argues that "despite the Reagan Administration's free-market rhetoric, its response to the debt crisis relied on government action. Ideologies aside, governments and international agencies acted quickly, pragmatically and effectively" (p. 27). He analyzes U.S. government involvement in debt rescheduling, in regulation of banking, and in direct foreign investment in developing countries. He also argues that "the same forces that drove the Reagan Administration to intervene in financial markets forced governments in the Third World to intrude more deeply into their own domestic economies" (p. 32).

[13] See Alexandra Gourdain Mitsotaki, "Les Accords Intergouvernementaux Relatifs aux Investissements," (Paris: OECD Development Centre, 1982).

# Chapter 6

# Host-Country Policies to Attract and Control Foreign Investment

## Stephen Guisinger

Policies that attract and control foreign direct investment have become the focus of considerable attention in both developed and developing countries in recent years, but for quite different reasons. For developing countries, the interest is prompted by the debt crisis: The poorer countries need additional foreign capital to fuel economic growth but cannot add more loans that call for fixed schedules of repayment. The flexibility inherent in dividend and capital repatriations makes foreign equity investment substantially more attractive than it has been in the past. Developing countries are eager to know what incentive policies can most efficiently attract the desired amount of capital and what controls on foreign investment can ensure that other national objectives—domestic ownership of key industries and balance-of-trade objectives, for example—are also attained.

The interest of the developed countries, which are primarily capital exporters, flows from a desire to have access to host-country markets. Increasingly, access is through local production rather than through exports. Investment controls that limit foreign participation in these markets can be as injurious as tariffs. Moreover, a number of developing countries impose restrictions that require firms to sell portions of their output in foreign markets and specify minimum amounts of inputs that the firms must buy in the host country. Some observers feel that these performance requirements, if left to multiply, could become a serious impediment to a liberal world trading environment.

Three basic questions lie behind this interest in investment incentives and performance: Do countries use investment incentives to compete for foreign investment capital? Do both incentives and performance requirements actually work? And if they do work, have they caused significant shifts in the international flow of trade and investment?

## Do Countries Use Incentives to Compete for Foreign Investment?

If this question is interpreted as "Do countries have at least one policy instrument that raises the profit of foreign investors?," the answer seems to be a definite "yes." Every country has at least one instrument—whether it is a cash grant, a tax holiday, or a subsidized loan—that benefits both domestic and foreign investors.

The question can, however, be interpreted another way: Do countries have at least one incentive that discriminates in favor of foreign investors relative to domestic ones? Although many countries have on occasion granted foreign firms incentives that were denied local investors, few have done so on a systematic basis.

But the search for evidence of such incentives misses the point. The context in which the question is normally posed calls for evidence about the *overall* impact of investment policies: Do incentives, on balance, outweigh disincentives, and is this net balance more favorable in one country than in others? The question has to be answered in relative terms.

Getting an answer to this question is difficult for two reasons. First, where does one draw the line between investment policies and other policies? Second, how does one sum up the influence of the wide array of investment policies into a single measure of attraction or repulsion?

The distinction between investment and other policies is not clear-cut. The array of policies that affect investment profitability can best be described as a spectrum. At one end are policies, such as cash grants, that have an obvious, direct impact on the profitability of individual investments. At the other end are policies, such as monetary policy, that affect investment profitability only indirectly and clearly cannot be termed investment policies. In the middle are policies that are difficult to classify.

Table 1 lists the complete array of investment incentive and disincentive measures available to a country and places them in one of four categories:

(1) measures affecting the revenues of an investment project;
(2) measures affecting costs of inputs purchased by an investment project;

(3) measures affecting the value of factors of production used by an investment; and
(4) measures affecting investment profitability but not classifiable in the other three categories.

No government uses all of these measures to implement investment policy. Coordinating the more than forty measures on the list would result in an administrative nightmare. Yet governments generally do use more than one instrument. A recent study of the policies employed in ten developed and developing countries in 1982 found that the national inventories of these measures ranged from a low of twelve to a high of thirty-five, with the average country relying on twenty-two incentive and disincentive measures.[1]

How a government selects a particular set of instruments from a large array of possibilities is a tantalizing question not addressed here. National investment policy portfolios appear to be the product of a country's history, size, and government organization, to name just a few determining factors. The large number of instruments observed in many countries may stem from the fact that old policies are hard to terminate when new ones are added or that competition to attract foreign investment has caused governments to adopt policy instruments they would otherwise prefer to do without. It is unlikely that each policy instrument is allied with a specific objective; many seem to be substitutes for one another, and therefore redundant.

The issue at hand, however, is not why governments choose particular policies but rather whether investment policies, taken together, repel or attract foreign investment. Up to this point, an implicit assumption has been that the effects of investment policies can be measured along a single dimension—the cumulative value of incentives less the value of disincentives—similar to the way in which the rate of effective protection provides a cardinal scale for assessing the strength of tariff protection. Yet, it is possible that investment policies may have multiple attributes, with the net incentive being just one of several that affect investors. If this is true, it is unlikely that a single measure will capture the total impact of these multiple attributes.

Information collected from a variety of sources—including responses to survey questionnaires on investment location decisions, personal interviews with investors, and the literature on foreign direct investment—suggests that six principal attributes of investment policies influence the location decision: the net incentive, the variety of incentives, stability of incentives, timing of incentives, investment promotion activities, and government services.

The net incentive is the aspect of incentive policies on which most analysts focus. For a proposed investment project, it can be

## Table 1. Classification of Incentives and Disincentives

| Incentives/Disincentives | Effect on After-Tax Return on Owner's Equity |
|---|---|
| Affecting Revenues | |
| Tariffs | + |
| Differential sales/excise taxes | + or − |
| Export taxes/subsidies (including income tax credits) | + or − |
| Quotas | + |
| Export minimums | − |
| Price controls (or relief from) | + or − |
| Multiple exchange rates | + or − |
| General overvaluation of currency | − |
| Government procurement preference | + |
| Production/capacity controls | + |
| Guarantees against government competition | + |
| Prior import deposits | + |
| Transfer price administration | − |
| Affecting Inputs | |
| Tariffs | − |
| Differential sales taxes (and exemptions therefrom) | + or − |
| Export taxes/subsidies (including utilities) | + or − |
| Quotas | − |
| Price controls | + |
| Multiple exchange rates | + or − |
| Subsidy or tax for public-sector suppliers | + or − |
| Domestic-content requirements (including R&D) | − |
| Prior import deposits | − |
| Transfer price administration | − |
| Transfer price administraton | − |
| Limits on royalties, fees | − |
| Multiple deductions for tax purposes | + |
| Cash or in-kind grants for R&D | + |
| Affecting components of Value-added | |
| Capital | |
| Direct subsidy | |
| Cash grant | + |
| Tax credits/investment allowances ⎫ Specify if reduces book value: | + |
| Subsidized leasing ⎭ taxable or not | + |
| Cost of capital goods | |
| Tariff/sales tax exemption on imported/domestic equipment | + |
| Prior import deposits | − |
| Local-content requirement for capital equipment | − |
| Limits on use of used equipment | − |
| Subsidized buildings | + |
| Subsidized cost of transportation | + |

Source: Stephen Guisinger and Associates *Investment Incentives and Performance Requirements* (New York: Praeger, 1985), pp. 2–3.

| Incentives/Disincentives | Effect on After Tax Return on Owner's Equity |
|---|---|
| Affecting Components of Value-added, continued | |
| Cost of debt | |
| Subsidized loans | + |
| Loan guarantees | + |
| Covering of foreign exchange risks on foreign loans | + |
| Priority of access (including limitations on foreign firms | + or − |
| Cost of equity | |
| Subsidized equity through public investment agencies | + |
| Exemption from capital gains taxes/ registration taxes | + |
| Dividend tax/waiver | + or − |
| Guarantee against expropriation or differential treatment | + |
| Limitations on debt/equity ratio | − |
| Controls/taxes on remitted dividends | − |
| Minimum financial/in-kind ratio | − |
| Corporate tax | |
| Tax holiday/reduction | + |
| Accelerated depreciation | + |
| Special deductions and valuation practices (inflation adjustment; multiple plant consolidation) | + |
| Tax sparing and double-taxation agreements | + |
| Loss-carry-forward provision | + or − |
| Contractual stabilization of rates | + |
| Labor | |
| Wage subsidies (including indirect, i.e., multiple deductions of wages for tax computations/reduction of taxes on labor) | + |
| Training grants | + |
| Minimum wage | − |
| Relaxation of industrial relations laws | + |
| Local labor requirements | − |
| Land | |
| Cash subsidy for purchase/rental | + |
| Exemption/rebate of taxes on land | + |
| Not Classified | |
| Limitations on foreign ownership | |
| Free-trade zones | |
| General preinvestment assistance | |
| Countertrade requirements | |
| Foreign exchange balancing requirements | |

conceived of as the increase in profitability (internal rate of return or net present value) that is attributable to all the measures listed in Table 1. Tariffs are included in this definition because governments occasionally substitute factor-based incentives (such as cash grants and labor subsidies) for commodity-based ones.[2] For example, the Board of Investment in Thailand has the authority to increase the level of protection from competing imports (including a complete ban on imports) and to lower tariffs on imported inputs as part of a negotiated investment incentive package that includes a tax holiday, with Board discretion over its length (zero to eight years). The Board has several different combinations of tariff and tax concession measures that can yield the same after-tax rate of return for investors.

*Variety of Incentives*. The notion that the mix of incentive instruments, quite independently from the actual net incentive received, may influence investment behavior does not fit well into international economic theory, but it can be explained by theories of management, especially organizational behavior and marketing. Some instruments may have more appeal; for example, tax abatements may be more intrinsically attractive to corporate decision makers than labor training grants—even though the impact on the after-tax rate of return is identical. Investors may prefer certain incentive instruments because their effects are not transparent to competitors and the tax-paying public. A large menu of incentives also gives investors maximum flexibility to design their own package.

*Stability of Incentives*. The stability of investment policies over time is an important consideration for investors. Although most incentive policies are fixed contractually prior to investment, governments nevertheless control other policies that can increase or decrease profitability during the course of the investment's life. A country's reputation for "obsolescing bargains"—for progressively watering down initial incentives with subsequent disincentives— may deter investors.

On the other hand, another type of policy instability can sometimes be a positive factor. For example, one automobile manufacturer invested in a European country on the assumption that government policies would eventually change in the direction of restricting entry for the products the manufacturer was exporting to that country. When that day came, the manufacturer wanted to be well established. The manufacturer thought that both current market conditions and existing incentives were inadequate, but the possibility of increased incentives in the future prompted his positive decision.

*Timing of Incentives.* The benefits and costs associated with a country's incentive and disincentive instruments are not distributed uniformly over time. Cash grants are disbursed quickly, whereas tariff protection is spread over the life of a project. Cash is generally more certain to be realized by the investor than are the benefits of tariff protection, which depend on the stability of government policies and the commercial success of the venture. Some countries, for example Belgium, provide incentives to new investments but impose disincentives (in the form of mandatory severance pay for employees) on investments at the end of their lifetime.

*Investment Promotion Activities.* Many governments spend large sums on investment promotion, including advertising, traveling delegations, and representative offices abroad. Ireland has more than ten offices in Europe, North America, and the Far East (including five in the United States), staffed with representatives that call on prospective investors. Like good marketers, these representatives "sell the sizzle, not the steak," and a full menu of incentives often provides the sizzle. Although promotion and incentives often appear as complements, they are ultimately substitutes, since governments must allocate funds between the two types of activities.

*Government Services.* For some projects, the provision of government services at less than full cost can be an important enticement. In many countries, buildings in industrial estates are provided at subsidized rates. Examples abound of governments building roads, bridges, ports, and housing projects to accommodate the plans of potential investors. In almost every case, these services have other users, so it is hard to identify the true subsidy element. Still, the capacity of a government not only to share the cost of infrastructure but also to see that services are delivered in the proper amounts and on time is regarded by investors as an important consideration in their investment location decision. The "one-stop shop" concept—the ability of one agency of government to negotiate and deliver incentive packages that include government services—is often attractive to prospective investors.

In summary, investment policies have at least six different aspects that appeal to investors. No single measure captures the impact of these six attributes on the potential investor. The relative strengths of these various elements are not known, making it difficult to analyze the effectiveness of any one element on invest-ment flows. The impact of the net incentive must be analyzed by controlling for the effects of the other five elements. It is commonly assumed that the net incentive dominates these attributes, but to date no evidence exists to confirm or reject this assumption.

## Do Incentives Work?

One often encounters the opinion, generally unencumbered by hard empirical data, that incentives do not work—or at least that certain incentives do not work. The arguments take various forms. One is that governments waste incentives on companies that were going to make an investment in the host country anyway. The cost of these windfall gains, so the argument goes, may exceed the benefits of any induced investment.

Another argument is that investors select host countries on the basis of real and enduring factors—such as market size and strength or labor and transport costs—rather than in response to artificial and fleeting factors, such as tax holidays and cash grants. One variation of this argument is that incentives may even be counterproductive, since the need to offer them is seen by investors as a sign of fundamental weakness in the host-country economy. Still another argument is that most non-tariff incentives—such as cash grants or tax holidays—are simply too small to matter much to investors.

The alleged insignificance of non-tariff incentives does not seem to be borne out in practice. Under reasonable assumptions, a one-time tax-free cash grant of 50 per cent of the value of an investment is tantamount, insofar as the investor is concerned, to a 30-per cent annual effective rate of protection over the lifetime of the investment.[3] This rate of effective protection means little unless it is put in perspective. The common external tariff of the European Economic Community provides Ireland, for example, with an aver-age effective rate of 27 per cent. The 50-per cent grant that the Irish government provides to selected new investments effectively adds another layer of protection, equal to that already existing from tariffs.

Although only a few countries offer cash grants ranging up to 50 per cent, many countries offer an array of other non-tariff incen-tives that come close to this level. Mexico grants tax credits to investments in priority regions and priority industries that amount to as much as 30 per cent of the value of the investment. The value of these tax credits, combined with subsidized loans and other fiscal incentives, can exceed 40 per cent of the value of investments.

Portugal recently proposed giving cash-grant equivalents of up to 40 per cent to help restructure its textile industry. France offers cash grants of more than 50 per cent to high-technology firms willing to locate in regions targeted for development.

## Empirical Studies of Incentive Effectiveness

One difficulty in conducting empirical studies of the effectiveness of fiscal incentives is that no country keeps a good record of the incentive measures granted to new investors. Whereas tariff protection is often granted through one instrument by one agency and applied uniformly to all firms in an industry, fiscal incentives are spread over many instruments, administered by a variety of agencies, and often applied at different rates to firms in the same industry. Sometimes good information exists on the use of one particular incentive instrument. At other times, complete information is available on incentives in a few selected investments. But neither of these provides the type of data needed to test hypotheses about the impact of the net incentive on investment decisions. In a study that we recently conducted under World Bank auspices, my colleagues and I attempted to bridge the data gap by collecting detailed information on seventy-four foreign investment projects directly from multinational enterprises in four industries—food products, automobiles, computers, and petrochemicals.[4] Numerous problems were encountered in obtaining data. Firms do not maintain complete records on incentives received in the past, nor do managers always have a clear concept of what is meant by the term "incentives." Some managers, for example, regarded tax holidays as investment incentives but treated accelerated depreciation strictly as an accounting convention.

Another problem was the definition of effectiveness. When countries compete for foreign investment, several of them often offer more or less the same investment package. The slight advantage that the incentives of one country may have over another's package generally makes little difference in the site selected. In surveys of the importance that decision makers attach to various factors affecting the investment location, other considerations—the cost of labor, infrastructure availability, proximity to markets—frequently rank well above incentives.

Can we conclude from such surveys that incentives are not effective? The answer would certainly be in the affirmative if one country could eliminate its incentives with no loss of foreign investment. Whether this is true or not depends on what other countries do. If they maintain their incentives, it would seem likely that the country dropping such measures would lose foreign investors. If, on the other hand, other countries follow the first one's lead, each country would more than likely maintain its share of investors. This dependence of outcomes on the strategies of other participants in a particular process is characteristic of "the prisoner's dilemma." In the case of incentives, the prisoner's dilemma often leads to competitive bidding in which all participants are left worse off than if no bidding had occurred. But the fact that granting incentives is not effective for all countries involved in bidding wars does not imply that any one country can withdraw with no injury to itself. Incentives may be effective in an asymmetrically perverse way: An increase in incentives may produce no net gain in competitive situations, but unilateral withdrawal may be highly detrimental to a country's inflow of foreign capital.

Inquiries into the effectiveness of incentives thus always beg the question: What do other countries do when one country raises or lowers its incentives? In the World Bank study, we chose an admittedly extreme basis for measuring the effectiveness of incentives. Respondents were asked the following hypothetical question: Would your firm have located in a particular country (i.e., where the seventy-four cases were in fact located) if no incentives (including market protection through tariffs) had been offered to you *and* if competitor countries maintained their incentive packages at their traditional levels? With the question posed in this manner, many respondents indicated that, in this hypothetical case, the absence of incentives would have affected their decision even though, in the real instance, the presence of incentives was not a major factor in their decision. In the absence of incentives, they would have chosen another location or would have served the host-country market through exports from existing production facilities in the home country or elsewhere.

Table 2 shows responses from the seventy-four projects surveyed. In twenty-four cases, respondents indicated that they would have stuck with their original decisions. Nine of the sixteen investments in food processing fell into this category, underscoring the importance of market or raw-materials proximity to the decision on location; for many firms in this industry, incentives are truly "icing on the cake." For the fifty cases in which incentive policies were decisive factors in the choice of investment location, twenty-four projects cited tariff and non-tariff barriers as important, and seventeen identified fiscal incentives as important.

In nine cases, firms indicated that it was the instability of investment policies, as described earlier, that motivated their in-

## Table 2. Dominant Influence on Location Decision

| Investment Orientation | Non-Policy Influence | Policy-related Influence | | |
|---|---|---|---|---|
| | | Policy Stablility | Commodity-based | Factor-based |
| Domestic market | 8 | 3 | 23 | 2 |
| Common market | 9 | 6 | 0 | 11 |
| Worldwide export market | 7 | 0 | 1 | 4 |
| Total | 24 | 9 | 24 | 17 |

Source: Stephen Guisinger and Associates, *Investment Incentives and Performance Requirements* (New York: Praeger, 1985), p. 49.

vestment location decision. Sometimes it was a threat—rarely made explicitly but frequently inferred from government behavior—that future import barriers would be coupled with restrictions on foreign investment; the clear implication was that a firm had best invest now or forfeit future opportunities. In other instances, governments hinted that new performance requirements would be imposed on existing foreign investments unless owners made additional investments in the host country. Studies using either survey techniques or data on existing incentive levels would not pick up these nine cases in which the government's power to vary incentives levels was the deciding factor.

Because the World Bank study did not follow stratified sampling procedures, few generalizations can be made about the comparative effectiveness of incentives among industries or across countries. Nor is it possible to conclude from the study that certain types of incentive instruments are more effective than others. This chapter already has emphasized the problems inherent in that line of inquiry. The study suggests, however, that the withdrawal of all incentives—an admittedly draconian step for most countries— would seriously impair the ability to attract new foreign investment, although this result depends on the assumption that the incentive policies of other competitor countries remain unchanged.

## Do Performance Requirements Affect Trade and Investment?

The third question is by far the most difficult. The prevalence of performance requirements is not hard to document, but their influence on investment decisions and on the pattern of foreign purchases and sales by an investment project is far more difficult to discern. The World Bank found that among seventy-four cases, thirty-eight were subject to trade-related performance requirements (typically, to export a certain fraction of their output). Other performance requirements included domestic content and trade balancing—the foreign-exchange cost of imported inputs must be offset by export earnings. No standard definition of performance requirements exists. The narrow definition of trade-related performance requirements comprises only those government restrictions that seek to reduce foreign-exchange costs or to raise foreign-exchange earnings of investment projects. Broader definitions include almost every form of government restriction on an enterprise, but most typically those that stipulate specific proportional requirements for ownership and employment based on national origin.

One problem of measuring the incidence of performance requirements encountered in the World Bank study was the use of implicit performance requirements administered through discretionary incentives. Many countries have created investment promotion agencies empowered to grant incentives to projects meeting certain criteria. The Industrial Development Authority in Ireland and the Economic Development Board in Singapore are notable examples. In lieu of explicit performance requirements on all new investment projects, these agencies reward projects designed to meet trade performance criteria and withhold incentives from those projects that do not. The World Bank study found an inverse correlation between market size and the imposition of formal performance requirements. Large developing countries, such as Brazil, India, and Mexico, have not delegated investment review and promotion responsibilities to a single agency, relying on decentralized decisions based on formal, automatic performance criteria applied uniformly to all investment projects. Small countries, such as Ireland and Singapore, do not explicitly impose domestic-content and export-minimum requirements on investors but prefer to exercise leverage through discretionary incentive policies.

Performance requirements act as turbochargers for incentive instruments. They magnify and redirect the rents from incentive measures by linking the receipt of incentive benefits to the fulfillment of certain performance criteria. The World Bank study found no investments subject to performance requirements that did not also enjoy substantial incentives, and it would be difficult to envisage these investments ever having been made if the requirements were present but the incentives absent. Governments use these incentive-generated rents to promote balance-of-payments equilibrium and import substitution. By stipulating quantitative targets for exports or domestic content in individual investments, these objectives can be served more efficiently. Performance requirements sidestep some of the prohibitions of the General Agreement on Tariffs and Trade (GATT) on export subsidization. But as Hufbauer and Erb have argued: "Perhaps now the concept of export subsidies should extend even further to cover the provision of licensing rights conditioned on export performance, such as the right of establishment or the right to apply for fiscal incentives."[5]

Another feature of the more broadly defined performance requirements is that they are designed to keep the incentive-created rents at home. If rents were merely exchanged among nationals of a country, only the income redistributive effects and the real resource costs of rent-seeking would provide cause for concern. However, when foreign investors are introduced into the picture, part of repatriated profits due to rents represents real resource losses. Governments seek to block these losses by stipulating limitations on foreign equity ownership and imposing ceilings on repatriation.

The World Bank study found that, of the thirty-eight investments subject to performance requirements, only four would have been located elsewhere (or would not have been made) were it not for the requirements. In these four cases, all in the automobile industry, the investors already had a substantial stake in the host country's market either through domestic production or exports. The investments were necessitated by the decisions of the governments to require that imports be offset with exports.

The study did not attempt to address the issue of trade distortions brought on by performance requirements because of conceptual and information gaps. To isolate the independent effect of performance requirements on trade patterns, a series of assumptions must be strung together. For example, in the absence of performance requirements, would the investment have been made at all? If so, what type of project would have been built? What kind of incentive package would the government have granted if performance requirements were not permitted?

Assumptions about these issues are critical because they determine the costs that performance requirements impose on firms. At present, only information about the number and type of performance requirements, by country and industry, is available. These are useful data, but they say little about the changes in firms' behavior induced by performance requirements.

Performance requirements may, indeed, have little effect in practice for several reasons. First, investors may meet the performance criteria without the need for the explicit requirements. In this case, they are simply redundant. Second, governments have on occasion relaxed performance requirements previously imposed on an investment in response to worsening external market conditions or internal shortages of intermediate inputs. Finally, requirements may not be enforced. Although legally binding, performance requirements are often regarded by governments as little more than good faith agreements that firms should do their utmost to achieve.

Although some analysts exaggerate the potency of performance requirements, these measures—including the implicit variety described above—are widely used by countries that have both the level of domestic incentives and the bargaining strength to make them stick. The problem is that researchers have no convenient method of measuring their impact in the same way that effective rates of protection measure the significance of tariffs. The number of performance requirements found in an industry or a country is irrelevant; number has no bearing on their aggregate strength. Until thorough case studies are compiled that convincingly detail the incentives and investment projects that would occur in the absence of performance requirements, their influence will remain in the realm of anecdote and speculation.

## Conclusions and Policy Implications

Investment incentives are a modern Hydra. The Herculean GATT severed the head of direct export subsidies, but now tax incentives, investment credits, and subsidized loans and performance requirements have sprung up to take their place. The number and complexity of investment incentives pose serious problems for anyone wishing to assess the importance of such measures.

Evidence of an indirect nature has been provided to show that the impact of investment incentives on the investor's rate of return may be quite important when compared with the levels of effective protection that many investors in both developed and developing countries enjoy. Thus, while any individual incentive measure may have a small effect, the cumulative effect of all incentive measures granted by a host country nevertheless may be substantial.

It also has been shown that out of a sample of seventy-four foreign investment projects undertaken by multinational enterprises in four industries (automobiles, chemicals, food products, and

computers) fifty—or two of every three investments studied—
would have been located in a different country if incentives had
been withdrawn (provided that all other countries maintained their
incentive systems at existing levels). This does not, however, suggest that countries can gain by increasing incentive levels, since
their actions may be matched by other countries, canceling out any
advantage that the increase momentarily gave the initiating country. The World Bank study, for which the survey was done, found
substantial competition among some countries for foreign investment, suggesting that, at least for these nations, policy changes in
one country more than likely stimulate changes in the policies of its
competitors.

If a "prisoner's dilemma" situation exists—with rounds of competitive bidding leading to no net change in any one competitor's
share of total foreign investment—each country has an interest in
limiting the use of incentive instruments. Clearly, investment incentives may have a role in promoting a higher aggregate volume of
investment worldwide; but once the appropriate volume of investment is attained, further incentives aimed at increasing one country's share may prove to be collectively futile. The Treaty of Rome
attempted to limit the use of incentives to influence investment
location by placing a ceiling on the cumulative value of incentive
awards equal to 75 per cent of the value of the investment. This
ceiling applied only to the least developed regions, and lower ceilings were imposed on more developed areas of the European Community. The Association of South East Asian Nations (ASEAN) also
has attempted to limit the use of incentives among its members.

The principal problem in all of these efforts to curtail the use of
incentives is one of negotiating enforceable agreements: The rewards from cheating can be substantial. The increased interest of
multilateral institutions such as the GATT, the World Bank, and
the recently proposed Multilateral Investment Guarantee Agency
in the problems of incentive proliferation may bring their powers of
enforcement to bear on the cheating problem. However, as this
chapter has emphasized, many conceptual and informational gaps
remain to be closed before any truly workable agreements can be
reached.

Another policy implication is that performance requirements
do not constitute a separate set of issues; rather, they determine
how the rents created by investment incentives are directed to
achieve social objectives. Performance requirements accelerate and
redirect the rents generated by incentive policies. Any attempts to
negotiate away performance requirements will very likely result in
compensating changes in host-country incentive policies, possibly
contributing further to distortions in trade and investment patterns.

# Notes

[1] Stephen Guisinger and Associates, *Investment Incentives and Performance Requirements* (New York: Praeger, 1985), pp. 5–8.

[2] The substitution between factor-based and commodity-based measures is discussed in Eric Bond and Stephen Guisinger, "Investment Incentives as Tariff Substitutes: A Comprehensive Measure of Protection," *Review of Economics and Statistics*, Vol. LXVII, No. 1 (February 1985), pp. 91–97.

[3] Stephen Guisinger, "Do Investment Incentives and Performance Requirements Work?," *The World Economy*, Vol. 9, No. 1 (March 1986), Footnote 7.

[4] Guisinger and Associates, op. cit.

[5] Gary Hufbauer and Joanna Erb, *Subsidies in International Trade* (Washington, D.C.: Institute for International Economics, 1984), p. 83.

# Chapter 7

# Investment Trends and Prospects: The Link with Bank Lending

David J. Goldsbrough

Although direct investment flows into developing countries generally continued to grow throughout the 1970s, their relative contribution to these countries' external financing was overshadowed by the rapid expansion in external borrowing, particularly from foreign commercial banks. The onset of widespread debt-servicing problems in 1982 caused a sharp decline in private lending, reflecting the banks' reluctance to add to their claims on many developing countries. Consequently, there has been considerable discussion of the extent to which increased foreign direct investment could help offset the decline in bank lending. In this paper, I consider the prospects for encouraging increased foreign direct investment flows—in the context of past trends and possible future market conditions and policies.

Foreign direct investment differs from other financing flows in that it involves a substantial element of managerial control. The actual form of the financial transfer varies considerably. In principle, all cross-border financing flows between a parent company and its affiliates are classified as direct investment; thus foreign direct investment may consist of new equity capital, reinvested earnings, or net borrowing from the parent company or other affiliates. In practice, a number of countries do not record data on reinvested earnings, and net borrowing from a parent company is sometimes included in external borrowing statistics. For developing countries that do collect data on reinvested earnings, such earnings appear to have accounted for an average of about two-fifths of all foreign direct investment inflows during the 1970s.

## Past Trends in Direct Investment

During the 1960s, recorded foreign direct investment accounted for well over half of all private capital flows from industrial to developing countries. By the late 1970s, however, it represented barely one-quarter of a much larger volume of flows, most of which were accounted for by medium-term bank lending and by suppliers' credits. The decline in the relative importance of foreign direct investment began in the late 1960s, when commercial bank lending to developing countries started to expand rapidly; it accelerated after the 1973–74 increase in oil prices, as non-oil developing countries financed most of their larger current-account deficits through external borrowing. In 1973, foreign direct investment still financed some 16 per cent of the combined current-account deficit and net accumulation of reserves of the capital-importing countries as a group, but it met only about 10 per cent of the larger financing needs in the late 1970s (see Figure 1)[1]. Nevertheless, foreign direct investment flows into capital-importing countries continued to grow in absolute terms, reaching a peak of $14 billion in 1981; at that time, they accounted for over one-quarter of global foreign direct investment flows, up from about one-fifth during the mid-1960s. As a result of the subsequent recession, they fell substantially—to about $10 billion in 1984, (in 1984 dollars), but were much less severely affected than was borrowing from private creditors.

An examination of long-term trends in foreign direct investment flows may help evaluate the likely prospects for encouraging a greater volume of such investment. During 1967–1984, investment flows to capital-importing countries grew at a trend real annual growth rate of 4.5 per cent (see Table 1). Within this global trend, however, direct investment patterns have varied greatly. Foreign direct investment flows to countries relying primarily on private creditors for their external borrowing (market borrowers) were large and had high trend growth rates, while flows to countries relying primarily on borrowing from official creditors (official borrowers) were small and tended to decline over the period. On a regional basis, flows to Asian developing countries have grown very rapidly; those to Latin American countries have grown more slowly; and flows to African countries have stagnated.

Although it is difficult to generalize about the economic characteristics that make a country attractive to foreign direct investment, much investment has been concentrated in countries that have large domestic markets, are rich in natural resources, or have

# Figure 1. Capital-Importing Developing Countries, Financial Flows, 1973–84[a]

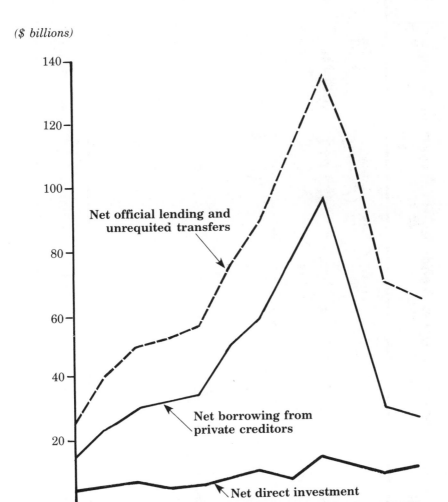

*($ billions)*

[a] Excluding reserve-related liabilities.
Source: *World Economic Outlook* (Washington, D.C.: International Monetary Fund, various issues.)

## Table 1. Capital-Importing Countries: Trends in Net Inflows of Foreign Direct Investment, 1967–84

| | Average Annual Inflow $ billions at constant 1980 prices | | | | Trend Real Annual Growth[a] Rate, 1967–84 |
|---|---|---|---|---|---|
| | 1967–70 | 1974–77 | 1981–82 | 1983–84 | |
| Capital-Importing Countries | 6.4 | 9.2 | 14.4 | 11.5 | 4.5% |
| *By Financial Criteria:* | | | | | |
| Market borrowers[a] | 4.7 | 7.4 | 11.7 | 8.7 | 5.3 |
| Seven major borrowers[b] | 1.9 | 3.4 | 5.9 | 3.3 | 6.4 |
| Official borrowers[c] | 1.2 | 0.9 | 0.8 | 0.5 | –6.4 |
| *By Region:* | | | | | |
| Africa (excluding South Africa) | 1.3 | 1.7 | 1.6 | 1.4 | –0.1 |
| Asia | 0.8 | 2.6 | 4.1 | 4.2 | 11.2 |
| Europe | 0.3 | 0.7 | 0.8 | 0.8 | 7.1 |
| Western Hemisphere | 3.3 | 3.7 | 7.2 | 3.9 | 3.7 |
| *By Income Level:* | | | | | |
| Smaller low-income countries[d] | 0.5 | 0.3 | 0.3 | 0.2 | –5.2 |
| Middle-income countries[e] | 5.9 | 8.9 | 13.6 | 10.5 | 4.7 |

Note: This table shows average annual net inflows of direct investment and the trend growth rate in these inflows for the group of capital-importing countries. The real trend growth rates are calculated by fitting time trends through observations for the period 1967–1984, using the price index of world trade in manufactures as a deflator. Indebted developing countries include all developing countries other than Iran, Iraq, Kuwait, Libya, Oman, Qatar, Saudi Arabia, and the United Arab Emirates.

[a] Capital-importing countries that obtained at least two-thirds of their external borrowing during 1978–82 from commercial creditors.

ᵇ Those with the largest total outstanding external debt at the end of 1984: Argentina, Brazil, Indonesia, Republic of Korea, Mexico, Philippines, and Venezuela.

ᶜ Capital-importing countries (other than China and India) that obtained at least two-thirds of their external borrowings during 1978–82 from official creditors.

ᵈ Comprises 41 countries whose per capita GDP, as estimated by the World Bank, did not exceed the equivalent of $410 in 1980. Excludes China and India.

ᵉ All other capital-importing developing countries, other than China and India.

Source: International Monetary Fund, *World Economic Outlook* (Washington, D.C., various years).

significant advantages for export-oriented manufacturing; in fact, five countries (Brazil, Indonesia, Malaysia, Mexico, and Singapore) accounted for about half of all foreign direct investment flows to capital-importing countries during the period 1973–1984. Countries without any of these characteristics generally have not been very successful in attracting foreign direct investment. On the basis of past trends, therefore, there would appear to be less scope for substituting foreign direct investment for bank lending in such countries, which include most of the official borrowers. However, even an economic setting that is potentially attractive to foreign direct investment does not necessarily lead to substantial investment inflows if policies toward such investment are generally restrictive; some countries that have large domestic markets (for example, India and Turkey) or that have substantial manufacturing exports (for example, Korea) until recently have attracted relatively little FDI.

The United States is the principal source of foreign direct investment in developing countries. At end 1982, it accounted for about half the total stock of foreign direct investment from industrial countries in developing countries, and it provided about 45 per cent of total foreign direct investment flows from industrial to developing countries over the period 1981–83.[2] The United Kingdom is the second most important source, accounting for some 11 per cent of the total stock at end 1982 and providing around 15 per cent of FDI flows during 1981–83. Foreign direct investment from Japan and Germany grew the most rapidly during the 1970s, but it also declined the most during the recent recession; at end 1982, these two industrial countries accounted for 8 per cent and 9 per cent, respectively, of the *stock* of industrial-country foreign direct investment in developing countries, and during 1981–83 they each provided about 10 per cent of foreign direct investment *flows*.

The factors underlying the 1982–83 decline in foreign direct investment flows to developing countries may affect prospects for resumed growth in such investment. For earlier recessions, there is some evidence that cyclical downturns might have had some lagged impact on the level of foreign direct investment inflows into developing countries—either because of a decline in profitable investment opportunities in the host countries or because of a reduced availability of investable funds. For instance, the downturns in economic activity in industrial countries in 1970–71 and 1974–75 were followed up to a year later by declines in the real level of foreign direct investment flows (see Table 2). The recent recession, however, had an even stronger impact on FDI flows, with the decline largely concentrated in Latin America. Information available from the capital-exporting industrial countries indicates that much of the decline was due to a large fall in reinvested earnings.

**Table 2. Capital-Importing Developing Countries: Changes in Net Inflows of Foreign Direct Investment During Recovery Phases of Last Three Business Cycles[a] (annual changes in percentages)**

| | 1971 | 1972 | 1973 | 1974 | 1975 | 1976 | 1977 | 1978 | 1982 | 1983 | 1984 |
|---|---|---|---|---|---|---|---|---|---|---|---|
| FDI Inflows to Capital-Importing Developing Countries (in constant prices)[b] | 25.1 | −16.3 | 33.7 | −3.8 | 11.9 | −21.4 | 3.0 | 15.6 | −5.2 | −23.0 | 7.1 |
| Real GDP of Capital-Importing Developing Countries | 6.2 | 5.1 | 7.3 | 4.5 | 5.1 | 4.2 | 6.3 | 5.7 | 2.0 | 1.7 | 5.0 |
| Real GDP of Industrial Countries | 3.7 | 5.6 | 6.1 | 0.6 | −0.6 | 5.0 | 3.9 | 4.1 | −0.2 | 2.6 | 4.9 |

[a] The troughs of the business cycles in industrial countries are generally regarded as having occurred around the third quarter of 1971, the second quarter of 1975, and the first quarter of 1983, respectively.
[b] Deflated by the price index of manufacturers in world trade.

Source: International Monetary Fund, *World Economic Outlook* (Washington, D.C.: various years).

Two interrelated factors accounted for this decline, and each of them may have rather different implications for future possibilities to substitute increased foreign direct investment for reduced bank lending. First, the cyclical factors discussed in the preceding paragraph must have reduced investment flows; the severity of the recent recession, particularly in Latin America, would help account for the greater impact on foreign direct investment than in earlier recessions. To the extent that cyclical factors accounted for the downturn, foreign direct investment could be expected to recover fairly quickly as output and profitability improved in the host countries. Such recoveries occurred after the two previous recessions (see Table 2). Second, part of the decline in foreign direct investment was probably due to a concern that the repatriation of earnings would be hindered by the host countries' foreign-exchange difficulties. In this case, it might be more difficult to substitute foreign direct investment for bank lending, since an improvement in creditworthiness would be a prerequisite for an expansion of both types of financing. However, direct investment generally involves a longer-term perspective than short- and medium-term bank lending, so that temporary payment difficulties might have somewhat less effect on FDI than on bank lending, provided that appropriate policies to correct external imbalance are adopted (an issue discussed later in this chapter).

Some observers have argued that the recent decline in foreign direct investment flows reflects a more profound shift in expectations concerning the profitability of investment in highly indebted developing countries and in the availability of alternative investment opportunities in industrial countries; both these changes could limit future flows of foreign direct investment to developing countries. Although it is difficult to distinguish changes in longer-term trends from cyclical fluctuations, I would argue that there is little evidence of any such fundamental deterioration in the prospects for foreign direct investment in developing countries as a group. However, the recovery in foreign direct investment flows that has taken place so far does appear to be a little slower than that which occurred following previous recessions; preliminary estimates for 1985 suggest that the growth in FDI flows may have slowed again—to a rate of about 1–2 per cent.

## Factors Affecting Substitution Possibilities Between Foreign Direct Investment and Bank Lending

The composition of private capital flows to developing countries is affected by developments in world markets, including shifts in the sources of net international savings between groups with different asset preferences, and by policies in the countries that receive the capital.

## Developments in World Markets

As a result of the two major increases in oil prices, the pattern of net international savings was radically altered for much of the 1970s. Net savings (i.e., the surplus of domestic savings over domestic investment) and the corresponding outflow of financial resources from industrial countries fell sharply; during 1974–81, net outflows of capital and unrequited transfers from industrial countries are estimated to have absorbed only about 0.75 per cent of their aggregate national savings, compared with roughly 2.5 per cent in earlier years.[3] Meanwhile, the oil-exporting countries accumulated substantial external assets, many of which were held in the form of official foreign-exchange reserves. Asset preferences that emphasized safety and liquidity led these countries to hold a significant portion of their assets in the form of relatively liquid deposits with international commercial banks, which consequently became major intermediaries in channeling funds to deficit countries. A relatively small part of these countries' assets were channeled into direct or portfolio equity investments in developing countries.

With the rapid disappearance of the current-account surpluses of the oil-exporting countries in the early 1980s, the influence of these countries' asset preferences on the composition of international capital flows began to decline. Portfolio preferences in the capital markets of the industrial countries, which are less exclusively concerned with relatively short-term, liquid investments, once again became predominant. Although any short-term effects of this shift cannot be distinguished from the impact of the recession and the widespread debt-servicing difficulties, this is one reason for believing that, in the medium term, the role of foreign direct investment in total private capital flows might become relatively more important.

A related issue is whether capital market constraints on investing companies, in terms of limits on debt/equity ratios or on the degree of foreign exposure, could impose a ceiling on the possible expansion in foreign direct investment flows. In practice, direct investment activities in developing countries represent such a small part of the total market capitalization in the principal source countries that it is unlikely that their expansion would encounter significant capital market restraints, at least on a global basis. For instance, at end 1982, the total value of corporate equities and of bonds outstanding in the United States amounted to some $1,720 billion and $571 billion, respectively; in contrast, the stock of U.S. direct investment abroad (at book value) was $222 billion, of which $52 billion, or less than a quarter, was in developing countries.[4]

## Developments and Policies in Individual Host Countries

Based on past experience, the degree to which foreign direct investment could replace bank lending would appear to vary widely between countries, depending on their resource endowment and economic structure. Nevertheless, even countries without substantial natural resources or large domestic markets can increase their attractiveness to foreign investors by pursuing more stable macroeconomic policies and by avoiding overly restrictive policies toward direct investment. In Africa, for example, the Ivory Coast, Kenya, and Swaziland have been moderately successful in attracting foreign investment, in contrast to the poor performance of many other countries in the region. Countries in which a large share of output and investment is controlled by the public sector would also seem to offer fewer prospects for foreign direct investment. Even in this case, however, there can be significant potential for the participation of foreign equity capital through various forms of joint venture arrangements with state enterprises (see, for instance, Chapter 6 in this volume). The experience of China, which has been quite successful in attracting foreign investment in recent years, shows that a system in which state enterprises account for a large share of output need not be an insuperable barrier to foreign direct investment.

As mentioned earlier, the onset of foreign-exchange difficulties in a country is likely to discourage inflows of foreign direct investment as well as of commercial credit, so that the adoption of macroeconomic policies designed to restore stability is likely to stimulate greater inflows of both types of capital. In this sense, movements in foreign direct investment and in bank lending will tend to be complementary. However, a host country's macro-economic policies can also affect the possibilities for substitution between foreign direct investment and bank credit. In particular, the underlying causes of the need for capital inflows affect the prospects for attracting foreign direct investment, since (unlike bank credit) it is generally directly linked with particular projects, and since most developing countries have fragmented capital markets that make it difficult to shift capital inflows among alternative uses. Consequently, foreign direct investment will more easily replace bank credit when macro-economic policies are such that capital inflows finance additional profitable investment rather than consumption or capital flight. For the same reasons, the volume of foreign direct investment inflows is likely to respond more quickly to an improvement in domestic output and profitability than would inflows of bank credit.

Of course, even at the level of individual projects, foreign direct investment and other forms of foreign capital complement each other to a considerable extent. Multinational firms generally do not finance projects entirely from their own funds. They also rely on borrowing from commercial banks (both in the host country and overseas) and trade credit; the presence of an internationally creditworthy firm can increase the possibilities for a project to attract such financing. However, multinational firms also have considerable scope for substituting between alternative forms of financing, and this substitution can be influenced by host-country policies. For example, tax policies and exchange controls on overseas remittances that discriminate against equity financing and in favor of loan financing are likely to discourage a substitution of foreign direct investment for commercial bank lending.

## Prospects for Foreign Direct Investment

The medium-term prospects for foreign direct investment will obviously depend considerably on output developments and on the types of macro-economic policies adopted in developing countries, but they will also be influenced more generally by the overall role of industrial countries as net suppliers of funds in international markets. It appears likely that, provided reasonable policies are pursued in most developing countries, foreign direct investment flows will show some cyclical recovery during the next few years and that their relative importance vis-a-vis private commercial credit will grow moderately over the medium term. However, it seems highly unlikely that the prospective improvement in foreign direct investment inflows into developing countries would be sufficient to offset more than a relatively small part of the sharp decline in commercial credit that occurred during 1982-84. Consequently, the total availability of foreign resources to developing countries over the medium-term future will probably be less than in the period 1974-81. This would reflect, in part, a return to a more sustainable level of capital flows following the period of recycled oil surpluses and, in part, the rise in the share of private savings channeled into the financing of fiscal deficits in many industrial countries.

These general considerations can be illustrated by using the latest medium-term scenarios for developing countries contained in the International Monetary Fund's *World Economic Outlook*.[5] Net inflows of foreign direct investment into the capital-importing countries are expected to show a partial cyclical recovery during 1986, growing by around 8 per cent a year in constant-price terms (using the index of world trade prices for manufactures as a deflator). This would be a relatively conservative recovery in foreign direct investment—at about the same pace as that following earlier recessions, even though the fall in foreign direct investment during 1982–83 was sharper than that experienced during earlier periods.

During 1987–90, the baseline medium-term scenario, which is drawn up on the assumption of the most likely policies in industrial and developing countries, supposes an annual growth of 3.25 per cent in net foreign direct investment inflows, or about 1.25 percentage points slower than the trend growth rate recorded during the period 1967–1984. In contrast, the average annual growth in real gross domestic product (GDP), at about 4.75 per cent, is about the same as that recorded over the period 1967-1984. The key features of the global economic environment underlying this scenario are: average real growth of GNP of just over 3 per cent a year in industrial countries; measures to reduce structural fiscal deficits in industrial countries by about 1 per cent of GNP; no increase in protectionism against developing-country exports; and a continuation of adjustment efforts in developing countries, resulting in a further reduction in fiscal deficits and a slower rate of credit expansion.[6] This scenario does not, however, assume any major change in policies vis-a-vis foreign direct investment. From a trough of $9.5 billion in 1983 (1983 dollars), FDI flows could reach $13.1 billion (in 1985 dollars) by 1987. On this basis, the real level of foreign direct investment inflows would regain the peak level of 1981 by around 1989. In contrast, available financing from private creditors is, in the absence of major efforts on the part of public authorities to expand it, likely to remain depressed during 1985 and 1986 and to grow by only 0.5 per cent a year in constant-price terms during 1987–90; trade financing would grow moderately, but net commercial bank lending would continue to decline in real terms. Moreover, official development assistance is assumed to remain constant in real terms because of budgetary constraints in industrial countries.

With these growth rates, during the late 1980s net foreign direct investment inflows would finance about one-quarter of the combined current-account deficits of capital-importing countries. In comparison, during 1979–81, the peak period of commercial bank lending to developing countries, net foreign direct investment inflows were the equivalent of about one-eighth of the much larger current-account deficits.

Alternative scenarios give a broad indication of the possible impact of the macro-economic policies of developing countries on trends in foreign direct investment inflows. Since the policies that underlie the baseline scenario are already quite favorable, the likely impact on foreign direct investment inflows—as well as on economic growth in general—of the adoption of worse policies is much greater than the likely impact of better policies. Worse macro-economic policies combining a sharp rise in fiscal deficits, faster monetary growth, and a loss of external competitiveness would be likely to cause a sharp decline in economic growth and to contribute to a poorer investment climate. The scenario supposes that such policies would reduce the average growth rate of real GDP in developing countries by a little over 1 per cent, but that they would have a much larger impact on foreign direct investment flows, which would now decline by around 1 per cent a year in real terms, or a total of 4.1 per cent a year from the base scenario, because of the adverse effects on the investment climate. In contrast, better policies—particularly with respect to exchange rates, interest rates, and administered prices—would improve the investment climate and could increase the annual growth rate of foreign direct investment inflows by 1 per cent, restoring it to about the trend growth rate achieved during 1967–1984.

It is interesting to compare these projections with responses to a survey of foreign direct investment intentions by 52 large multi-national companies conducted in 1983 by the Group of Thirty.[7] In this survey, 22 per cent of respondents expected their real foreign direct investment flows to non-oil developing countries to be higher during the period 1983–87 than during 1978–82, whereas 7 per cent of respondents expected their FDI flows to be lower. (Other respondents expected no change.) These results suggest that the real value of foreign direct investment flows during 1983–87 would be higher than during 1978–82, whereas the *World Economic Outlook* baseline scenario suggests a slight fall. The survey was, however, conducted before the full extent of the decline in FDI flows during 1982–84 was realized, and the firms covered—although large—still accounted for less than half the total stock of foreign direct investment.

These global projections do not distinguish likely regional variations in the growth of foreign direct investment. My own view is that, as in the past, foreign direct investment flows to Asian developing countries will grow considerably faster than those to other country groups, and that, without dramatic changes in policies, flows to African countries will continue to lag behind those to other areas. The largest uncertainty concerns prospects for foreign direct investment in Latin America. Flows to this region were the most severely affected during 1982–84; nevertheless, reasonable prospects now exist for a moderate recovery over the next few years as output and profitability improve. This, however, will require macroeconomic policies that reassure foreign investors that external financial balance can be maintained over the medium term.

## Notes

Note: The views expressed in this paper are those of the author and should not be interpreted as necessarily indicating the position of the International Monetary Fund.

[1] The classification of developing countries as 'capital-importing' countries, 'market borrowers,' and 'official borrowers' used in this section follows International Monetary Fund, *World Economic Outlook* (Washington, D.C.: October 1985). See the footnotes to Table 1 for precise definitions.

[2] Data on the stock of FDI from industrial countries are taken from International Monetary Fund, *Foreign Private Investment in Developing Countries*, Occasional Paper No. 33 (Washington, D.C.: 1985), Table A.3, p. 43; data on FDI flows during 1981–83 are taken from Organisation for Economic Co-operation and Development, *Development Cooperation, 1984 Review* (Paris: 1984), Tables II.I.6 to II.I.8, pp. 254–59.

[3] See International Monetary Fund, *World Economic Outlook* (Washington, D.C.: April 1985), Supplementary Note 9, pp. 188–93.

[4] Figures on the outstanding stock of U.S corporate equities and bonds are from Board of Governors, Federal Reserve System, *Flow of Funds Accounts* (Washington, D.C.: 1984); figures on U.S. direct investment are from U.S. Department of Commerce, *Survey of Current Business* (Washington, D.C.: August 1984).

[5] International Monetary Fund, *World Economic Outlook*, April 1985, op. cit., Chapter III, pp. 72–96.

[6] A detailed list of the environmental and policy assumptions underlying the various medium-term scenarios is given in International Monetary Fund, *World Economic Outlook*, April 1985, op. cit., Table III-3, p. 86.

[7] Group of Thirty, *Foreign Direct Investment, 1973-87* (New York: 1984); see responses to Question 6.

**About the Overseas Development Council and the Contributors**

The Overseas Development Council is a private, non-profit organization established in 1969 for the purpose of increasing American understanding of the economic and social problems confronting the developing countries and of how their development progress is related to U.S. interests. Toward this end, the Council functions as a center for policy research and analysis, a forum for the exchange of ideas, and a resource for public education. The Council's current program of work encompasses four major issue areas: trade and industrial policy, international finance and investment, development strategies and development cooperation, and U.S. foreign policy and the developing countries. ODC's work is used by policy makers in the Executive Branch and the Congress, journalists, and those concerned about U.S.-Third World relations in corporate and bank management, international and non-governmental organizations, universities, and educational and action groups focusing on specific development issues. ODC's program is funded by foundations, corporations, and private individuals; its policies are determined by a governing Board and Council. In selecting issues and shaping its work program, ODC is also assisted by a standing Program Advisory Committee.

Victor H. Palmieri is Chairman of the ODC, and J. Wayne Fredericks is Vice Chairman. The Council's President is John W. Sewell.

# The Editors

*Investing in Development: New Roles for Private Capital?* is the sixth volume in the Overseas Development Council's new series of policy books, U.S.-Third World Policy Perspectives. The co-editors of the series—sometimes jointly and sometimes alternately, collaborating with guest editors contributing to the series—are Richard E. Feinberg and Valeriana Kallab. Theodore H. Moran is guest editor of this volume.

**Theodore H. Moran** is Landegger Professor and director of the Program in International Business Diplomacy at the Georgetown University School of Foreign Service. He is also professor and member of the Executive Council of the Georgetown University School of Business Administration. A former member of the Policy Planning Staff of the Department of State with responsibilities including investment issues, Dr. Moran has since 1971 been a consultant to corporations, governments, and multilateral agencies on investment strategy, international negotiations, and political risk assessment. His publications include many articles and five major books on the issues explored in this volume. He is a member of the ODC Program Advisory Committee.

**Valeriana Kallab,** is vice president and director of publications of the Overseas Development Council and series co-editor of the ODC's U.S.-Third World Policy Perspectives series. Before joining ODC in 1972 to head its publications program, she was a research editor and writer on international economic issues at the Carnegie Endowment for International Peace in New York. She was co-editor (with John P. Lewis) of *U.S. Foreign Policy and the Third World: Agenda 1983* and (with Guy F. Erb) of *Beyond Dependency: The Third World Speaks Out.*

**Richard E. Feinberg** is vice president of the Overseas Development Council and co-editor of the Policy Perspectives series. Before joining ODC in 1981, he served as the Latin American specialist on the Policy Planning Staff of the U.S. Department of State, and as an international economist in the Treasury Department and with the House Banking Committee. Dr. Feinberg is the author of numerous books as well as journal and newspaper articles on U.S. foreign policy, Latin American politics, and international and economic and financial issues. His most recent book is *The Intemperate Zone: The Third World Challenge to U.S. Foreign Policy* (1983).

# Contributing Authors

**Joseph M. Grieco** is assistant professor of political science at Duke University. During 1985-86, he was German Marshall Fund Fellow and Paul-Henri Spaak Research Fellow at Harvard University's Center for International Affairs. In 1986-87, he will serve in the Office of the United States Trade Representative as an International Affairs Fellow of the Council on Foreign Relations. Dr. Grieco is the author of *Between Dependency and Autonomy: India's Experience with the International Computer Industry* (1984).

**Dennis J. Encarnation** is assistant professor at the Harvard Business School, where he specializes in international political economy and the management of international business. He has served as a consultant to multinational corporations, host government agencies, and the World Bank. Dr. Encarnation's first book, drawing on his overseas experience, examined bargaining relations involving multinationals, the state, and local enterprises in India. His current research examines the motivations and consequences of cross-investment between the United States and Japan.

**Louis T. Wells, Jr.,** is Herbert F. Johnson Professor of International Management at the Harvard University Graduate School of Business Administration. Dr. Wells serves as consultant to the governments of several developing countries on issues concerning trade and foreign investment; he is also adviser to management schools in Latin America and Asia. He is the author and editor of numerous journal articles and books, including *Third World Multinationals, Technology Crossing Borders* (edited with Robert Stobaugh), and (with Raymond Vernon) *The Manager in the International Economy.*

**Vincent Cable** is a special adviser in the Economic Affairs Division of the Commonwealth Secretariat, with particular responsibility for research and policy development on foreign investment and international debt. Prior to joining the Secretariat, he was deputy director of the Overseas Development Institute, London. Dr. Cable has served as consultant on trade and industrial policy to several international organizations; special adviser to the British Trade Minister; researcher on Latin American economic integration; lecturer in economics at Glasgow University; Treasury official in Kenya; and in the diplomatic service of the United Kingdom. Dr. Cable has published widely on trade and development issues and was also editor of *Development Policy Review.* His latest book is *Protectionism and Industrial Decline.*

**Bishakha Mukherjee** is senior economics officer in the Commonwealth Secretariat's Economic Affairs Division. Her work has focused on foreign investment policy, developing-country debt, and international capital markets. She was a research assistant while a doctoral candidate at the London School of Economics and has had varied experience in journalism and business.

**David Glover** is associate director of the Social Sciences Division at the International Development Research Centre (IDRC) in Ottawa, Canada. His work involves the management and coordination of research projects in economics and rural development—projects carried out by institutions in developing countries with financing from IDRC. Prior to joining IDRC, Dr. Glover carried out research on new forms of foreign involvement in Latin American agriculture.

**Charles P. Oman** is a principal administrator at the Organisation for Economic Co-operation and Development (OECD) in Paris, where he is responsible for research on North-South investment issues at the Development Centre. Before joining the OECD in 1978, he was for four years first visiting professor and then associate professor of economics at the Graduate School of Business Administration (ESAN) in Lima, Peru. He worked for the Ford Foundation in Lima in 1973. Dr. Oman is the author of a number of books and articles in the fields of development economics and international investment. He is currently setting up a research project on changing international investment strategies and industrialization in developing countries.

**Stephen Guisinger** is professor of international management in the School of Management of the University of Texas at Dallas. Dr. Guisinger has served as a consultant to the World Bank, the International Finance Corporation, the United Nations Centre for Transnational Corporations, and other international institutions. He is the author of *Investment Incentives and Performance Requirements* and other works on trade and investment policy.

**David Goldsbrough** is presently a senior economist in the Asian Department at the International Monetary Fund; his previous assignment was in the Research Department of the IMF's Developing Country Studies Division. He has also served in the Ministry of Finance and Economic Planning of Swaziland. Mr. Goldsbrough's published articles have focused on the role of foreign direct investment in the external adjustment process and on the responsiveness of international trade of multinational corporations to changes in aggregate demand and relative prices. He is also the author of the IMF's Occasional Paper, *Foreign Private Investment in Developing Countries* (1985).

# Overseas Development Council

## Board of Directors*

**Chairman: Victor H. Palmieri**
*Chairman, The Palmieri Company*
**Vice Chairman: J. Wayne Fredericks**
*Ford Motor Company*

Marjorie C. Benton
*Chairman of the Board*
*Save the Children Federation*

William H. Bolin
*San Francisco, California*

Thornton F. Bradshaw
*Chairman of the Board*
*RCA Corporation*

William D. Eberle
*President*
*Manchester Associates, Ltd.*

Thomas L. Farmer**
*Prather, Seeger, Doolittle and Farmer*

Roger Fisher
*Harvard Law School*

Stephen J. Friedman
*Executive Vice President*
*E. F. Hutton & Co., Inc.*

John J. Gilligan
*Chairman, Institute for Public Policy*
*University of Notre Dame*

Edward K. Hamilton
*President*
*Hamilton, Rabinovitz,*
*and Alschuler, Inc.*

Frederick Heldring
*Deputy Chairman*
*Philadelphia National Bank*

Susan Herter
*Santa Fe, New Mexico*

Ruth J. Hinerfeld
*Former President, The League*
*of Women Voters of the USA*

Joan Holmes
*Executive Director*
*The Hunger Project*

Robert D. Hormats
*Vice President*
*International Corporate Finance*
*Goldman, Sachs & Co.*

Jerome Jacobson
*President*
*Economic Studies, Inc.*

William J. Lawless
*President*
*Cognitronics Corporation*

C. Payne Lucas
*Executive Director*
*Africare*

Paul F. McCleary
*Associate General Secretary*
*General Council on Ministries of the*
*United Methodist Church*

Robert S. McNamara

Lawrence C. McQuade
*Executive Vice President*
*W. R. Grace & Co.*

William G. Milliken
*Former Governor*
*State of Michigan*

Alfred F. Miossi
*Executive Vice President*
*Continental Illinois National Bank*
*and Trust Company of Chicago*

Merlin E. Nelson
*Kleinwort, Benson (International)*

Jane Cahill Pfeiffer
*Former Chairman, NBC, Inc.*

John W. Sewell**
*President*
*Overseas Development Council*

Daniel A. Sharp
*Director, International Relations*
*and Public Affairs*
*Xerox Corporation*

*Board members are also members of the Council.
**Ex Officio.

# Council

Robert O. Anderson
*Atlantic Richfield Company*

Robert E. Asher
*Washington, DC*

William Attwood
*New Canaan, Connecticut*

Marguerite Ross Barnett
*The City University of New York*

Douglas J. Bennet
*National Public Radio*

Edward G. Biester, Jr.
*Judge, Court of Common Pleas
Doylestown, Pennsylvania*

Jonathan B. Bingham
*Former Member, U.S. House of
Representatives*

Eugene R. Black
*Scandinavian Securities
Corporation*

Robert R. Bowie
*Washington, DC*

Harrison Brown
*Albuquerque, New Mexico*

Lester R. Brown
*Worldwatch Institute*

John C. Bullitt
*Shearman & Sterling*

Goler T. Butcher
*Howard University Law School*

Frank C. Carlucci
*Sears World Trade, Inc.*

Lisle C. Carter, Jr.
*Verner, Liipfert, Bernhard,
McPherson and Hand*

Kathryn D. Christopherson
*Louisville, Kentucky*

George J. Clark
*Citibank, N.A.*

Harlan Cleveland
*Hubert H. Humphrey Institute of
Public Affairs
University of Minnesota*

Frank M. Coffin
*Chief Judge, United States Court of
Appeals for the First Circuit*

John C. Culver
*Arent, Fox, Kinter, Plotkin & Kahn*

Ralph P. Davidson
*Time Incorporated*

Richard H. Demuth
*Surrey & Morse*

William T. Dentzer, Jr.
*Depository Trust Company*

John Diebold
*The Diebold Group*

Albert Fishlow
*University of California at Berkeley*

Luther H. Foster
*Alexandria, Virginia*

Arvonne Fraser
*Hubert H. Humphrey Institute of
Public Affairs
University of Minnesota*

Orville L. Freeman
*Popham, Haik, Schnobrich,
Kaufman & Doty, Ltd.*

Richard N. Gardner
*Columbia University School of Law
and International Organization*

Peter C. Goldmark
*Times Mirror Co.*

Katharine Graham
*The Washington Post Company*

James P. Grant
*UNICEF*

Arnold C. Harberger
*University of Chicago*

Theodore M. Hesburgh, C.S.C.
*University of Notre Dame*

Philip Johnston
*CARE*

Peter T. Jones
*University of California at Berkeley*

Vernon E. Jordan
*Akin, Gump, Strauss, Hauer & Feld*

Nicholas deB. Katzenbach
*IBM Corporation*

Philip H. Klutznick
*Klutznick Investments*

J. Burke Knapp
*Portola Valley, California*

Peter F. Krogh
*Georgetown University*

Geraldine Kunstadter
*New York City Commission for the
United Nations*

Walter J. Levy
*Research & Social Service
Foundation*

George N. Lindsay
*Debevoise & Plimpton*

Harald B. Malmgren
*Malmgren, Inc.*

Edwin M. Martin
*Population Crisis Committee*

William McSweeny
*Occidental International*

John W. Mellor
*International Food Policy Research
Institute*

Robert R. Nathan
*Robert Nathan Associates*

Rev. Randolph Nugent
*General Board of Global Ministries
United Methodist Church*

Joseph S. Nye
*John F. Kennedy School
of Government
Harvard University*

Richard Ottinger
*Pace University Law School*

Daniel S. Parker
*Charleston, South Carolina*

James A. Perkins
*International Council for
Educational Development*

John Petty
*Chairman and Chief Executive Officer
Marine-Midland Bank, N.A.*

James J. Phelan
*The Chase Manhattan Bank, N.A.*

Samuel D. Proctor
*Rutgers University*

Charles W. Robinson
*Energy Transition Corporation*

William D. Rogers
*Arnold & Porter*

J. Robert Schaetzel
*Washington, DC*

David H. Shepard
*Cognitronics Corporation*

Eugene Skolnikoff
*Massachusetts Institute of
Technology*

Davidson Sommers
*Webster & Sheffield*

Joan E. Spero
*American Express Company*

Stephen Stamas
*Exxon Corporation*

C. M. van Vlierden
*San Francisco, California*

Alan N. Weeden
*Investment Banker*

Clifton R. Wharton, Jr.
*State University of New York*

Thomas H. Wyman
*CBS, Inc.*

Andrew Young
*Mayor, Atlanta, Georgia*

George Zeidenstein
*The Population Council*

Barry Zorthian
*Alcade, Henderson, O'Bannon & Rousselot*

194

## ODC Program Advisory Committee

Overseas Development Council
1717 Massachusetts Ave., N.W.
Washington, D.C. 20036
Tel. (202) 234-8701

*A New Series from the Overseas Development Council*

# U.S.-THIRD WORLD POLICY PERSPECTIVES

*Series Editors: Richard E. Feinberg and Valeriana Kallab*

This new ODC policy series expands and diversifies the issue coverage provided by the ODC in its respected *Agenda* policy assessments, *U.S. Foreign Policy and the Third World*—now published every other year as part of this series. In the new series, the Overseas Development Council singles out for policy analysis issues that merit priority attention on the U.S.-Third World policy agenda. Each volume offers a variety of perspectives by prominent policy analysts on different facets of a single policy theme. The series addresses itself to all who take an interest in U.S.-Third World relations and U.S. participation in international development cooperation—in the U.S. government, Congress, international institutions, U.S. corporations and banks, private U.S. education and action organizations, and academic institutions.

*Series Editors:*

**Richard E. Feinberg** is vice president of the Overseas Development Council. He previously served as the Latin American specialist on the Policy Planning Staff of the U.S. Department of State, and as an international economist in the Treasury Department and with the House Banking Committee. His most recent book is *The Intemperate Zone: The Third World Challenge to U.S. Foreign Policy* (1983).

**Valeriana Kallab** is vice president and director of publications of the Overseas Development Council. Before joining ODC in 1972, she was a research editor and writer on international economic issues with the Carnegie Endowment for International Peace in New York.

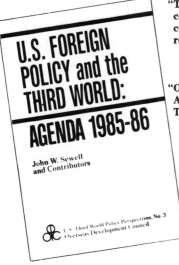

"These volumes have the virtue of combining cogent and comprehensive analysis with constructive and practical policy recommendations."

—Lawrence A. Veit
Brown Brothers Harriman & Co.

"ODC continues its important contribution to American understanding of U.S. interests in the Third World's economic and social progress."

—Governor Richard F. Celeste
(Peace Corps Director, 1979-81)

*ODC's Agenda—
now part of this
new series*

# U.S. FOREIGN POLICY AND THE THIRD WORLD: AGENDA 1985-86

*John W. Sewell, Richard E. Feinberg, and Valeriana Kallab, editors*

> "high-quality analysis . . . has made the ODC's *Agenda* series necessary reading for anyone interested in American foreign policy or development issues"
> —Joseph S. Nye
> Professor of Government and Public Policy
> John F. Kennedy School of Government
> Harvard University

> "This year's volume begins with an interesting balance sheet of the Reagan administration's 'reassertionist' approach . . . All [chapters] are full of ideas . . . for policy-making."
> —*Foreign Affairs*

The Overseas Development Council's 1985-86 *Agenda*—the tenth of its well-known annual assessments of U.S. policy toward the developing countries—analyzes the record of the Reagan administration's first term and identifies the main issues currently looming in this area of U.S. foreign policy. The losses and gains of the administration's "reassertionist" approach are tallied both in terms of its own expressed objectives and in terms of broader, longer-term criteria for advancing U.S. economic, security, and humanitarian interests in the Third World.

**Contents:**

**Overview: Testing U.S. Reassertionism: The Reagan Approach to the Third World**
**Paul R. Krugman**—U.S. Macro-Economic Policy and the Developing Countries
**Richard E. Feinberg**—International Finance and Investment: A Surging Public Sector
**Steve Lande and Craig VanGrasstek**—Trade with the Developing Countries: The Reagan Record and Prospects
**John W. Sewell and Christine E. Contee**—U.S. Foreign Aid in the 1980s: Reordering Priorities
**Anthony Lake**—Wrestling with Third World Radical Regimes: Theory and Practice
**Stuart Tucker**—Statistical Annexes

John W. Sewell has been president of the Overseas Development Council since January 1980. From 1977 to 1979, he was the Council's executive vice president, directing ODC's program of research and public education. Prior to joining ODC in 1971, he was with the Brookings Institution, and served in the U.S. Foreign Service. A contributor to several of ODC's past *Agenda* assessments of U.S. policies and performance in U.S.-Third World relations, he was also recently a co-author of *Rich Country Interests and Third World Development* and of *The Ties That Bind: U.S. Interests in Third World Development*

ISBN: 0-88738-042-5 (cloth)          $19.95
ISBN: 0-87855-990-6 (paper)          $12.95
1985                                 242 pp.

# BETWEEN TWO WORLDS:
# THE WORLD BANK'S NEXT DECADE
*Richard E. Feinberg and contributors*

In the midst of the global debt and adjustment crises, the World Bank has been challenged to become the leading agency in North-South finance and development. The many dimensions of this challenge—which must be comprehensively addressed by the Bank's new president assuming office in mid-1986—are the subject of this important volume.

As mediator between international capital markets and developing countries, the World Bank will be searching for ways to renew the flow of private credit and investment to Latin America and Africa. And as the world's premier development agency, the Bank can help formulate growth strategies appropriate to the 1990s.

The Bank's ability to design and implement a comprehensive response to these global needs is threatened by competing objectives and uncertain priorities. Can the Bank design programs attractive to private investors that also serve the very poor? Can it emphasize efficiency while transferring technologies that maximize labor absorption? Can it more aggressively condition loans on policy reforms without attracting the criticism that has accompanied IMF programs?

The contributors to this volume assess the role that the World Bank can play in the period ahead. They argue for new financial and policy initiatives and for new conceptual approaches to development, as well as for a restructuring of the Bank, as it takes on new, systemic responsibilities in the next decade.

**Contents:**

**Richard E. Feinberg**—Overview: The Future of the World Bank
**Gerald K. Helleiner**—The Changing Content of Conditionality
**Joan M. Nelson**—The Diplomacy of the Policy-Based Lending:
  Leverage or Dialogue?
**Sheldon Annis**—The Shifting Ground of Poverty Lending
**Howard Pack**—Employment Generation Through Changing Technology
**John F. H. Purcell and Michelle B. Miller**—The World Bank and Private International
  Capital
**Charles R. Blitzer**—Financing the IBRD and IDA

**Richard E. Feinberg** is vice president of the Overseas Development Council and co-editor of the U.S.-Third World Policy Perspectives series. From 1977 to 1979, Feinberg was Latin American specialist on the policy planning staff of the U.S. Department of State. He has also served as an international economist in the U.S. Treasury Department and with the House Banking Committee. He is currently also adjunct professor of international finance at the Georgetown University School of Foreign Service. Feinberg is the author of numerous books as well as journal and newspaper articles on U.S. foreign policy, Latin American politics, and international economics. His most recent book is *The Intemperate Zone: The Third World Challenge to U.S. Foreign Policy* (1983).

ISBN: 0-88738-123-5 (cloth)                                              **$19.95**
ISBN: 0-88738-665-2 (paper)                                              **$12.95**
**June 1986**                                                            **208 pp.**

# THE UNITED STATES AND MEXICO: FACE TO FACE WITH NEW TECHNOLOGY

*Cathryn L. Thorup and contributors*

Rapid technological advance is fast changing the nature of the relationship between the industrial countries and the advanced developing countries. This volume explores the meanings of this change close to home—as it affects the U.S.-Mexican relationship.

What is the impact of the new technology on trade, investment, and labor flows between the United States and Mexico? Will development of a stronger Mexican industrial sector constitute an aid or a threat to specific U.S. industries? While demand for the middle-technology goods that countries such as Mexico can produce is growing in the United States, the debt crisis and the high dollar make procuring the high-technology capital goods necessary for this effort difficult and expensive.

An overview essay explores the impact of technological change upon conflicts between the economic and political objectives of the two countries and ways in which the coordination of national policies might be maximized. The authors—representing a mix of government and business experience in both countries—offer specific recommendations on improving the efficiency of bilateral economic interaction, reducing the adjustment costs of technological change, and avoiding diplomatic tensions between the two nations.

Contents:

**Cathryn L. Thorup** is director of the Overseas Development Council's U.S.-Mexico Project, a policy-oriented, Washington-based forum for the exchange of ideas among key actors in the bilateral relationship. She is the author of many articles on conflict management in the U.S.-Mexican relationship, on Mexico's attempts to diversify its foreign investments, on the Reagan administration and Mexico, and on U.S.-Mexican policies toward Central America.

ISBN: 0-88738-120-0 (cloth)                                    **$19.95**
ISBN: 0-87855-663-6 (paper)                                    **$12.95**
**October 1986**                                               **224 pp.**

# DEVELOPMENT STRATEGIES RECONSIDERED

*John P. Lewis and Valeriana Kallab, editors*

> "First-rate, comprehensive analysis—presented in a manner that makes it extremely valuable to policy makers."
> —Robert R. Nathan
> Robert Nathan Associates

Important differences of opinion are emerging about the national strategies best suited for advancing economic growth and equity in the difficult global adjustment climate of the late 1980s.

Proponents of the "new orthodoxy"—the perspective headquartered at the World Bank and favored by the Reagan administration as well as by a number of other bilateral donor governments—are "carrying forward with redoubled vigor the liberalizing, pro-market strains of the thinking of the 1960s and 1970s. They are very mindful of the limits of government." And they are "emphatic in advocating export-oriented growth to virtually all comers."

Other prominent experts question whether a standardized prescription of export-led growth can meet the needs of big low-income countries in the latter 1980s as well as it did those of small and medium-size middle-income countries in the 1960s and 1970s. They are concerned about the special needs of low-income Africa. And they see a great deal of unfinished business under the heading of poverty and equity.

In this volume, policy syntheses are proposed to reconcile the goals of growth, equity, and adjustment; to strike fresh balances between agricultural and industrial promotion and between capital and other inputs; and to reflect the interplay of democracy and development.

**Contents:**

**John P. Lewis,** guest editor of this volume, is professor of economics and international affairs at Princeton University's Woodrow Wilson School of Public and International Affairs. He is simultaneously senior advisor to the Overseas Development Council and chairman of its Program Advisory Committee. From 1979 to 1981, Mr. Lewis was chairman of the OECD's Development Assistance Committee. He has served as a member of the U.N. Committee for Development Planning. For many years, he has alternated between academia and government posts, with collateral periods of association with The Brookings Institution and The Ford Foundation.

ISBN: 0-88738-044-1 (cloth)  **$19.95**
ISBN: 0-87855-991-4 (paper)  **$12.95**
1986  **208 pp.**

# HARD BARGAINING AHEAD: U.S. TRADE POLICY AND DEVELOPING COUNTRIES

*Ernest H. Preeg and contributors*

U.S.-Third World trade relations are at a critical juncture. Trade conflicts are exploding as subsidies, import quotas, and "voluntary" export restraints have become commonplace. The United States is struggling with record trade and budget deficits. Developing countries, faced with unprecedented debt problems, continue to restrain imports and stimulate exports.

For both national policies and future multilateral negotiations, the current state of the North-South trade relationship presents a profound dilemma. Existing problems of debt and unemployment cannot be solved without growth in world trade. While many developing countries would prefer an export-oriented development strategy, access to industrialized-country markets will be in serious doubt if adjustment policies are not implemented. Consequently, there is an urgent need for more clearly defined mutual objectives and a strengthened policy framework for trade between the industrialized and the developing countries.

In this volume, distinguished practitioners and academics identify specific policy objectives for the United States on issues that will be prominent in the new round of GATT negotiations.

Contents:

**Ernest H. Preeg,** a career foreign service officer and recent visiting fellow at the Overseas Development Council, has had long experience in trade policy and North-South economic relations. He was a member of the U.S. delegation to the GATT Kennedy Round of negotiations and later wrote a history and analysis of those negotiations, *Traders and Diplomats* (The Brookings Institution, 1969). Prior to serving as American ambassador to Haiti (1981-82), he was deputy chief of mission in Lima, Peru (1977-80), and deputy secretary of state for international finance and development (1976-77).

ISBN: 0-88738-043-3 (cloth)          **$19.95**
ISBN: 0-87855-987-6 (paper)          **$12.95**
**1985**                             **220 pp.**

# UNCERTAIN FUTURE: COMMERCIAL BANKS AND THE THIRD WORLD

*Richard E. Feinberg and Valeriana Kallab, editors*

> "useful short papers by people of differing backgrounds who make quite different kinds of suggestions about how banks, governments and international bodies ought to behave in the face of the continuing debt difficulties"
> —*Foreign Affairs*

> "the very best available to academia and the general public . . . on the criteria of reader interest, clarity of writing, quality of the research, and on that extra something special that sets a work apart from others of similar content"
> —James A. Cox, Editor
> *The Midwest Book Review*

The future of international commercial lending to the Third World has become highly uncertain just when the stakes seem greatest for the banks themselves, the developing countries, and the international financial system. Having become the main channel for the transfer of capital from the North to the South in the 1970s, how will the banks respond in the period ahead, when financing will be urgently needed?

The debt crisis that burst onto the world stage in 1982 is a long-term problem. New bank lending to many developing countries has slowed to a trickle. The combination of high interest rates and the retrenchment in bank lending is draining many developing countries of badly needed development finance. While major outright defaults now seem improbable, heightened conflict between creditors and debtors is possible unless bold actions are taken soon.

New approaches must take into account the interests of both the banks and developing-country borrowers. No single solution can by itself resolve the crisis. A battery of measures is needed—reforms in macroeconomic management, in the policies of the multilateral financial institutions, in bank lending practices as well as information gathering and analysis, and in regulation.

**Contents:**

**Richard E. Feinberg**—Overview: Restoring Confidence in International Credit Markets
**Lawrence J. Brainard**—More Lending to the Third World? A Banker's View
**Karin Lissakers**—Bank Regulation and International Debt
**Christine A. Bogdanowicz-Bindert and Paul M. Sacks**—The Role of Information: Closing the Barn Door?
**George J. Clark**—Foreign Banks in the Domestic Markets of Developing Countries
**Catherine Gwin**—The IMF and the World Bank: Measures to Improve the System
**Benjamin J. Cohen**—High Finance, High Politics

ISBN: 0-88738-041-7 (cloth)    **$19.95**
ISBN: 0-87855-989-2 (paper)    **$12.95**
**1984**    144 pp.

# ADJUSTMENT CRISIS IN THE THIRD WORLD

*Richard E. Feinberg and Valeriana Kallab, editors*

**"major contribution to the literature on the adjustment crisis"**
—B. T. G. Chidzero
Minister of Finance, Economic Planning
and Development Government of Zimbabwe

**"The adjustment crisis book has really stirred up some excitement here"**
—Peter P. Waller
German Development Institute (Berlin)

**"good collection of papers"**
—*Foreign Affairs*

Just how the debt and adjustment crisis of Third World countries is handled, by them and by international agencies and banks, can make a big difference in the pace and quality of *global* recovery.

Stagnating international trade, sharp swings in the prices of key commodities, worsened terms of trade, high interest rates, and reduced access to commercial bank credits have slowed and even reversed growth in many Third World countries. Together, these trends make "adjustment" of both demand and supply a central problem confronting policy makers in most countries in the mid-1980s. Countries must bring expenditures into line with shrinking resources in the short run, but they also need to alter prices and take other longer-range steps to expand the resource base in the future—to stimulate investment, production, and employment. Already low living standards make this an especially formidable agenda in most Third World nations.

What can be done to forestall the more conflictive phase of the debt crisis that now looms ahead? How can developing countries achieve adjustment *with growth?* The contributors to this volume share the belief that more constructive change is possible and necessary.

Contents:

**Richard E. Feinberg**—The Adjustment Imperative and U.S. Policy
**Albert Fishlow**—The Debt Crisis: Round Two Ahead?
**Tony Killick, Graham Bird, Jennifer Sharpley, and Mary Sutton**—
The IMF: Case for a Change in Emphasis
**Stanley Please**—The World Bank: Lending for Structural Adjustment
**Joan M. Nelson**—The Politics of Stabilization
**Colin I. Bradford, Jr.**—The NICs: Confronting U.S. "Autonomy"
**Riordan Roett**—Brazil's Debt Crisis
**Lance Taylor**—Mexico's Adjustment in the 1980's: Look Back Before Leaping Ahead
**DeLisle Worrell**—Central America and the Caribbean: Adjustment in Small, Open
Economies

ISBN: 0-88738-040-9 (cloth)  **$19.95**
ISBN: 0-87855-988-4 (paper)  **$12.95**
**1984**  **220 pp.**